DIGGING DEEP

A Journey into Southeast Asia's past

T0284501

Foreword

Almost fifty years to the day since I ventured forth on my first archaeological fieldwork in Southeast Asia, the Covid crisis struck, bringing to an end any prospect of further excavations, travel or attendance at conferences. More than one colleague then encouraged me to reflect on those five decades, and set down for the record, how it happened.

Taking the bait, I decided to go back to bedrock and describe how I came to be an archaeologist. My interest was stimulated by my Uncle Strachan in his quest for locating old Wimbledon House, and my brother Richard for getting us both onto digs. I thank them for this, combined with my gratitude for the endless support from my parents. My early formal studies at London University Institute of Archaeology brought me into contact with Sheppard Frere, who taught me how to excavate and continued to advise and encourage me into his 99th year. At Cambridge, I owe a considerable debt of gratitude to Grahame Clark, Glyn Daniel and my PhD supervisor, Eric Higgs.

My two co-directors Rachanie Thosarat and Amphan Kijngam have made my fieldwork both possible and infinitely rewarding. Literally hundreds of Thai villagers have shared with me the excitement of discovery. The funds needed to run an excavation have come from many Institutions, and I thank in particular, the Marsden Fund, Earthwatch and its Research Corps, the National Geographic Society, the University of Otago, the Ford Foundation and the Australian Research Council.

I thank all those who have worked with me as friends and colleagues over the years. Bill Solheim, Donn Bayard and Chet Gorman encouraged me to start. The discoveries we have made would hardly have been possible without the dedication of Nancy Tayles and her team of bioanthropologists, my son Tom with his dating expertise, and Bill Boyd's reconstruction of environments. I have so enjoyed working alongside a legion of graduate students many of whom have gone on to their own archaeological careers, including Nigel Chang, Dougald O'Reilly, Helen Heath, Oli Pryce and Carmen Sarjeant.

Writing a book like this is pretty straightforward, particularly with daily diaries from 1955 on the bookshelf to refer back to. Publishing it is quite another, and I thank Narisa Chakrabongse and her team at River Books for making it all possible.

DIGGING
DEEP

A Journey into Southeast Asia's past

CHARLES HIGHAM

RIVER
BOOKS

For my wife Polly
By keeping the fires burning at home,
she made my fieldwork possible

First published in Thailand in 2021 by
River Books Press Co., Ltd.
396/1 Maharaj Road, Phraborommaharajawang,
Bangkok 10200 Thailand
Tel: (66) 2 224-6686, 2 225-0139, 2 622-1900
Email: order@riverbooksbk.com
www.riverbooksbk.com

Editor: Narisa Chakrabongse
Production: Narisa Chakrabongse
Design: Ruetairat Nanta

ISBN 978 616 451 058 6

Front cover: It was with quite a sense of achievement that we completed our
excavation at Khok Phanom Di.

Printed and bound in Thailand by Sirivatana Interprint Public Co., Ltd.

Contents

Tony & Eileen Higham, Mum and Dad, whose support of my academic and sporting endeavours was unwavering.

One | Beginnings

1944 was an important year for my family. My father was in France, serving as an engineer on the staff of Field Marshall Montgomery, having landed at Normandy on D+10. His letters home reveal negotiations to buy his older brother Strachan's house in Leopold Road, Wimbledon. Mum and we three small boys were then living in North Wales, and when the sale was finalized, we took the train to London and finally by taxi, drew up outside a three-storied Victorian family home. My initial memory was the paper tape stuck on the windows to minimize bomb damage, and the stressed faces of a family of Polish refugees my uncle had given shelter to. I was five years old. The V1 and V2 rockets were then assailing London, and the parade of shops at the bottom of our road were bombed and boarded up. I began my schooling at Wimbledon Park County Primary School. I was throughout an average pupil, and ended up in the top of two classes that had to go through the first major test, long since abandoned, known as the 11+ exam. My older brother Richard had already passed his, and was in his first year at Raynes Park County Grammar School for boys. This examination divided young boys and girls into two groups. Those who passed were given entry to a grammar school, those who did not went to a secondary modern school. The former were academic and played rugby, the latter trained more for manual careers and played football.

I sat my 11+ exam in morning and afternoon sessions at nearby Wimbledon College. This was a Catholic boys school, run by Jesuit priests. One of these, my invigilator, declared over lunch break that a boy had forgotten to put his name on the exam script during the morning. He then singled me out as the culprit. I felt I had no chance of passing, and when, six weeks later, the headmaster announced the half dozen or so who had passed, my name was missing. I strongly suspect that my Mum took up action stations behind the scenes, because I was soon summoned to the Grammar School for an interview. I nervously waited in the secretary's office until ushered in to be confronted by the Headmaster, Mr Henry Porter, and two officials from County Hall. They asked me a few questions, I cannot recall any of them, and I then took the bus home. About a week later my headmaster, Mr Shrive, called for me and said, "well, you are a Grammar School boy now". I rushed home elated to tell Mum, but she was not at home. I knew that she would be out for a walk and ran down Dora Road to find her pushing my new young brother in a pram. We shared the exciting news, but, of course, she already knew, Mr Shrive had rung her.

In 1950, in my new school uniform, I nervously arrived for my first day at Raynes Park Grammar School. I was about a year younger on average than my peers, and school reports during my first few years varied from average to awful. In one particularly devastating return my mathematics teacher recorded that I was 32nd in a class of 32, with the comment "He is still miles behind the rest, but there is still hope". Mum sent me to a tutor to try and help. I was placed in the less academically gifted class that was taught geography, whereas Richard was in the select group learning Greek. However, I was interested in history and this was further stimulated by my first experience at excavating.

My uncle Strachan had moved to a fine detached house on Wimbledon Hill close to the All England tennis courts. Ten years older than my father, he had met with great success as a director of Longmans Green publishers. My father was an architect, and travelled up to Westminster to work in the Department of Housing and Local Government. Post-war years were austere, and raising four young boys greatly strained his income. Uncle Strachan, however, was not only wealthy, but generous. His spare time interest was to research the history of Wimbledon House, built by William Cecil in the reign of Queen Elizabeth, owned in turn by Queen Henrietta Maria, and finally demolished and replaced with a new mansion by the first Duchess of Marlborough. He was anxious to find out where the mansion had stood, and summoned Richard and me to help. Armed with a spade each, we three went into the garden of a large house in Arthur Road, and he set us to work, digging down in a chosen spot. Before long we encountered fragments of Tudor brick,

then bricks in situ, forming the corner of a building. He was delighted, declaring that this must be part of the orangery from which he could reconstruct the location of the entire palace (Higham C.S.S. 1962). I think I must have been about 13 when this took place.

My home, 50 Leopold Road, Wimbledon.

My Uncle Strachan, whose generosity meant so much.

The Grammar-school boy. I might have been cheerful for the picture, but my school reports were awful.

At the age of 10, I had to sit the 11+ exam to secure entry to Grammar School. I just made it.

At about this same time, the BBC initiated a programme on television called "Animal, Vegetable, Mineral". Chaired by Dr Glyn Daniel, a Cambridge archaeology don, it involved three visiting experts challenged by various museums to identify a succession of objects in their collections. One prominent expert was Sir Mortimer Wheeler, who seemed to have an uncanny knack of getting things right. The programme took off in popularity and was a regular feature until 1959. Sir Mortimer was voted TV personality of the year in 1954, and Glyn Daniel had the same award a year later. The programme was thus very popular and we at home were avid viewers. In 1955, Richard came across a call for volunteers to join a dig at a place called Snail Down, near Upavon in Wiltshire. It was to be directed by Nicholas Thomas from the Birmingham Museum, and Charles Thomas from Cornwall. Our application was accepted, and Dad delivered us to an ex-army Nissen Hut that was to be our accommodation.

The site turned out to be one of a row of Bronze Age round barrows on the Salisbury Plain about 12 km north of Stonehenge (Thomas and Thomas 2005). They were located in a military zone used for tank training, and the barrows were excellent mounds for tanks to rumble over. It was one of those memorably hot summers, and we reveled in the new experience of digging. Nick and Charles were excellent company and always ready to offer advice as we learned the ropes and grew in confidence. The plan was to strip the entire barrow down to the natural chalk, leaving baulks in place to record the stratigraphy. It was one of those summers of long since when every day was sunny and hot, and I recall to this day discovering my first of many thousand post holes. I found a potsherd that Vincent Megaw identified as being Iron Age. On our return to school in the autumn, Richard gave a talk to the school history society, and he and I hatched a plan for further diggings.

On fine days, I cycled to school, a distance of about five km, but when raining, I took the 604 trolley bus. The closest stop to home just off Wimbledon High Street led into Alexandra Road, and on alighting there one afternoon, I stopped to look into the window of an establishment known as Peter's Carrier Cycles. They sold and serviced the bicycles young men and boys used to deliver groceries. I noticed there for sale, an NSU Quickly. This was in effect a little motor cycle with a 49 cc motor, supplemented when necessary, as in climbing a steep hill, by pedals like an ordinary bike. It cost in the region of £60, far more than I could possibly afford on 10 shillings a week pocket money. I really wanted it, and immediately began saving every penny I could lay my hands on. My Mum helped by knitting jerseys and bit by bit we accumulated sufficient for the necessary deposit, the balance to be paid off by regular instalments. I proudly took delivery of a machine that was to open up a new vista of archaeological opportunities. Richard saved up too, and before long we were both mobile.

Our plan was to try and join a dig in France. Again, Mum took the lead, writing to Dr Glyn Daniel in Cambridge for his advice. He replied at once, encouraging us to write to Professor André Lerou-Gourhan at the Musée de l'Homme in Paris. His response was also favourable. Yes, he wrote, your sons can join me on the École de Fouilles at Arcy-sur-Cure this summer. The only impediment was money. We needed £60 each to cover all our costs. So each Sunday, I mounted my NSU Quickly and rode from Wimbledon to Richmond, to sell Walls ice cream on the Thames towpath.

My trusty NSU Quickly. It took me to all my early digs, including Arcy-sur-Cure in France.

Some days were chilly; on 29th April 1956, I sold £2 2s 9d worth, and was paid by commission 17 shillings. The following Sunday was warmer and I sold £18 worth to earn 35 shillings. All the cash went into a stationary box, and by the 9th May we had accumulated £34. Bit by bit, we saved the money, but as the time to depart drew closer, we were still quite a way short. I hope with no devious intentions, I found myself visiting my Uncle Strachan at about this time, and in his typically jovial manner he asked how I was and what I was up to. I told him of our plans and savings, and when I finished, he reached into his pocket and pulled out his wallet. It contained a thick wad of beautiful white £5 notes, from which he peeled sufficient for our trip and handed them to me. This was the first time I really appreciated the generosity of a benefactor, it was a lesson that I was to reflect upon over the years.

André Leroi-Gourhan replied to our letter saying that we could join him digging at Arcy-sur-Cure. I will never forget his welcome and support.

And so, on the 30th July 1956, we set off on our mopeds for Lydd, crossed the channel by air, and took two days to trundle down to the site, about 100 miles south of Paris. Looking back, I do wonder how much Mum and Dad must have worried about us, aged 16 and 17, setting off like that into the blue. There, we pitched our tent along the banks of the Cure, and joined the excavation team. There were two other English volunteers, John Coles, later my teacher at Cambridge, and Charles McVean. Otherwise, the entire summer involved listening, trying to understand, and, by degrees, speaking French. It was essentially a school of archaeology for young students from Paris, and our objective was to excavate a 4m-deep sequence covering the Mousterian to the late Upper Palaeolithic (Leroi-Gourhan 1961).

It was a memorable experience. Richard and I began in the Grotte de L'Hyène. This was a tunnel complex with a deep stratigraphic sequence that began with Clactonian stone tools, followed by layers containing Neanderthal tools of the Mousterian tradition, together with the remains of mammoth, chamois and rhinoceros. It was dark and cold, and at lunchtime we crawled out into the welcome summer warmth for food, liberally enhanced with the local red wine. All then retired for a much-needed siesta, to be awakened for further digging in the mid afternoon by the sound of Mongolian bagpipes played by Professor Leroi-Gourhan, 'Le Patron'.

After a week or so apprenticeship in the dark Hyaena cave, we were moved to the much more salubrious Grotte du Renne. This was the prime focus of the 1956 campaign, and we made some dramatic finds. My particular moment came when I helped to trace a row of mammoth tusks, dug into the front of the cavern – presumably to hold some sort of structure against the glacial wind. We were tutored to take the greatest care to record every artefact within the cave, and every bucket removed went down on a wire to the river's edge to be screened. Having meticulously recorded and removed the Aurignacian occupation layers, we worked our way down into the Neanderthal sequence, one which was to raise a considerable controversy because there were so-called Chatelperronian remains, worked bones and ornaments that might or might not have been manufactured by Neanderthals. This issue rose to a head many years later, when my son Tom radiocarbon dated those artefacts.

Most evenings, there were lectures on the Upper Palaeolithic cultures of this region and beyond, and we made several excursions, one to the 9th-century abbey at Vezelay, another to visit and sample the local vintages. But the abiding memory of that long, hot summer was the excitement of discovery. One Sunday Le Patron

Snail Down, Wiltshire, my first excavation. We completely opened a Bronze Age round barrow.

I look down at the excavation of the Grotte du Renne at Arcy-sur-Cure. What a summer that was.

In the Grotte du Trilobytes at Arcy-sur-Cure, 1956. I am in the centre at the back peeling potatoes and talking to André Leroi-Gourhan on my right.

announced that he would take us deep into the Grotte du Cheval. When we reached the entrance, it turned out to be a tiny, locked metal door, just about big enough to squeeze through. One by one we were invited in, head first and down a sharp slope. It was not for the faint hearted. Ahead of me was Marie-Cecile, a large French girl, and behind was Richard, broad shouldered and standing well over 6 feet tall. There were times when the tunnel was so narrow I had to breath out to wriggle through, and other times when the cave swelled into a large chamber. After what seemed an eternity we reached the point 100

In the gloom of the Grotte de L'Hyène, Arcy-sur-Cure in the summer of 1956.

metres from daylight, where under the light of a torch, we could see the dim outlines of painted animals, a horse, a bear and hand prints of the artists. What a magic moment!

On the 25th August at 9.30 in the morning Richard and I left Arcy in driving rain for an 11-hour journey south to Geneva. We stopped for just 20 minutes for lunch and again at the customs post after we climbed up and over the Jura Range. Our objective was our Uncle and Aunt's villa on the shore of Lake Geneva, where we had stayed for summer holidays in 1951. After a week of fishing and local visits I set off south to join up with Richard and his pen friend in Lyon before setting forth, again on my own, for Wimbledon and home. I returned to join the sixth form at school, and Richard to commence his two years national service with the Grenadier Guards. The sixth form involved three subjects taken at GCE (General Certificate of Education) Advanced Level. My chosen subjects were History, Geography and English literature. The syllabus for the first of these was 17th century Europe, I cannot recall what I learned in Geography, but the English course remains fresh as in those days, when we studied the metaphysical poets of the 17th century, particularly Donne and Marvell, and the later poems of Dryden and Pope.

My headmaster was an Oxford man and he had an honours board set up in the school hall for the names of boys who had been awarded a scholarship or exhibition at Oxford or Cambridge. In 1956, four names were added, one being Peter Parsons, who entered Christchurch as an open scholar, and ended up the Regius Professor of Greek, described by a colleague of mine as the finest classical scholar of his generation. My brother Richard was down to go up to Wadham to read Greats after National Service, and it was therefore not surprising when one day my father took me aside and said "My boy, it is time for you to apply to University, Oxford or Cambridge". I must as an aside, reiterate that I was about a year younger than my peers in the sixth form. They discovered girls earlier than I, so while they were partying, I continued solidly working. And actually I enjoyed the History and English. I read beyond the minimum, for example a biography of Wallenstein, a general in the Thirty Years War, called "Soldier under Saturn". I learned metaphysical poems be heart, particularly Marvell's "To his Coy Mistress". However, during the course of 1956/7, a neighbour and friend of my mother's, Mrs Naylor, asked Mum to knit a jersey for her daughter Judy. This brought mother and daughter to our home for fittings, and I fell head over heels for Judy. My diaries describe her as my "dream girl". None of my overtures was successful. She declined every invitation I made. In retrospect, this was helpful, because I had no particular interest in looking elsewhere, and continued with my steady application to study while my friends were enjoying themselves. I thus began to find myself top of the class.

Aged 17, I applied to Oxford and Cambridge, and was offered a place at St. Catharine's College Cambridge for the autumn of 1959.

W.F. "Peter" Grimes, Director of the Institute of Archaeology, who let me in aged 17 to study for a Postgraduate Diploma. This portrait is exactly how I remember him.
© UCL, Institute of Archaeology.

There remained one further problem. Oxford and Cambridge required GCE Ordinary Level passes in a Latin and Mathematics. I had the former, but had failed the latter by three marks. Appreciating my plight, Mr High, one of the mathematics teachers at school, said he would give me tuition three times a week during his lunch break. This is the sort of incredible kindness one never forgets. I retook the exam in the autumn, along with Sam Cohen, who had missed the summer exam through illness. After it was over, we compared our answers. None tallied, and I knew Cohen to be pretty good at maths. A few weeks later he and I were summoned to the headmaster's office. The pass mark, for some arcane reason, was 47%. I felt doomed to failure, as Mr Porter looked up and announced "I want to congratulate you both on passing. Cohen, you got 94% and Higham, you got 49%".

The door was now open to apply to Oxford or Cambridge, and I asked Dad how to. He told me to write to the Master of each chosen college to request admission. He then arranged for me to spend a weekend in Cambridge with Gwilym Jones, a close family friend and lecturer in Social Anthropology. Gwilym showed me round the colleges and explained to me how each is independent, and one needs to gain admission to one of them to enter the University. I fell in love with Cambridge, the ancient colleges, the manicured courts, and the fact that they were still lived in. I bought a postcard featuring the coats of arms and foundation date of each college, and this was the basis of my choice of colleges to apply to: I chose those with the most complex coats of arms, Queens' and Gonville and Caius, as well as Trinity due to my family connections; Selwyn and St Catharine's because a boy at my school had been admitted to each, and I thought this a good omen. I knew little of Oxford, but wrote off nevertheless, to Oriel and St Edmund Hall, the latter because they had a reputation of favouring good rugby players, and I was then playing in England schoolboy trials.

I applied to read Archaeology and Anthropology at Cambridge, and History at the other place in the absence of an archaeology course. One by one the college's replies came back. Gonville and Caius required a £1 non refundable deposit, which went away in the form of a postal order. Shortly after, they wrote that I was not wanted. St Edmund Hall asked me up to Oxford for an interview on the 20th March 1957. I took the 9.45 train and was looked over for 15 minutes by the Principal, the Revd. Dr John Kelly. It went well until I gave him an honest answer when he asked about my Latin, at which point a cloud seemed to cross his sunny face, but he did ask me back to take an entrance exam in early July. I really liked Teddy Hall, writing "I really would love to go there, it is quite sweet and so old". Selwyn also asked me up for an interview, there was no talk of an entrance exam since archaeology was not on any school curriculum and it was assumed I knew little about it. On the 6th May, I unwisely set off into a strong headwind on my NSU Quickly, but disaster struck in Royston when the chain came off. I arrived late with grease all over my hands, to be looked over by the senior tutor, the Revd. Donald Hardy. He made no attempt to disguise his irritation at my timekeeping before sending me to a second interview with the archaeological air photographer, Dr Kenneth St Joseph, known to all as Holy Joe. It was a sombre three hours on my NSU going home to Wimbledon, confirmed on the 14th May by a brief rejection slip.

Ten days later, I wisely took the train to Cambridge for an interview at St Catharine's College. At 1.45, after a strong cup of coffee, I nervously knocked on the door of Mr T.R. Henn's rooms, C2 staircase in the main court. A voice in the distance asked me into his study, where he sat with his back to me for the entire interview. He then sent me to the Archaeology Department to be interviewed by Dr Jack Goody, who after about ten minutes offered me a boiled sweet and noted that the next train to London was imminent.

St. Catharine's College, Cambridge.

FROM THE SENIOR TUTOR
T. R. Henn, c.b.e., m.a.

TELEPHONE 59445

TRH/NS

31st May, 1957.

Dear Mr. Higham,

With reference to your interviews with myself and Dr. Goody on 24 May, I am glad to be able to tell you that the Admissions Committee think you would be a suitable candidate. We are therefore prepared to offer you a definite admission to read Archaeology and Anthropology in October 1960, subject to your withdrawal from the other Colleges with which you are negotiating; and also subject to a satisfactory performance in the G.C.E. at "A" level this Summer. As soon as you let me know these results we shall be prepared to confirm your admission.

Yours sincerely,

The short letter that changed my life, on June 1st 1957.

I returned to Wimbledon to await Mr Henn's verdict. It took a week. On the 1st June, at 8.00 am, Richard brought me a small blue envelope with a Cambridge postmark. I was still in bed and ripped it open. It was the offer of a place at St Catharine's, with two conditions. I had to perform satisfactorily in my forthcoming advanced level examinations and withdraw from all other applications to other colleges. The latter was easy, the former problematical. I rushed into Mum and Dad's room to give them this wonderful news. Richard had always succeeded in everything he touched, which probably made me far more competitive than was good for me. His entry to Oxford was anticipated, mine to Cambridge was a surprise.

I went that day to the school summer fête and told my history master. He looked at me with mild incredulity. But I buckled down with increased commitment to my studies, I was not going to let this opportunity slip. Exams took place just three weeks later and on the 16th August I heard the results: 60% for History, 56% for English and 46% for Geography. Mum wrote a letter to St Catharine's, informing them in no uncertain terms that I had passed, and we waited once again for their verdict. The reply came from the newly appointed Senior Tutor, the Revd. Canon Christopher Waddams, and all was well. I was still wanted.

I was then 17 years old, and destined like all my classmates for two years National Service. Then came a bolt from the blue. Harold Wilson's government announced the end of military conscription, and all young men born on or after the 1st October 1939 were not needed. I was born on the 19th. The next question was, whatever would I do for the next two years? Again, Mum and Dad swung into action. They discovered that the Institute of Archaeology in the University of London offered a two-year postgraduate diploma. Mum contacted the secretary and on the 11th September, we three found ourselves at St John's Lodge in Regent's Park for an interview with the secretary, Mr Edward Pyddoke. Twelve days later I returned to be interviewed by the new director, W.F. "Peter" Grimes, who had just succeeded Gordon Childe as Director. He could see no reason why I should not benefit from two years studying for a Postgraduate Diploma. There was a range of topics from which to choose. Max Mallowan, husband of Agatha Christie, and Kathleen Kenyon taught Middle Eastern prehistory. Freddie Zeuner covered the Palaeolithic and John Evans, newly appointed in place of Gordon Childe, European Prehistory. In the end we opted for the archaeology of the provinces of the Roman Empire, under Sheppard Frere. This choice was made because I did not want to cover the same ground that I was going to study at Cambridge. The fees were £30 a year, just about the sum I had saved from a labouring job. And so, on the 2nd October 1957, I drove my NSU Quickly up to London to meet Professor Frere, and begin my University career.

St John's Lodge, where I began my studies of Roman archaeology in October, 1957.

Two | The Institute of Archaeology
1957-1959

The Institute was housed in St John's Lodge on the Inner Circle of Regent's Park. It is a grand Palladian building dating back to 1812, that had a succession of lordly owners, including the 3rd Marquess of Bute, then reputedly the richest man in the world. When sold to the Brunei royal family in 1994 for £40 million, it was the most expensive house in Great Britain. However, between 1937 and 1958, it was the home of the Institute of Archaeology, founded by Sir Mortimer and Tessa Wheeler. One walked through a grand entrance into a hall giving immediate access to the library. The basement housed the photography studio run by Maurice Cookson, "Cookie", and his assistant Mrs Conlon. Mr Stewart taught surveying, and there was a conservation laboratory under the aegis of Ione Gedye and Henry Hodges. That most vital of venues, the tearoom, was located on the ground floor, while upstairs there were staff offices, to which I was ushered to meet Mr Sheppard Frere, who was to teach me all about the Romans. The students for the Postgraduate Diploma were distributed across the various specialities from Roman to Palaeolithic to Middle Eastern and European prehistory. I was one of just two in Frere's Roman class, the other being John Ellison, a classics graduate from Oxford. But we all joined forces to attend the practical courses on photography, conservation and surveying. Hence, my first lecture on the 3rd October by Mr Cookson was attended by eight students. There were rather more for Mr Frere's lectures because we were joined by classics students from nearby Bedford College.

The Institute was very welcoming. The tearoom was egalitarian, staff and students mingled. The course I followed reflected Sir Mortimer Wheeler's resolve that we should be well grounded in the practical as well as the academic sides of the discipline. Conservation included sticking together sherds into a whole pot. We surveyed round the Institute building to the background noise of the lions in the nearby London Zoo. Cookie had been Wheeler's site photographer for years. He used a big mahogany box camera and rightfully imparted the imperative to photograph only the clearest and cleanest targets. He used half-plate film, and explained the importance of stopping down to f45 in order to ensure everything was in focus, and exposed the camera by lifting off the lens hood for about one third of a second, manually. I wonder how he would have adapted to the digital photography I use

Maurice Cookson, "Cookie", taught us photography. He used a large mahogany box camera and exposed the film by manually removing the lens hood for about 1/3rd of a second. Any of my archaeological photographs in this book reflect his teaching.

Cookie at work at Verulamium, only after we had spent hours cleaning his target.

today, but I owe him a considerable debt for his sometimes rather abrasive criticism of some of my earlier efforts. Mrs Conlon was always on hand to counter his critical barks with soothing encouragement.

Mr Frere was a formidable scholar with a Cambridge classics degree and considerable experience excavating Roman sites, including post-war Canterbury. I found too, that my course also covered the British Iron Age as a prelude to the Roman annexation. John Ellison and I were given tutorials in his office, and these included translating Roman inscriptions. The first of these somewhat forbidding experiences involved him placing in front of us a Latin inscription to translate. My problem was that the Romans were very parsimonious when it came to using marble, and abbreviated almost every word. So my first text began with the letter L. I looked at it long and hard while his eyes bored into me, until I suggested, tentatively, "50?" "Oh, Glory!" he murmured. I should have said Lucius, someone's name.

I went up to the Institute most weekdays on my NSU Quickly, through Battersea Park and Hyde Park. On Monday 21st October, I arrived to find everyone there in mourning, for on the 19th October, my 18th birthday, Gordon Childe had died in his native Australia. It was only a few months since he had

The Institute of Archaeology staff when I went up for my interview in 1957. Gordon Childe is in the centre of the front row, flanked on his right by Max Mallowan and his left by Freddie Zeuner. To Mallowan's right, sit Sheppard Frere, Kathleen Kenyon and Maurice Cookson. © UCL, Institute of Archaeology.

retired on reaching the age of 65, and as the news seeped out, it seemed that he had fallen to his death from a cliff top in the Blue Mountains known as Govett's Leap. Those in the know at the Institute were aware of his depression, ill health and resolve to commit suicide. Fifty-one years later I paid a pilgrimage to Govett's Leap. We booked accommodation via the internet and found to our surprise that the house had been the childhood home of Gordon Childe. The owner had a photograph of him in his mother's arms in the garden, so Polly took a photo of me in exactly the same spot.

Sheppard Frere as I remember him at Verulamium. His influence on my own excavations was profound.

I greatly enjoyed my first term. It ended on the 8th December, and the next day I began my holiday job to pay the necessary £23 for my fees by working at the Post Office. The new term began with a setback. On my way home I unwisely cut between a stationary bus and the kerb when the lights turned green and the bus turning left, hemmed me against a metal railing. I was untouched, but my trusty NSU Quickly was badly damaged. Going up for lectures now involved a borrowed bicycle that took me 50 minutes, or by train in bad weather. It was a great relief to have it repaired on the 7th March, for £5-19-0d. The term otherwise went with a swing, with lectures, essays and visits to the British Museum. Mr Frere gave my essay on towns in Roman Britain B++ which was pleasing. The principal event this term, however, was the move from St John's Lodge to the splendid new building in Gordon Square. The official opening was performed by Queen Elizabeth the Queen Mother, and the day before the ceremony, a palace official visited to brief us on protocols. My friends and I were positioned in the conservation laboratory, and were informed that she would enter it at 2.15. "Don't hold her in conversation, and if she chooses to talk to you, agree with what she says and address her as Maam, rhyming with dam". The following day she arrived into the laboratory late, looking radiant and surrounded

I played rugby for London University and was awarded my "purple".

by a cohort of academics in full regalia, including Sir Mortimer Wheeler. As it happened, she chose to address me, asking what I was doing. "Restoring some Roman Iron, Maam," I replied. She didn't show very much interest in this exercise, but her eyes brightened as she went on "Aren't the trees looking lovely in Gordon Square". Indeed they are, Maam, was my response, as she and the escort moved on to the next room.

The new building greatly energized staff and students. On six floors, it was designed specifically for us, and remains the home of the largest Department of Archaeology in Britain. We were then an independent institution within the University of London, but since it has been absorbed into neighbouring University College. The vital tea room was located in the basement then, the library on the first floor, and we Romanists on the second. Ione Gedye and Henry Hodges ran the conservation lab on the 6th floor, and Cookie had a new photography facility. We were a stone's throw from the British Museum, and the London University students' union, where I had regular visits to the gym and swimming pool, and after some trials, played rugby for the University.

I was very fortunate to have the opportunity to increase my experience excavating while studying at the Institute. Max Mallowan was then involved in fieldwork at Nimrud where at Fort Shalmaneser in the palace built by Ashurnasirpal II (883-859 BC), he had recovered an astonishing cache of ivories. These were brought back to the Institute and I often visited the restoration laboratory for a close up look. I decided to try my luck and knocked on Mallowan's office door to ask if I could join him at Nimrud. He rather reminded me of a teddy bear and with a kindly smile, he said I could, but I would need to raise the money.

I had been working as a labourer during the university break for seven shillings and hour, and this was never going to meet the costs involved. So early in April, I biked down to Sussex to join Mr Frere at the Roman villa of Bignor. This is one of the finest villas in England, and my first day was spent tracing a fallen wall over a corridor with fine mosaics. The following day it was snowing hard but we could dig after lunch and had the excitement of finding my first Roman coin minted in the reign of Constantius 2nd. Back at the Institute, the practical side of the course involved a remarkable prediction of things to come many years later, when I made a mould for casting a socketed bronze axe.

The summer of 1958 was spent digging. I began as a volunteer at Verulamium, the Roman city on the outskirts of St Albans in Hertfordshire. A main road that ran right across the ancient city was being widened and Mr Frere was in charge of a major excavation that incorporated shops that fronted Watling Street, and the residences behind. It was an area sandwiched between the forum and the theatre. I and others pitched our tents in an adjacent field. I learned a great deal about excavating during this and subsequent seasons there, under the eagle eye of Mr Frere. On the 14th July, I noted that I was beginning to understand stratification a bit better. We worked our way down from the latest occupation buildings in stone

Nicholas Thomas aloft at Dane's Camp, Conderton Hill in 1958.

until we reached a thick layer of burnt daub that resulted from the sacking of Verulamium in 61 AD by Queen Boudicca. Under this lay the remains of the first city with no coins earlier than the destruction date. It was a momentous experience for me, having learned about her courageous revolt against the Roman domination of her tribe, the Iceni, to find myself handling the very buildings she had burnt to the ground. Mr Frere employed a technique that I was to follow myself many years later, opening a large area excavation without dividing it into small squares divided by baulks.

On the 25th July, I left for Dane's Camp near Tewkesbury. Now known as Conderton Hill, it is an Iron Age hill fort on Bredon Hill being excavated under the direction of Nick Thomas (Thomas 2006). It is a wonderful

Digging at Strawberry Hill, Pembrokeshire in the summer of 1958.

At Lipari or the Aeolian Islands, Sicily. Professor Bernabo Brea is lecturing to us. I look interested. To my left is David Trump and immediately behind, John Evans. Rose Thomson is at the far right.

location with commanding views over the surrounding countryside. Our base was a stone barn, but I and most others slept under canvas and walked up daily to the hillfort. I excavated in a series of Iron Age pits, and helped uncover the stone wall foundations of the Iron Age houses. One day we were visited by Martin Aitken, a young scientist from the Oxford Research Laboratory for Archaeology and the History of Art. He came with a new contraption called a proton magnetometer, which by magic could identify subterranean disturbances. I think this was the first time it had been used in the field, and I was deputed to hold the sensor and move it over the ground as Martin sat with the receptor taking the readings. He then created a plan of the site with directions as to where to dig. As if by magic, it pinpointed invisible features that invariably turned out to be pits or house foundations.

We also experienced the unpleasant domination of a quartet who seized control of the social side of the excavation. Led by a nasty fellow who kept a sharpened trowel in a holster and jabbed we serfs with it when it suited him, we were required to build a wall of hay bales in the barn to divide the team, he and his three mates sleeping on the other side and being waited on by us at meal times. When my brother Richard joined us one late afternoon, I warned him of this domestic scene. His army training with the Grenadier Guards must have primed him for action. We had just served the four with pumpkin soup for dinner, as Richard picked up a large drumhead cabbage and lobbed it over the straw bale wall. It landed fortuitously on their tureen of hot soup and sprayed it all over the place. He with the sharp trowel soon appeared, his tool at the ready, but Rich picked him up by the scruff of his neck and seat of his pants and unceremoniously took him outside and dunked him in the horse trough. He then marched back indoors, leaned on the bale wall and toppled it onto their hideaway. Peace was restored. The barn and trough were still there half a century later when I paid a visit.

From Dane's Camp I travelled 164 miles west to Dale in Pembrokeshire, where Peter Grimes was involved in the excavation at another Iron Age site known as Strawberry Hill. The team was based at the Dale Fort Field Centre, but on my arrival the director, John Barrett, told me that it was full, and directed me to a local farmer who allowed me to pitch my tent in one of his fields. It turned out that Peter Grimes was a friend of the Barrett's and regarded this excavation season as his annual holiday. So when Richard turned up, Grimes asked him to direct the dig while he dealt with correspondence and the London Times in a local hostelry. We found little, but Richard had a stroke of good fortune. One evening we went to a local beach as the sailing boats from a regatta were coming in to land. John Barrett and his daughter Jane were hauling theirs onto the sand, and Richard went to help. He asked the daughter if she would fancy a ride home on the pillion of his Lambretta, and she agreed. In due course I was best man at their wedding.

It took 12 hours to motor home to Wimbledon, and start my labouring job to earn the fees for my second year at the Institute. When term began in the New Year of 1959, one of John Evans's students Gladys Pike told me that she was chosen to join students from Oxford, Cambridge and Edinburgh to visit the Lipari Islands in the spring. The Lipari or Aeolian Islands lie off the northern coast of Sicily, and with her encouragement, I approached Professor Evans to see if I could join the chosen group. I explained to him that I was intending to study Neolithic, Bronze and Iron Age archaeology at Cambridge, and that this would be a most useful experience for me. He was kindness itself, and agreed that I could be in the London group. Apparently the trip was promoted by the Italian Government to encourage tourists to the region, but I had to find £30 for my own expenses. Mum's knitting swung in action, and on the 18th March, I joined a group of undergraduates at Victoria Station, together with John Evans, Glyn Daniel and Stuart Piggott. We stopped overnight in Rome, where my aunt picked me up and gave me my first tour of the Eternal City, including the Forum and Colosseum. The following day we crossed the Strait of Messina to the main island and booked into our hotel. What a contrast from the gritty east wind we had left behind at Victoria Station. I opened the shutters in my room and breathed in the perfume of orange blossom on a warm spring day. I have never forgotten that moment and to replicate it I have my own orange and lemon trees under my study window in New Zealand. We were given a civic welcome, followed by a performance by a local dance group under the stars overlooking the sea.

Our hosts had laid on for us a three-masted sailing ship, to take us to the other islands and visit archaeological sites outlined to us by Professor Bernabo Brea. Lipari was a major source of obsidian, that was widely traded in the Mediterranean and as we sailed from one island to the next, I was reminded that here is the classic sea crossed by Odysseus. Polyphemus the one-eyed giant is clearly Stromboli, the volcano that throws out rocks at passing sailors. Scylla and the swirling Charybdis are in the Strait of Messina. We all agreed that Circe must have lived on Panarea, and as for the floating islands, we noticed that in the morning low cloud at sea level gave the mirage that the islands were, indeed, floating. I also came better acquainted with my Cambridge friends. Euan McKie went on to work in the Hunterian Museum in Glasgow. Rose Thomson was the daughter and granddaughter of Nobel prizewinners, and Nick David ended up doing his archaeology in Canada. It was an excellent learning curve for me. On the 26th March, Rose and I studied the earliest Neolithic pottery from Castellaro, the previous evening Professor Evans gave me a one on one conversation on the Neolithic occupation of Southern Italy. This was the grounding I needed, for the day before our departure for London, I was called on to give a presentation on this very topic, my diary recording that "I spent the

62 years later, I visit the bathhouse at Bignor that Barry Cunliffe and I had worked in under the direction of Sheppard Frere.

most nerve-racking ten minutes of my life this afternoon when I had to get up and declaim on the Neolithic on Lipari before four of the most illustrious scholars of the day on this subject". I was told afterwards that it was "good".

This was soon followed by a second season at Bignor villa. This time Mr Frere set me to work clearing some fill in an outbuilding, I think part of the baths complex. The site had been excavated the previous century and was owned by a Captain Tupper, who charged visitors a small entrance fee. Mr Frere dispatched another volunteer to speed up my assignment. It turned out to be Barry Cunliffe, the future Professor of European Prehistory at Oxford. We hit it off at once; he was a cheerful person to work alongside, and we discovered that we were both destined for archaeology at Cambridge in the autumn. I then returned to Wimbledon and the countdown to my final exam for the Postgraduate Diploma. These commenced on June 8th with six exams in three days. The questions on the Roman Provinces were answerable, those on Iron Age and Roman Britain less so. On the 26th June, I was grilled for half an hour in a viva exam by Mr Frere, Peter Grimes, Kathleen Kenyon and Ian Richmond. There was in retrospect little reason to feel any tension, I was never to be awarded a diploma and I never heard officially of the results. But Mr Frere did say four days after the viva that I had done alright and he wrote a letter stating that I had passed. In the meantime, I was back working as a labourer to garner sufficient money to launch myself into further excavations.

This involved another excursion to France. Mr Frere had organized an expedition to dig at the Camp du Charlat, another Iron Age hill fort just south of Ussel in the Department of Corrèze. It was Richard's long vacation from Oxford, and we decided to travel there with me riding pillion on his Lambretta. This turned out to be a disaster, for it broke down in Paris and needed a long time to effect repairs. Our only option was to travel to Ussel by train. We checked timetables at the Gare d'Austerlitz, and then decided to visit the Roman gallery at the Louvre before our evening departure. There, of all people, I bumped into Bill Manning, another student at the Institute who was heading to the dig as well. He was travelling with a Mrs Dodson, who had two spare seats in her car. What luck! We suggested that we take a route via Arcy-sur-Cure, and that evening, we stopped in Vermenton. They went to a hotel, we had strictly limited funds, but we had suggested Vermenton because we knew that André Leroi-Gourhan had a holiday house there. At about 10.00 pm we knocked on his door to be accorded a royal welcome. Bearskin rugs were laid out on the kitchen floor for us to sleep, and in the morning there was an excellent breakfast on their sunny terrace. Having visited the Roman theatre and walls at Autun, we heaved up in Lyon for a less comfortable night on a park bench, to be awoken in the early hours when a water sprinkler was activated. We then were driven to Ussel where Mr Frere greeted us in his hotel and drove us in his Rolls Royce to the farm where we camped.

It was a really splendid dig. High summer in Central France, a river to swim in each evening, and a fascinating rampart of *murus gallicus* to excavate. We were a

On the ramparts at the Camp du Charlat. I am on the left in the foreground opposite John Ellison. Brother Richard is far right.

Opposite page: After a day's digging at the Camp du Charlat. I am peeling potatoes, John Ellison helps while Richard struggles with the primus stove surrounded by the farmer's children.

small team and Mr Frere was on top form. I wrote that "it is a life one dreams of in the long winter months, I am serenely happy here". Each evening we activated the primus and cooked for ourselves, supplemented by peaches from the farm orchard and milk just ten minutes from their cows. Mr Frere had some money left over and he offered us each £5 to backfill our square, followed by an invitation to join him in the Hotel de la Boule d'Or in Bourges for dinner on his way back to England. Anne Grosvenor-Ellis, one my contemporaries at the Institute, was one of our team. She drove a Triumph TR3 sports car and in typical form, Richard organized with her a tour of France with me squeezed into the dicky seat at the back. So we three joined Mr Frere and his three middle-aged lady admirers there for a sumptuous meal and our first night sleeping in a bed for some weeks. Then our archaeological tour began, to Périgueux for the Romano-Gallic temple to Vesunna, and the amphitheatre. Then to Lascaux for an unforgettable hour seeing the real cave paintings before the replica was constructed for tourists, Le Moustier, and Combarelles before finding a camping spot and all three of us squeezing into our tent.

That was quite a summer tour. We drove down to Albi, and on to the see the walls of Carcassonne, to Narbonne, the site of Rome's first colony in Transalpine Gaul. We watched wild bulls in the Camargue, visited the amphitheatre at Arles and swam under the Pont du Gard. "What sight seeing", I wrote, "dreams come true." On the 30th July, we reached Arcy-sur-Cure to be greeted by our old friends and get back into digging in the Gravettian layers of the Grotte du Renne.

My hope, on returning to the next season at Verulamium, was to be invited by Mr Frere to be one of his site supervisors. This was not to be, but the next best thing

Leaving Arcy-sur-Cure after roaming round France. I am in the back seat of Anne Grosvenor-Ellis's Triumph TR3.

was to be included as one of his paid workers rather than as a volunteer. I soon found that this had pluses and minuses. Although earning £7.10.0d a week, I was also assigned the least interesting tasks. Nevertheless over time this regime was relaxed and I had some fascinating times working both in the residential quarter of the city and, briefly, also in the theatre. There were some very exciting discoveries. Gavin Brown and I found ourselves peeling off the thin layers of clay floor that a Roman family had laid down in their back living room when we

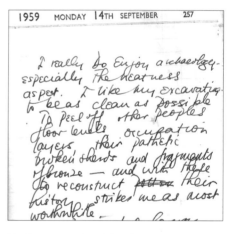

My diary entry as I ended my happy two years at the Institute reveals that my enthusiasm for archaeology was undiminished.

exposed the outline of a pit that the new floor had concealed. We excavated its contents and in one afternoon, found about 35 tiny coins. On another occasion we helped to excavate the deep deposits that filled a well. The pottery at the base was in pristine condition, and it was in the inky depths that Professor Frend from Cambridge found the bronze statuette of Venus that occupies pride of place in the

Verulamium Museum today. We also found a corn-drying furnace, that caused me a problem because Mr Frere, assuming that I was fluent in French, had tasked me with translating his description of the excavation to a delegation from the VI International Classical Congress. Fortunately I then had a French girlfriend and a fevered phone call provided me with the words "furneaux sécher le blé.

Another highlight was a visit on the 9th September from Sir Mortimer Wheeler, who had excavated at Verulamium before the war. He was shown round by Mr Frere as we all had our heads down doing our best. In those days, we never screened what we had excavated. Having placed all the finds in a tray, we put the rest into a wheelbarrow for the dump. Frere and Wheeler reached my square, and Frere picked up a large piece of Samian ware from my finds tray. "It has a fresh break, Charles", he said, "where is the rest of

Felicity Wild and I helped Martin Aitken, who brought his proton magnetometer to Verulamium, and in a few hours, we traced a defensive ditch across the length of the Roman city.

it?" I looked up hopelessly. He rummaged in my wheelbarrow and pulled out the other half. "Be more careful in future" he commanded. To this day I am sure I saw a frisson of sympathy on Sir Mortimer's distinguished face. This event followed an entry in my diary at the time: "I really do enjoy archaeology, especially the neatness aspect. I like my excavating to be as clean as possible. To peel off other people's floor levels, occupation layers, their pathetic broken sherds and fragments of bronze and with these to reconstruct their history strikes me as most worthwhile".

I rate my time at Verulamium as the most valuable chapter in my early training to be a field archaeologist. I learned the basics of stratigraphy, excavated a rare *lararium* where Romans kept their household gods in a niche. I prised away the destruction layer left by Boudicca and kept a sharp eye open for coins. My immediate site supervisor was a rather fierce lady called Marion, and she insisted that I troweled with the right technique, once loudly declaiming "No no no no no!" when I didn't. On the 25th of September 1959 I finished at Verulamium after being involved there for 45 days. It had been a wonderful summer of fieldwork, but as the days shortened, and the mist over the Hertfordshire fields brought a chill into the morning air, I also had another objective. After digging all day, I ran the complete circuit of the Roman walls in order to get as fit as possible for the impending rugby season.

The iron portals of St Catharine's College, Cambridge, swung open for me in October 1959.

Three | A Cambridge Undergraduate

Dad advised me that at Cambridge, one works in the morning and the evening, and plays in the afternoon. I was a serious-minded 19-year-old when Mum and Dad drove me up on the 4th October 1959. I had two ambitions. My wider family had a consistent record of excelling academically, and I felt pressure to do well in my exams. I also badly wanted to be selected to play rugby against Oxford University, and thus become a Cambridge blue. This ambition was sharpened when, during my first term, brother Richard was given his Oxford blue playing against us and winning 9-3. My college, St Catharine's, found digs for all first year undergraduates except scholars. Mine were at 36, Langham Road, where we met my landlady Mrs Murkin and her son Bernard. I was given the ground-floor room facing the street for my living room, and the bedroom above it. The house was somewhat damp and despite an ancient ceramic vessel for hot water in my bed, I soon developed rheumatic aches. Mrs Murkin had to keep a time sheet showing that I was in residence before 10 pm each night unless I had a valid reason approved by my tutor, who had the remarkable name of Augustus Caesar. I had breakfast in my digs supplied by Mrs Murkin, and lunch and dinner in hall. The latter was a formal occasion requiring a jacket, tie and my college undergraduate gown.

James Neill and Co. on the corner of King's Parade and Silver Street supplied my college blazer, a gift from my grandmother that I still wear on occasion. Mum and Dad gave me my scarf and gown. There were about 100 freshmen in my year, all young Englishmen. Through rugby training and chatting over lunch, about half a dozen of us became close friends, and met from time to time in the digs of Richard Walduck for tea and crumpets, because he lived closest to college. As a grammar-school boy I had mixed feelings about the effortless superiority I had encountered from public schoolboys in Surrey county rugby circles, but I found my new friends who came from Harrow, Tonbridge, St Paul's, and Eastbourne good company. We were warned by our Senior Tutor not to form cliques, so we called ourselves "the clique".

Cambridge was then in its twilight years as a bastion of Victorian antipathy towards women. My tutor had a proud boast that since the college's foundation in 1473, the only woman to have dined in hall was Queen Victoria, not because she was the Queen Empress, but because she was the Chancellor's wife. There was a rigid regulation banning women in college beyond 10.00 pm. If one escorted a lady

Glyn Daniel declined to supervise me, as I was not from St John's College. But we were to become firm friends, and years later I was to become a Fellow of St. John's.

past the porter's lodge after 10.00 pm there was a fine of one shilling a minute. If after 10.30 pm, you had a date with your tutor to explain. College gates were closed shut at 10.00 pm, and anyone locked out had the option of trying to climb in somehow undetected, or incur the wrath of your tutor by knocking on the front door and being reported.

Lectures began during my first week, and took place in the Department of Archaeology and Anthropology. I soon met up with Barry Cunliffe, who had been given a choice set of rooms in the second court of St John's. We struck up a good friendship and I was often there. Our subject matter during the first term ranged from palaeolithic archaeology to ethnography and social anthropology. I was committed to at least two essays a week, which were assessed when I met my supervisor. Early that term I made my way to the third court of St John's and climbed the staircase to knock on the door of Glyn Daniel's rooms. I asked him if he would supervise me. "Are you a Johnian?", he responded. Of course I wasn't, and he declined to assist. I did, however, have the good fortune to chat with Paul Ozanne, a third year archaeologist in my college, who urged me to seek out his wife Audrey in the Archaeology Department. She took me under her wing. We two met at least once a week, when I would read her my latest essay before she commented. I soon fell into a routine. Lectures and reading during the morning, then cycling down to my college for lunch before heading for the rugby ground or the squash courts. By 4.00 pm I would be in the library before dinner at 6.00 and then, usually, cycling back to Langham Road to read or write before turning in hardly ever later than 10.00 pm.

This routine did not extend into all the weekend. On the 24th October a friend from the Institute, Hannah Williams, came up for the weekend and we went punting. Barry Cunliffe hosted another Institute friend and the four of us had dinner and wine in his rooms that evening. While my academic work progressed smoothly, rugby didn't. Two other freshmen in my college who played in my position, hooker, were preferred to me and I languished in a lower college team. My progress was also derailed when, only three weeks into the term, I arrived back at Langham Road to find that Mrs Murkin had died. I had to find alternative accommodation, and did so before I went down with a bad case of flu. When I arrived at my new digs following my recovery, I found that my landlady there had also died. I then tracked down a perch in 96, Mowbray Road where Miss Nash made me welcome. It was a warm and most comfortable home for the rest of the academic year but so far out of the centre of town that I was given a permit to use my NSU Quickly by the Motor Proctor.

The end of the term brought my first college bill for accommodation, subsistence and incidentals. The entirety was met by the County Major Scholarship given me by my county, Surrey. It even had a clause stating that there was sufficient in the grant to cover my costs during the vacations. My Uncle Strachan had died in 1958. He established a trust in his will, of which I was a beneficiary. On the 8th January 1960 I was given the first of many instances of generosity, and set

October 1959, an Indian summer, punting on the Cam with my friend from the Institute, Hannah Williams.

My rowing eight. We won our oars. I am seated, second from the left. To my right is Gavin Simpson, who told me about the Great Chesterford Celtic mirror as I was going to my practical exam with Glyn Daniel.

this grant aside with a visit to Greece during the summer on my list of plans. Following Glyn Daniel's course on the history of archaeology, I often went up to the British Museum library and requested original books to read, including, for example, William Camden's *Britannia*, published in Latin in 1586. I had a small hard-backed notebook in which to record relevant sentences from this and other key sources for future references, thinking of impending summer examinations.

The second, or as it is known at Cambridge, the Lent term, began on the 13th January. Our archaeology lectures were given by Roy Hodson, Charles McBurney, Glyn Daniel and the Disney Professor, Grahame Clark. We also went to social anthropology lectures by Edmund Leach and Reo Fortune, and physical anthropology was taught by Jack Trevor and Don Brothwell. Illustrations were projected via glass slides manually by one of the Department technical staff. Gone were the egalitarian days I had enjoyed at the Institute, where I could sit and chat at the same table as the professors. Lectures were formal affairs, we had to wear jacket, tie and gown, and stand when the lecturer entered. Grahame Clark's great interest was the Scandinavian Mesolithic, a topic that did not excite me, nor I think anyone else in the class. Apart from Barry, my contemporaries included several others who went on into professional archaeological careers, including Paul Mellars and John Nandris. I also befriended David Clarke, Derek Roe, Martin Biddle, Bob Rodden, Judy Wilkins and Glyn Isaac, all a year ahead of me. My essays covered a wide range of topics, including the Wessex culture, Megalithic tombs and Neolithic B in Britain. After on of my essays, Audrey Ozanne gave me hope for the summer exams when she concluded that "If you continue like that, you will get a first". She then gave me an enormous essay assignment on the Beaker Culture, as I wrote, leaving me no spare time. Four days later I read it to her, and again, I recorded that it was "much admired". Things were going well on that front, but rugby was a big frustration as I languished in a lower college team playing out of position.

The third or Easter term began on the 19th April. Rugby turned to rowing, and I volunteered for an eight of complete beginners that metamorphosed into the St Catharine's 4th May boat. This involved regular training on the Cam for the May bumping races that involve about 12 college eights in succession starting simultaneously 1.5 lengths apart, with the objective of catching up and bumping the boat ahead. If successful, positions are changed the following day. Four bumps in four days and each member of the crew is awarded one's oar, painted with the college crest and the names of the crew and cox.

Glyn Daniel was lecturing to us on Mohenjo-Daro and Mycenae, Yehudi Menuhin came to speak to the college Shirley Society. There were regular meetings of the Archaeological Field Club, addressed by visiting luminaries. We heard Jimmy Mellaart talk about Çatal Höyük, and Louis Leakey on his latest finds at Olduvai Gorge. But the impending examinations were my principal concern. At Cambridge, one sits Part One of the tripos at the end of one's first year, Preliminary Exam to Part 2 a year later and Part Two, finals to finish one's degree.

I had made copious notes on my reading, and had a growing pile of essays. I also compiled a small hard-backed notebook with what I called "observables", mainly quotes to incorporate into an exam essay. The exam also involved a practical exam in which one was ushered into Glyn Daniel's office to be confronted by him sitting behind a table covered with a green cloth on which sat about a dozen objects. One was then asked to identify each. Half way through the term, Audrey Ozanne, who worked in the Department as a museum curator, asked me after one

The first page of my book of observables.

Queens' College Cambridge, the President's Lodge. Maria and I watched a performance of the Midsummer Night's Dream there during a balmy evening in June 1960.

of our meetings to accompany her into the Museum's reserve collection and opened a drawer containing red painted potsherds. "These", she declared, "are Cucuteni A ware from Niuezviszka on the Upper Dneister". I made a mental note, despite the fact that this observation bore no relationship to the topic of my latest essay discussion.

I worked consistently on my revision for part 1 exams, interspersed with rowing, tennis and squash. A week before they began I had a major disappointment, missing out on the ballot for rooms in college during my second year, whereas all my friends were successful. Following the ballot, the Dean said that he had kept back a handful of rooms in case any of we gentlemen got a first. There was an element of subdued laughter among we unfortunates at this remote possibility. So I was resigned to being out in digs again while all my friends would enjoy life in college rooms. There were six three-hour exams over three days, ending on the 1st June, the third anniversary of my receiving that letter admitting me to St Catharine's. I noted at the time that I did my best on a turning wicket, but ended with the feeling that I might be given a lower second. However, there was one bright spot. After the written exams, Glyn Daniel held his practical test. On my way to his office for my turn I bumped into a college friend Gavin Simpson, who told me that a Celtic mirror had been found last week at the village of Great Chesterford. Glyn sat behind his table laden with artefacts and he asked me to identify them one by one. We soon came to a sherd of painted pottery. The conversation that followed went like this. "This is a sherd of painted pottery". "Indeed it is" he said. I continued "May I go on? I believe that it is Cucuteni A ware, probably from Niuezviszka on the upper Dneister". He looked at me with astonishment, and next up, showed me a photograph of a Celtic mirror which I identified as such. "You won't know where this is from" he said. My reply: "It was found last week in Great Chesterford".

Once all the exams were over, rowing took pride of place, but I also needed to find a partner for the college May Ball. On the advice of my friend Richard Walduck, I ventured to a Mrs Hudson's home where she hosted and taught English to Italian girls and there I met Maria Borello. She was so beautiful. She accepted my invitation, and the Ball was memorable, followed by my punting her up river to Grantchester for breakfast in the garden made famous by Rupert Brooke's poem "The Old Vicarage, Grantchester". I saw a lot of Maria, we went to a performance of Romeo and Juliet in the beautiful cloister court of Queens' College, built during the lifetime of Shakespeare. Two days later as she and I were leaving St Catharine's, my tutor, Augustus Caesar, drove into the car park. He stopped the car, wound down his window and summoned me. I remember his precise words to this day: "Well boy, you are in danger of a first". Maria and I left to visit King's College next door, and his words began to sink in. I wrote that the result was far beyond my wildest dreams. And I would have rooms in college after all, not to mention a college prize to buy books, with an inscribed plate with the college arms to place within. Soon a letter arrived from the Senior Tutor to say that I had been elected a minor scholar of the college, which meant some welcome funding and a place on the roster to read the Latin grace before dinner in hall. Other letters then began to arrive from my uncles, aunts and school house master. Barry Cunliffe and Paul Mellars also took firsts. Glyn Daniel asked me to call on him in St John's and suggested that for

part II I should specialize in Neolithic, Bronze and Iron Age Europe, while Charles McBurney had me round for tea and recommended the Palaeolithic option. I chose the former.

In my study at Mowbray Road, preparing for my Part 1 exam.

My rooms for my third year in Walnut Tree court, E8. They are the three dormer windows at the top right. Far from the madding crowd, they date to 1634.

Whereas the Institute of Archaeology in London stressed the importance of practical experience excavating, Cambridge left it rather to individual initiative. Charles McBurney was then actively involved digging the massive cave of the Haua Fteah in Libya and this attracted those studying his Palaeolithic course, but neither Glyn nor Grahame Clark were involved with fieldwork. Thanks to my Surrey County scholarship and my Uncle's generosity, however, I could plan a long vacation visiting Greece. Richard and I booked tickets on a chartered German student train that left Victoria Station on the 16th July. I had seen a lot of Maria in the interval between the May Ball and our departure, including lunch with her parents, who had flown over from Turin for her 21st birthday celebration. Her mother kindly invited my to stay with them during their summer break in Venice on my way back from Greece.

It took three or four days chugging through Germany, Austria and the Balkans before we finally reached Athens. Our objective was to explore the major sites and after the Parthenon and Cape Sounion, we bussed to Nauplion to visit Epidaurus, Mycenae and Tyrins. We were almost the only visitors at Mycenae, it was open to all, no fences and no ticket office. The Greeks were so hospitable, we pitched our tent wherever we paused for the night, and travelled by bus. After Delphi we slept on the deck of the Crete ferry and found our way to Knossos. There, John Evans was digging into the Neolithic layers and he welcomed us with an invitation to stay in the Villa Ariadne, built by Sir Arthur Evans in 1906 as his personal base. Richard and I knocked on the front door to be greeted by the same quartet who had dominated the social scene at Dane's Camp until their leader was dunked in a horse trough. This did not stop us from assisting with the excavation until the time came to move on to Mallia, Gournia and over the island to Phaestos. All good things come to an end and we were soon heading north. I alighted in Munich, took the train to Venice and was met there by Maria. Roaming Venice before it was overwhelmed by tourists was pure magic. We combined hours on the beach at the

Lido with visits to the churches, art galleries and St Mark's. She and I finally parted company at the railway station for my trip back to London and my second year at Cambridge. I never saw her again.

The new academic year saw the arrival of two new members to our Neolithic, Bronze and Iron Age group, Crown Princess Margrethe of Denmark and Colin Renfrew. He had studied Natural Sciences in his first year after two years in the Royal Air Force for National Service. It was soon apparent that he was a force to be reckoned with. I found him excellent and stimulating company, although away from the Department, he made waves in the political arena and rose to become President of the Union Society, whereas I played rugby and rowed. Audrey Ozanne and Judy Wilkins were my supervisors and I continued to meet the deadlines for my essays and obtain their approval. During one of his lectures, Glyn Daniel said that David Trump was looking for volunteers to join him excavating a Maltese Neolithic temple in the spring, and I put my name down immediately. Judy also told me that her fiancée, Bob Rodden, had undertaken a site survey for Neolithic sites in Macedonia and was applying for funds to excavate it the following summer. Bob had come to Cambridge from Harvard to undertake doctoral research, and he and I struck up a good friendship. On the other hand, I found that Barry Cunliffe, with whom I had been on such good terms during the previous year, was now regularly cutting me dead when we met in the Department. I couldn't for the

At Knossos, we met with my London professor John Evans where he was digging down into the Neolithic layers, and we stayed at the Villa Ariadne.

What a thrill it was, after Glyn Daniel's lectures, to visit Mycenae before the crowds found it. There was no entrance kiosk and we scrambled over the site in the manner of Lord Byron.

life of me figure out why, he had always been such jovial company. He was totally dedicated to his archaeology, and was planning a major excavation at the Roman palace of Fishbourne, near Chichester.

My Aunt Florence had generously opened an account for me at Heffers Bookshop worth £5 a term. When a book cost about 15/- to £1, it was a great help and I bought among others Glyn Daniel's Megalithic Tombs of France. I wrote

At Skorba in Malta, we opened one of the famous Neolithic temples. We were a small team led by David Trump, seated beside his wife Bridget.

We celebrated Grahame and Molly Clark's 25th wedding anniversary in the hills of Macedonia. Sybil Whinney is at the far left.

that day "One day I will write a book like that, and won't I be proud". My rugby had also, at last, turned a corner. I fought my way into the college 1st team for the inter-college cup competition. In the semi final, we were up against Christ's College, and no one gave us a chance as they had several blues. Against all odds, we triumphed, and I managed to score our only try. This took us into the final, where we beat Pembroke to win the cup. This in itself was memorable, but even more significantly, I had been noticed, and was invited to play for the LX club, that is the University 2nd XV, with the promise of a trial for the University itself in the autumn. Things were going well.

John Nandris and I flew to Malta during the March vacation to join David Trump's excavation at Skorba, a Neolithic temple (Trump 1966). This is one of the last temples to have been excavated. We removed a lot of loose rubble as we worked our way down to the in situ walls. On the 30th March I managed to trace one of the apse walls in the central area. Ultimately, some of the massive stone uprights were found to be nearly 3.5 metres high. Under the temple foundations ran a wall dating back to the earliest Neolithic settlement at about 5000 BC. Not only were we able to spend our days excavating but we also visited all the other major Maltese temples including Hal Saflieni and Tarxien that collectively have been added to the list of World Heritage sites. I recorded that my time spent at Skorba was quite invaluable in learning about the Mediterranean Neolithic.

The Easter term was, as a year earlier, dominated by rowing and preparation for the Preliminary Exam to Part 2 of the tripos. It was traditional to leave the pressure cooker of Cambridge for a few days to take a field trip, and we all went down to Salisbury for three days with Glyn Daniel to visit Avebury, the Sanctuary, and Durrington Walls. I wandered round Salisbury Cathedral with Princess Margrethe

Left: At Nea Nikomedia, we stayed in the incomplete Veroia Museum. Here I am drawing pot rims with some local help.

Below: We wandered round Greece, plied with tomatoes. At Mallia we four found ourselves alone on the beach.

At Nea Nikomedia, we traced house foundations and burials. It was a prelude to my later excavations at Non Ban Jak.

and her companion, Countess Armfeld. We had an amusing time being shown round the Pitt-Rivers Museum by Captain Pitt-Rivers, the grandson of the famous General before moving on to Stonehenge. On my return to Cambridge I was buoyed by finding an invitation to play in the University senior's rugby trial in October. But the biggest trial on my immediate horizon was the examinations. One of my revision techniques was to learn the names of impossibly difficult European prehistoric sites to work into any essay that might be relevant, and these included Tiszapolgar-Basatanya, Pusztaïstuanhásá and Hoenheim-Suffelsweyersheim. I worked solid 10 hour days in the final week, interrupted by some further excellent news. All 2nd-year undergraduates in my college were asked to complete a form giving their preference for rooms in the final year. I scoured the college and found in Walnut Tree Court, the rooms of my dreams. The building dated to 1634, and right at the top was a set accessed by its own little winding staircase, that led on into a low living room with oak beams and dormer windows, beyond which was a bedroom and tiny study. It was quiet, very private and looked out over an ancient walnut tree in one direction, and Queens' College in the other. And the Dean assigned the set to me.

There were two written exams on the 29th May, and then freedom set in for a few days until we all had a practical exam. I chatted with Colin Renfrew after, concluding in my diary that "He is rather bright". After all the festivities of May week, that included all the top four college eights winning their oars, including my own, I returned home to Wimbledon to prepare for my summer in Greece, when on the 17th June a note arrived from my tutor saying simply, "Bless you, the only first".

Bob Rodden had been successful in his application for National Science Foundation funding for the excavation of Nea Nikomedia, a Neolithic settlement in Macedonia. There was one proviso, that the fieldwork involve our Professor,

Grahame Clark. We had several meetings in his home in preparation, and on the 27th June, I met up with Sybil Whinney, one of our team, at Victoria Station for the long train journey to Thessaloniki. We all lived in the shell of the Veroia Museum, that was under construction. It included Geoff Movius, the son of the Harvard Professor Hallam Movius, Colin Renfrew and John Nandris. The site comprised a large occupation mound, part of which had been removed by a bulldozer that left the early occupation layers intact. This made it possible to open a fairly large area excavation. We drove out daily to the site, and soon began to uncover wall foundations, living floors and ovens. Grahame and Molly Clark finally arrived after he managed to break the axle of his Mercedes en route. They stayed in a hotel and normally reached the site mid morning. We knew he was coming from the multi-coloured umbrella to provide him with shade. Grahame did no digging himself, but sat and watched while Molly from time to time provided him with a moist cloth to wrap round his head to keep him cool. On one memorable day we all drove up to Nausa in the hills to a taverna in the woods to eat and dance and celebrate the Clarks' silver wedding anniversary.

As we edged down closer to the natural substrate, we were able to detect the walls of an early Neolithic house (Rodden et al.1996). These were fabulous days. Then we uncovered the top of a circular pit which Bob asked me to delve into. Before long I was gingerly trowelling round a human skull, that was soon revealed as a woman, interred in a crouched position holding newly-born twins. I rate my experience at Nea Nikomedeia as a vital grounding to the similar mounded occupation and mortuary sites I have since excavated in Thailand. We opened a large area devoid of baulks, and we scraped clean each freshly exposed surface to identify the wall foundations, postholes, floors, pits and grave silhouettes. The major difference is that in Greece we had no roof, and the sun would soon turn subtle colours a uniform grey. After the dig was over, Sybil and I met Richard and Jane and trained down to Athens and on to Crete for further explorations. A few days were spent in Mallia, where we camped in the olive grove of a wonderful Greek family that plied us with grapes and tomatoes, and had the entire beach to ourselves. I understand that the whole area is now given over to bars and nightclubs for the hordes that descend each season.

I couldn't resist returning to Verulamium and more excavations on my return from Greece. We were now a small team, finishing off down in the lowest layers, and when complete, I helped backfill our square by moonlight. This sandwiched with playing rugby for my London club team, Rosslyn Park, and doing all I could to get fit for the senior rugby trial on my return to Cambridge. I settled in quickly and happily to my new rooms at the top of old E staircase, and counted down the days to the trials. There were four teams involved and I found myself in the fourth

Twenty minutes before the start of the 1961 Varsity Match, we went out for a team photo. The tension was almost unbearable.

of these, meaning I had only a remote chance of impressing the selectors. The day before the trial game I called on Colin Renfrew, who occupied a flat overlooking King's College chapel. I wrote that "He is a remarkably clear thinker, and I much admire him not only for this, but his kindness and sense of humour".

The trial went far better than I could ever have hoped. I scored two tries in the first 10 minutes and at half time the University vice captain singled me out for advice. The University and LX teams are posted in the window of Ryder and Amies clothing shop in King's Parade, and the following morning, I could see a group of interested people looking on. I went down praying that I had made it into the LX club, and was disappointed not to see my name. I then looked to see whom they had selected to play for the University on the next Saturday, and was astonished to see me listed. I was simply over the moon but also full of trepidation. I must confess that turning to an essay on the coming of iron to Central Europe was difficult to concentrate on the day before my first game for the University. This was the theme of the entire term, trying to keep up with work towards my finals while training daily and playing twice a week under the dark cloud that I might have a bad game and be dropped. They were terribly worrying and frustrating days. It was for me a baptism of fire. Within a span of seven days, I played against the Welsh, English and Scottish international front row. Academic work took a decided back seat as the University team had an unbeaten run culminating in my being selected to play against Oxford on the 12th December. Twickenham was packed to the rafters with 68,000 spectators. The sound was deafening. Thirty minutes into the match I charged down an Oxford kick, and scored in the corner. I will never forget that moment. After the tightest of contests we triumphed 9-3. One side of my ambitions was achieved, my rugby blue. Now I had to think about finals.

It was during the ensuing months that I came under the influence of Eric Higgs. He was a Director of Research in the Department and as part of the course, we had to go to his office, christened "the Bone Room" to learn how to identify animal bones to species. He was a former hill sheep farmer in Shropshire, and came late to archaeology with the conviction that what mattered in prehistory was how people managed their economy. To this end, it was vital to be able to reconstruct their subsistence and one way of doing this was to give detailed analyses to assemblages of animal bones from occupation and mortuary contexts. I found this and his way of giving the impression that one really mattered with his piercing blue eyes, appealing. I was drawn to this approach and spent a lot of time learning skeletal anatomy and the differences in form between horse and cow, sheep and goat, deer and human bones. By February, he was mentioning to me his plans to take an expedition to Greece in the summer to seek evidence for Neanderthal settlements. A week later, Grahame Clark supported my application to undertake doctoral research, but that of course, depended on a good exam result.

My supervisor that term was John Coles. We had met back in 1956 at Arcy-sur-Cure, and by now he was lecturing in the Department. He greatly approved of my essays, which as I wrote at the time, "I try so very hard to grasp firmly the facts basic to the essay and give a really lucid explanation, in which not a word is wasted and every sentence carries its punch line." My essay on the early Bronze Age in Scandinavia he praised to the skies and kept it to go through in his own time. I was also given a boost when Eric Higgs gave me the page proofs for the first edition of Science in Archaeology to check for him. This gave me access to a lot of unpublished information that turned out to be relevant during the final exams. I also hunted out little-known European journals, many in German, to try to increase the database on which I relied when composing essays under exam conditions.

It was an indescribable relief when I heard the final whistle in December 1961. We won 9-3 in front of 68,000 spectators to become the first Oxford or Cambridge team to win every game we played. I watch while Nick Drake-Lee has the ball.

One of these included yet more impressive sites of the Hungarian Bronze Age, such as Hodmeszovaszahelybaksokert.

The weeks leading up to finals were, in effect, like a carefully planned military exercise in which every possible question was researched and the basic facts written down on revision cards to be learnt by heart for instant recall. One only had three hours in each exam to answer about four questions. A chance meeting with Augustus Caesar in college saw him ask me how many hours a day I was working. I told him never less than eight or more then eleven. He told me never to go beyond six. On the day before the finals began I went out into the countryside to sit in a cornfield and go through my revision cards. During the course of the afternoon, I began to develop such a pain in my right shoulder that I called on Dr Trevor Wilson at his home, it being a Sunday. Trevor had treated injuries suffered by the members of the university rugby team and was a personal friend. He diagnosed a winged scapula, and indeed, my shoulder blade projected like a wing when I moved my arm. He prescribed a painkiller, there was nothing else that could be done. That night I lay in such pain that sleep never came. I heard the dawn chorus and went into two three-hour exams suffering accordingly. My right arm jabbed with pain all day when I dipped my fountain pen into the ink well. And I had to endure this for 21 hours of writing, seven three-hour written papers from Monday to Thursday lunchtime.

On the Tuesday evening I called on Colin Renfrew. It was the night before our special topic paper, the Megalithic of Western Europe, Glyn's pet subject on which he had lectured most of the year. However, as we found out later, he went on an archaeological tour of Bulgaria before the questions were set, and this task was undertaken by Terence Powell from Liverpool, one of our external examiners. Colin and I tortured ourselves by setting questions neither of us could answer. The following morning in the exam hall, virtually identical questions filled the exam paper, such that we glanced round at each other, shrugged our shoulders and simply got on with it. My diary that night records that the exam was "utterly appalling, bearing no relation to the lectures on the subject by Dr Daniel. It was dreadful, but is over". All that was left was the viva exam, chaired by Grahame Clark. All that I can remember is his laconic remark that "I see you have done your homework on the Hungarian Bronze Age." Indeed I had.

Then, it was all social mayhem with parties, dinners, and all the diversions that are May Week in Cambridge. My friends, the clique, had a farewell dinner of roast peacock prepared by the college chef. The following day it was a party hosted by Rhys Jones, who was to contribute so much to Australian prehistory. Interspersed with rowing again in May bumping races, I had lunch with Colin in the Union, and met a girl Jenny on the towpath watching the rowing, whom I invited that evening to the college May Week concert. We saw a fair bit of each other. Fifty years later, she sat opposite my son Tom at an Oxford college feast, and seeing a facial likeness, asked if he was related to me. Then Colin, Geoff Movius and his wife Cathy came to my rooms for breakfast that lasted for over two hours. But all this jollity could not disguise the fact that the exam results were looming ever closer. If history was anything to go by, there was either no first in part II of the tripos, or at most one. Typically, Eric Higgs confidentially whispered to me that four of us were in contention. He loved to tease. Two days later, I found myself in the Department and overheard Grahame Clark's confiding to Warwick Bray, then a graduate student, "marvelous news, five firsts this year". I was concealed behind a huge cast of a Maya stela from Copan, and when they had turned a corner, I emerged to be confronted by Mr Morley, the Department photographer. Come with me, he said, and took me into the Secretary's office. She was actually typing the class list and I looked over her shoulder. Under Class One, there were five names: Gavin Brown, Colin Renfrew, Barry Cunliffe, Paul Mellars, and me. I immediately cycled round to Colin's flat and told him the news, then to my rooms to down a glass of Cyprus sherry.

St Catharine's made me a senior scholar with my rooms on E staircase for another year. Aunt Florence gave me £70 for my forthcoming Greek fieldwork. On the 30th June my St Catharine's cohort marched down King's Parade to the Senate House to have our degrees conferred by Sir Ivor Jennings followed by the college garden party. Then I had a quick change, went down to 35, Panton Street and got into the back of Eric Higgs's landrover for the long drive to Greece. Rhys Jones, David Calvocoressi and I were his team, he called us his running dogs, to hunt down the Balkan Neanderthals. We arrived in Greece after a 16-hour day on the road from what was then deepest Yugoslavia. Eric scorned official camping grounds, and we had camped in a suitably remote spot when we awoke about midnight to find ourselves in the middle of army manoeuvres. We hastily packed and moved south. Our objective was to undertake a site survey to find Neanderthal settlements and, naturally, caves were a principal focus. It was all a bit like Arcadia. We camped beside the nearest available river and swam after the heat of the day, slept under the stars on camp stretchers, and by day, we three were used by Eric to search. His fieldwork technique involved driving slowly until he saw what might be something interesting, then stopping and sending us to investigate. Looking back, he made a pretty serious error of judgement by never asking the Greeks if they had ever heard of or seen anything of potential interest.

The first fortnight drew a complete blank. So he decided to split us into two groups. I took a landrover with Rhys and David with instructions to survey a particular valley, with the order to meet him a week hence at a predetermined

We climbed over a bluff and encountered deep gullies at the base of which Mousterian stone tools were visible. Our quest for the first Neanderthals in the Balkans was over.

village. On the first morning of our recce, I awoke in the Paramythia Valley, stretched and picked up a stone. It was a nicely flaked scraper. We had come across a dried-out lake bed, round the shore of which were numerous concentrations of stone tools. At the rendezvous a week later, we proudly presented our collections to Eric, who sniffed at them and declared them too late to be of interest. Nor had he found anything, so he declared, "We will drive south to Arta" and off we set. Half way to Arta, we were stopped by a red traffic light due to road repairs. We running dogs always sat in the back of the landrover, and David asked one of the road workers in Greek "Έχετε σπήλαια εδώ' or 'are there any caves round here?' 'Ναι, ναι' came the answer, 'yes, over there', pointing to a steep rise beside the road. I shall never forget the exchange that followed. 'Eric, there are some caves round here, shall we have a look' said David. Eric's reply 'Oh, alright, it is about lunchtime'. So Rhys and David were sent over the slope in one direction, and I in the other, with instructions to return in half and hour.

I climbed up and turned to the left, there were no caves, and I returned empty handed. Eric and I waited and before long, the others turned a corner and came towards us. Rhys had his sun hat upturned in his hands and wore a seraphic smile. The hat was brimming with white flaked stone artefacts. Eric looked down, I can still see his expressionless face as he picked up and examined them, one by one. Even I could tell, they were Mousterian. Bingo. "We will stop here" is all Eric said. Lunch forgotten, we all scrambled up the slope and turned right, to encounter deep ravines cut into a bright red soil, eroded by the rains after the goats had cleared the vegetation. Metres down, at the base of these gullies, more white flakes were poking out of the soil. It was like Christmas, as we collected more stone tools and returned to the landrovers.

We had a permit to survey, not to excavate. So our next step was to track down the Ephor of Antiquities in Ioannina to inform him of this groundbreaking discovery. It was quite a long drive to his office, which was closed, so we sought him out at home. His wife told us that he was excavating at Actium, scene of the crucial clash between Augustus and Mark Anthony. So on we drove into the evening and finally found Dr Sotiris Dakaris, the Ephor. He was a classical archaeologist but obviously highly intrigued by this discovery in his bailiwick. "Collect me tomorrow and take me there" he said. We were strictly prohibited from excavating or moving artefacts, so had no option but to drive back to the site with our precious finds. It was in the small hours by now, and it was by moonlight that we restored the site to its original condition. Then we drove back to Actium, collected the Ephor in the early morning, and returned once again to the find spot.

There, we encouraged him to find the precious Mousterian tools, guiding him down into the ravines and congratulating him as he rediscovered our points, side scrapers and burins. Eric knew that the British School, which had just three excavation permits a year to distribute, would always favour classical archaeologists, so he cunningly suggested that Dr Dakaris might wish to excavate here, with Eric as his co-director. This was soon arranged, and excavations the following year resulted in "Dakaris, Higgs, Hey and Tippet 1964, The climate, Environment and Industries of Stone Age Greece Part 1", the first of many publications on our site, Kokkinopilos, that continue to this day with news that there is an excellent cultural sequence that commenced over 200,000 years ago.

We continued our survey, down to Arta, and then to Delphi. Eric was determined to make this one of our sites, so he sat in the landrover smoking, with his back to the oracle, while we hunted out a couple of flints, and we were on our way to Thessaly. Tired by a long day as a hunting dog, I hitched a lift on a passing donkey to the outskirts of Larisa. Then up to Salonika and we turned right to Thrace. Suddenly Eric brought the landrover to a halt. "We are going home" he said. Rhys grabbed his rucksack and jumped out, saying he was going to explore Turkey. We turned and headed for Dover.

The Neanderthal tools were pure white. It was like Christmas, so many presents.

I met Polly on the 24th March 1963. We drove up to Cambridge to admire
the daffodils but I had eyes only for her.

Four | A Research Student

I returned to Cambridge in October to begin my doctoral research. The state scholarship paid all my expenses and Eric Higgs was my supervisor. When I asked him for his advice on a suitable topic, his reply came in two words, "Try Norway". I went as far as buying a Norwegian dictionary but my enthusiasm for that country soon ran into the sand. Meanwhile, Colin Renfrew was planning to excavate at Sitagroi in Greece and Paul Mellars was tracking down the stone tool assemblages of the Mousterian Neanderthals in the Dordogne. Barry Cunliffe remained so distant that I am not sure what topic he chose to pursue. My own plan was to track down assemblages of animal bones from European Neolithic sites in order to reconstruct their economies. Leading questions involved the ratio of domestic to wild animals, which species were raised and which were hunted, was there a pattern to how cattle or sheep or goats were selectively killed, were they raised for meat or traction, what do the species tell us of the environment. I began by looking at likely sites in Britain that included a visit to Avebury to see Isobel Smith, but before long, began listing possible museums and departments on the continent that might have collections I could study, and heard back from Belgium, the Netherlands, Germany and Switzerland. It soon became apparent that to get to these institutions, I would need a car. But having relied entirely on my NSU Quickly for transport, I had no driving licence, so I booked in for driving lessons in Cambridge.

Rugby too dominated the term, though being a blue, the stress was greatly reduced. I missed three games through injury, but we were again successful at Twickenham, by 14-0. Following this game, I was asked if I would be available to tour New Zealand with the England team the following year, and I was selected to travel down to Gloucester for the 2nd England rugby trial. I was beginning to think and hope that perhaps I might one day be an England international. Dr Lucan Pratt was then the Senior Tutor of Christ's College and a fanatical supporter of University rugby. If a candidate for admission had a strong rugby record, his chances of success rose significantly. In early November, I was enjoying a cocktail party in his college and he confided that I should apply for a Research Fellowship in Christ's. Looking back, I must have been completely idiotic not to have done so. It would have given me all the benefits that come with a college fellowship: rooms in college, dining privileges, financial support not to mention the academic mana. Colin was then, for example, a research fellow at St. John's. I think I declined the invitation through misplaced loyalty to St. Catharine's. That was a crossroads where by turning right rather than straight on, I think I would have had a quite different career.

The Lent term of 1963 was bitterly cold. My exercise included skating on the River Cam. As the term progressed, my plans for a research trip to the continent matured. My itinerary began in Brussels, and then the Biologisch-Archaeologisch Institute in Groningen, where Anneke Clason told me that she had some interesting samples to look at. Then, it was to Schloss Gottorf in Schleswig before going to the Zoologisches Museum in the University of Zurich. The only issue now was a vehicle. My mother identified a Ford Escort 100E estate car on a friend's advice, costing £200.00, far beyond my means. Again, the trustees of Uncle Strachan's bequest lent a hand and the car was mine for £160.00. It had a major plus. The back seat let down flat to allow me to extend a mattress and sleep there. This was to prove a great benefit on my travels, but I still had to pass a driving test and obtain a licence. Until then, I could only drive if someone with a licence was with me, so on the 24th March, Richard and his wife Jane suggested that we three go up from their flat in Welwyn Garden City to Cambridge to give me driving practice. At the last minute that Sunday morning, Richard suggested that he invite Pauline, who worked in his office. She agreed on the telephone and we went over to collect her in Hertford Heath. We four enjoyed a lovely spring day, admiring the daffodils on the backs, lunch in a Chinese restaurant and a movie. Pauline (Polly) and I were married the following year.

My initial search for large, well-provenanced samples of faunal remains in England returned little of value. In those days, animal bones were not retained and analysed as they are today. Indeed, at Verulamium they were not kept for any form of analysis. I paid visits to various museums, and looked at some small collections but they were all insufficient for my purposes. So I looked increasingly to the continent, and having heard of the samples I needed from Professor Magnus Degerbøl in Copenhagen University, applied for a Danish Government scholarship. An interview at the Danish embassy ensued and on the 1st April I heard by letter that I had been successful. However, Degerbøl soon wrote that all the collections would be unavailable for a year because they were moving into a new museum. On the same day, I had my first acquaintance with a new-fangled device known as a computer. Chris Petrie, an expert in the Shell Department of Chemical Engineering, helped me with a program that would rapidly provide me with the means, variations and confidence limits of bone measurements. This computer cost £60,000. The new Ferranti Jupiter on order cost about £1,000,000.

On the 9th April, I cleared a vital hurdle by passing my driving test. I was now free to venture onto the continent and just eight days later I took the ferry to Ostend and ended up in the home of Mr Jean Verheyleweghen in Brussels. He had

I arrived at Schloss Gottorf on a wet Sunday afternoon, and was given sumptuous accommodation. Sadly there was little there of interest to me.

excavated at the Neolithic flint-mining site of Spiennes. Unfortunately, again there was insufficient material. So I drove on, again by prior arrangement, to Groningen and the Biologisch-Archae-ologisch Institut where I had been informed by Dr Anneke Clason that she had available, the large samples that I so badly needed. I settled down happily in the Groningen camping ground and spent all day working on a sample from the site of Vlaardingen. At last I had what I needed. But it was a false dawn. Dr Clason began to show anxiety at my enthusiastic hours poring over the bones, and after a week or so, told me that I should move on and not use them in any way, they were her sole responsibility. Disappointed, I went to see the Director, Dr Waterbolk, in the hope of finding a resolution but to no avail. I had no option but to move on again.

My next port of call was the Schleswig Museum. I drove across north Germany on a rainy Friday to arrive outside the magnificent Schloss Gottorf, a stately castle on an island with an impressive wooden gateway well locked after closing hour. I knocked on the little postern door and was admitted by a watchman. He rang the director and gave me the telephone. The voice at the other end welcomed me with the news that the guest suite was at my disposal. The prospect of a night in the car evaporated as I was led along a long corridor to total comfort, a hot shower and equipped kitchenette. I could have stayed there all summer had the collections suited my purpose, but they didn't. So 48 hours later I set off on my last throw of the dice: Switzerland. Two days and 657 miles later, I arrived in Zurich and found a campground on the lake shore. The following day I arrived at the Zoologisches Museum of the University of Zurich to meet Dr Hanspeter Hartmann-Frick. He was a schoolteacher with an interest in identifying animal bones, and a major publication under his belt from the site of Eschner Lutzengüetle in Liechtenstein.

I had fallen on my feet. Hanspeter unreservedly welcomed me, and took me up into the *Estrich*, the museum roof space where were stored box upon box of animal bones from the Swiss Neolithic lake village of Egolzwil 2. My spirits were high. The director of the Museum, Hans Burla, gave me the run of the institution and asked Marco Schnitter, one of his junior colleagues, to show me the ropes. He took me to the University Studentenheim, where I could buy breakfast, lunch and dinner. I found a practically deserted campground on the shore of the Greifensee Lake about half an hour from central Zurich, and I embarked on the analysis of Egolzil 2, beginning with the very large sample of cattle bones. At this juncture I also received an encouraging letter from Grahame Clark. Up to this point I was concentrating only on the early Neolithic, but he suggested that I cover the Bronze and Iron Ages as well and look out for significant changes in economic behaviour over time. This opened up the need to look at a lot more samples and I threw myself into it all. One drawback was that I worked in the gloomy space right under the roof, their storage area. It was windowless and very hot in summer. Each lunchtime I took the cable car down to the railway station to buy yesterday's Daily Telegraph to keep in touch with home news, and almost without exception, every day there was a letter from Polly.

On the 27th May, I had an appointment with Professor Emil Vogt, the Director of the Swiss National Museum. It began worryingly when he told me that the stratigraphy of Egolzwil 2 was not reliable and then went on to describe how he had just finished excavating another Neolithic lake village on the shore of the same lake known as Egolizwil 4. The complete assemblage of bones had been sent to Hanspeter Hartmann-Frick for analysis. I returned to the museum and decided to ask him if he would allow me to take over, and with great magnanimity, he agreed. But my sojourn in Zurich was about to end. Polly flew out on the 10th June to Geneva, and I went down to collect her at the airport.

We drove along the southern shore of Lake Geneva to Fionnay, where I wanted to see the native ibex in the Alpine foothills. Then we climbed up to 7000 feet to camp in the snow and awake in our little tent to the sight of chamois and

Each evening I drove out to the Greifensee from Zurich, extended the mattress and slept in my car. I particularly remember the smell of the mown meadow.

Polly and I drove up into the Alps to camp above the snow line and observe some of the animals I was identifying from the Swiss Lake Villages: chamois and ibex.

marmottes. It was very cold, and we made coffee from snow boiled on my primus stove. By day the sun warmed and we sunbathed beside a glacier and watched lots of chamois. I maintained that this all helped me interpret my faunal samples, but I was in fact much more interested in talking to Polly. The following fortnight still provides intense memories: we camped by the Pont du Gard, followed the Mediterranean coast to Toulouse and Albi and headed north to the Camp du Charlat and the welcoming French farmer family. Thence to Bourges and Chartres cathedral, Rouen and the boat crossing to Dover. On the 25th June we were back at her home in Hertford Heath. When I finally returned to Wimbledon, I told Mum and Dad that Polly and I were going to get married, but I hadn't actually asked her.

I returned to England in June because I was a member of the combined Oxford and Cambridge rugby team for a tour of Africa. This involved a pretty tough training week in Oxford, where I stayed in St Edmund Hall, then taking our flight to Entebbe in Uganda. Over the following six weeks we played there followed by Kenya, Zambia, Zimbabwe and South Africa. In many ways it was a fascinating experience in practical social anthropology. Africa was then still in the thralls of colonialism. Zambia was Northern Rhodesia and Zimbabwe was Southern Rhodesia. Harare was Salisbury. When there, we voted on a visit to a game park or the ancient Zimbabwe archaeological site. The vote went 24-1 for the game park. On the morning of departure, it was shrouded in heavy mist so we all bussed to Zimbabwe and for me at least it was a memorable day. South Africa was deep in apartheid. In Pretoria, there was a notice outside the grounds saying that blacks were only allowed in the ground if they were nannies accompanying white children. In Durban and Cape Town, the blacks could stand behind the posts, but in Bloemfontein, heart of Afrikanerdom, not even nannies were allowed.

I returned to Zurich in late August, to continue in my identification and measuring of the bones from Egolzwil 4. I was anxious to be able to distinguish between cows, bulls and steers, and obtain age profiles as a means of reconstructing

My Danish government scholarship provided me with a nice shared flat in central Copenhagen. It was centrally heated, the winter was bitterly cold.

how the Neolithic occupants were organizing their husbandry. For example, was a spike in mortality among young cattle the result of autumn slaughter, and was the structure of the adult herd mainly cows. Did they maintain oxen for traction? Also, how much hunting was undertaken, and for what species? Things went well on arrival. Professor Burla let me sleep in the museum, so there was no travel to and fro. He also offered me a job in the museum when my PhD was finished. At the same time Eric Higgs wrote saying he was working on Professor Clark to have me appointed his research assistant. To cap it all, Professor Vogt arranged to pay me £6 a week while I worked on Egolzil 4. I really was working very hard now, trying to finish my analyses before Christmas. I finished Egolzil 4, nearly 3,000 bones, by mid October and then turned to the several other sites that came to my attention as news of my presence and interests spread through the Zurich archaeological community and I was invited to expand my analyses. I did not complete all I needed, but took to the road and drove home in early December.

Denmark

After a much needed few weeks catching up, and on Christmas Day becoming engaged to Polly, I geared up for my time in Copenhagen. On the 1st February 1964, I drove to Harwich and boarded the Kronprinz Frederick bound for Esbjerg. The Danish Government scholarship provided me with accommodation in a sixth floor flat that I shared with three others. The Zoological Museum was brand new and I was given my own study adjacent to a store room packed with the bone samples I needed to replicate what I had done in Zurich. Professor Degerbøl welcomed me, and his colleague Ulrik Møhl guided me through the archive. One of my abiding memories of my time in Copenhagen was the bitter cold. Four inches of snow fell on my first day driving to the museum. But the weeks passed quickly as I worked my way through the faunal remains, most of the sites coming from Langeland. Mr Møhl found a nickname for me, "the bulldozer". I was hell-bent on getting all the data I felt I needed for my PhD and then getting home.

I was increasingly aware that to make a proper interpretation of all the cattle bones I had measured, I would need a comparative sample. Mr Møhl did some research and found that there was an abattoir that could help. So I drove there by arrangement and collected boxes of the distal limbs of cattle of the Red Danish breed, some from cows and others from steers. They were packed with formalin and as I drove back to the museum, and the fumes made me feel rather giddy, but I just made it back in one piece. Then with some help I defleshed them all and found them of immense value in my various interpretations. This, for example, involved making sense of a sample of 20,000 bones from just one site, Troldebjerg.

As winter turned into spring, I made plans to visit the sites I had analysed, and so in May I said farewell to my friends in the museum after four months and drove to Langeland. I wanted to see how each site was situated relative to the sea, rivers and soils, and the aspect of the land, an approach that Eric Higgs was keen on pursuing. This proved to be very useful, and from Langeland I headed for Esbjerg and my return home. I really wanted to stay back in Cambridge, but my conscience dictated a final drive down to Zurich. I needed to look at a couple more samples and visit some of the sites. So on the 5th July, decidedly unwillingly, I set forth once again. I was able to complete the analyses of the new sites, and drove to Austria and Liechtenstein to visit some of them. I then drove to Bern to discuss my findings with Dr Stampfli, whose work at the site of Burgaschisee matched mine. Then I drove to Geneva to examine further samples. But on arrival in the camping ground,

I decided that if I didn't have enough for a PhD dissertation by now I never would. So I awoke very early on the 22nd July determined to drive until I reached home. I made it as far as Arras and slept in a little hotel, and the following day I made it back to Wimbledon.

My college provided us with a ground floor flat in Panton Street, with the white door. This was our first home.

Married Life

I was tantalisingly close to playing rugby for England.

A month after my return, Polly and I were married. Dr Stanley Aston, bursar of St Catharine's had just converted two Victorian houses in Panton Street into flats for graduate students, and we were lucky enough to be able to move straight in. Polly soon found a job with the Ministry of Animal Health nearby, that covered all our domestic expenses, including £5 a week rent. I settled down to absorb my data and commence making sense of it all. This involved preparing mortality frequencies based on the dentition of the various species, coefficients of variation for samples of dimensions taken from the same bone, and working on the shape of bones to determine which were male or female, wild or domestic. This I applied to all the sites I had analysed, and prepared the ground for identifying changes in animal husbandry, the relative importance of hunting against raising domestic stock, and adaptation through changing environments based on pollen analyses. The Swiss Lake Villages are famous for the survival of organic material. For example, at one of my sites there was a building containing deposits of cow dung riddled with fly pupae. This suggested that the cattle were folded within the village during the cold winter months.

Our marriage survived an early hiccup in our domestic lives when I went to Smithfield and returned with the frozen distal limb bones of 30 cows and 30 steers from Australia. Over several weeks, I rendered these down in a large copper containing boiling water and spread the bones out in our back yard to dry. The smell was not conducive to a harmonious relationship, but we survived due entirely to Polly's forbearance, and I used the resulting data extensively in my interpretations.

I needed to apply statistical analyses to the samples, and I reverted again to a computer, housed in the Department of Chemical Engineering. It was a behemoth of banked winking valves into which data were fed by having holes punched into a reel of yellow paper tape. I could book this monster for half-hour slots that first involved programming it with a huge reel of yellow tape that had to be fed in, followed by the shorter lengths containing my data. After a lot of blinks from the valves, results were fed into a typewriter. I never had any meetings with my supervisor Eric Higgs. When I had completed some draft chapters, I gave them to him for comment. My only feedback was when he stopped me in the street and wound down the window of his landrover, looked at me with his piercing blue eyes, and declaimed "be careful of the word random", before driving on. One of my college friends, Anthony Roberts was much more helpful with advice, and I

We moved into our own home in Barrington, overlooking the village green, and flanked by the River Cam. All was idyllic, and in early 1966 Tom was born. The only problem was, I wanted to be an archaeologist.

was also stopped when in St Catharine's one day by Michael Message, a young Fellow. He had noted my name down in the computer booking form, and asked what I was doing. It seemed to interest him and he asked to see my draft chapters. After a week or so we passed each other again, and he said to me, "there is no point putting your neck on the slab and asking your examiners to chop it off". Thereafter we met regularly and we went through my text line by line, suggesting changes here and there. It was a most helpful learning curve for me that ultimately led to a joint publication (Higham and Message 1971).

By early 1965, Polly and I faced a dilemma. My State Scholarship was due to expire after the statutory three years and I still needed a few months to complete my dissertation. I was at another crossroads in my life and took the wrong turning. The situations vacant in *The Times* advertised for an editorial post at the Cambridge University Press. My Uncle Strachan and one of my cousins had both been publishers and, in a particularly badly advised move, I decided to apply. Unfortunately, I was offered the post and in October I joined the Press on a salary of £1,200 a year. My first month was spent in the London office learning how to market books, and then the other appointee, Anne Mather and I, shared an office in the Pitt Building, just over the road from St Catharine's. In fact from the Pitt Building I could look over at my window when I was there in my 2nd year. My job was to talk to potential authors in the social sciences and persuade them to offer a manuscript for consideration by the Press Syndics. These were about 15 august gentlemen representing a cross section of the major disciplines, essentially a board of directors. The chairman was Sir Frank Lee, Master of Corpus Christi College. Sir Alan Hodgkin from Trinity was a Nobel Prize winner. Sir Gordon Sutherland was Master of Emmanuel and Alec Vidler, who looked very like a reincarnation of the Deity, was Dean of King's. Each month they foregathered in the Oriel Room of the

Professor Björn Kurtén came over from Helsinki for my PhD viva, and didn't ask a single question of me.

Pitt Building and we editors would circulate papers describing possible books for publication. Dick David was Secretary to the Syndics, that is in essence the Managing Director of the Press. A man of ruggedly handsome mien, Wykehamist, Shakespearean scholar and botanist, he was welcoming and kind. He allowed me time from my duties to represent Eastern Counties at rugby.

This and my regular games for my new club, Bedford, seem to have come to the attention of the England selectors. I had the temerity again to think that I might become an England international. Following a game against arch rivals Coventry, the press gave me a good write up for my performance against the England hooker Bert Godwin, and the following weekend Eric Evans, an England selector, came to watch our next game with his eyes focused on me. I was selected to play in the next England trials, and I got very close, but not close enough to be selected, being invited to be a reserve for the match against France.

My salary and steady employment meant that Polly and I could now consider buying a home of our own. I scoured Cambridge Building Societies and after a clutch of rejections, secured agreement for a mortgage up to three times my annual income from the Halifax Building Society. We went hunting for a house to suit our needs, and chose an end of terrace in the village of Barrington, with a view over the biggest village green in East Anglia. It cost £4500 and we needed a 10% deposit which we did not possess. Once again I turned to Uncle Strachan's trust and the necessary funds, augmented by Polly's superannuation refund from her old job in Welwyn Garden City, sufficed. We moved in as I began with the Press, it was about 20 minutes from Cambridge on my NSU Quickly. The security of a job and our own home led naturally to Polly's first pregnancy. In February 1966, our son Tom was born.

On the surface, all was just fine, but deep down, it wasn't. I was still having to finish my thesis, and spent weekends, lunchtimes and tea breaks putting finishing touches to various chapters. My heart sank not long into my brief tenure at the Press when Anne Mather looked across her desk at me and said, "The novelty is beginning to wear off, isn't it?" Then a package arrived on my desk from the University of Sheffield. Colin Renfrew was by now a recently appointed lecturer there and the package contained his doctoral thesis for me to edit and take to the Syndics for publication. It crystallised my mind. I am an author, not an editor. I went up to the Department and poured out my woes to Eric Higgs. Again, his answer was brief and direct: "Write to Jack Golson in Australia and Peter Gathercole in New Zealand

and ask them for a job". Jack was then head of the Archaeology Department at the Australian National University, and Peter likewise at the University of Otago. It was in February 1966. I had been at the press for four months. Polly had just given birth to Tom. I wrote to Peter Gathercole enquiring if there was a vacancy in the Department of Anthropology for a lecturer. Somehow Australia did not appeal as much as New Zealand, but both countries were being populated by Cambridge archaeologists. Jack and Peter were the pioneers. John Mulvany was an Australian native with a Cambridge qualification. Rhys Jones was already at Sydney and Peter Bellwood was on the brink of going to Auckland.

Arguably the most abrasive man I have ever met, Professor Fred Shotton, FRS, did me one immense favour by not offering me a lectureship at Birmingham University.

Everything was transacted by airmail, and after a wait of about three weeks, I received a reply from Peter, affirming that there was indeed a vacancy for a lecturer in archaeology. I suspect that the Cambridge mafia then swung into action. Peter had been at Peterhouse, Grahame Clarke's college. Grahame was dead set on colonising new or growing archaeology departments with his protégés. He knew Otago – his two sons were there, one at the university, the other a farm cadet. He would have written for me a golden reference and before long, I had a formal offer on a salary of NZ£1350 a year. Yet, there was still a dilemma. Were Polly and I, and our new son Tom, really prepared to leave behind everything we held dear, our new home, or friends in the village, our parents and relatives, and go to the nether regions of the world? At this juncture, we were thrown a potential lifeline. The University of Birmingham advertised a lectureship in European Prehistory. It was right up my street and I enthusiastically applied.

The wait for news from Birmingham was punctuated with my PhD viva examination. These had a fearsome reputation. David Clarke told me that his was a gruelling three-hour interrogation. Eric Higgs asked me if I had any ideas on an external examiner, and I suggested a Finnish specialist, Björn Kurtén. I didn't know him but he had published papers that matched my topic. He accepted, and was asked if a viva exam was necessary. He answered yes, and I found myself summoned to Grahame Clark's rooms in Peterhouse. I was invited to sit and Clark turned to Kurtén asking him to lead with a question. Kurtén looked a bit blank, and said he had nothing to ask. Nor had Grahame. I was offered a glass of sherry and ten minutes later, left for home thinking it was either a very good or very bad thesis or, perhaps, neither had read it. Shortly thereafter I received confirmation from the registry that I had passed and my graduation date was arranged.

An envelope postmarked Birmingham in due course arrived. I was invited to an interview. News spread through the Department, and the buzz was that I had a very strong chance of being appointed. Colin was of course, now at Sheffield. Barry was lecturing at Southampton. John Nandris had taken up a post at the Institute of Archaeology, and Glyn Isaac was at Berkeley. David Clarke was a research fellow at Peterhouse. Perhaps now it was my turn. Polly and I made a solemn pact. If I were appointed to Birmingham, I would happily accept it, and if not, we would go to New Zealand.

In order to arrive fresh and vibrant at the interview, I travelled to Birmingham by train, changing at Ely and Coventry. I arrived with a mild headache, perhaps it was the tension, my future life was about to be determined. There were three on the short list and we sat in a room with little if any conversation. Lawrence Barfield sat opposite me, I didn't really know him at all, he was a year or two ahead of me at Cambridge and I heard that his PhD was on Italian prehistory. There was also a young woman whom I did not know then or since. A registry official entered the room and invited me in first. I found myself seated at the end of a long table, flanked by members of the Department, I assumed, with the chairman at the end. He introduced himself as Professor Shotton, a geologist who had sourced Neolithic axes to the original stone quarries. He looked at me with ill-disguised disdain and fired not a question, but a statement thus: "Ah Higham, I have been wondering for some time why you chose such an eccentric PhD topic". I began my response "I don't think it is eccentric because…" but he rudely cut me short. "But I do". He then riffled through the folder in front of him, it must have contained a copy of my CV. "Ah, I see you play rugby. What position?" "I am a hooker". With a smile to the audience he responded "I thought that was a form of Turkish pipe". The interview crawled along at ground level thereafter. I was asked what foreign languages I spoke by an archaeologist on the staff there called Peter Gelling, and he sniffed when I responded that I spoke French. After ten forgettable minutes, the torture came to an end and I was asked to wait in the adjacent room while the other two had their turns at being grilled.

Before long, we three sat to await the verdict as the committee pondered our futures. Then the registry man re-entered and asked for Mr Barfield. My last hope lay in the remote possibility that we two rejects might also be called in for supplementary questions but even this died when I heard laughter from next door. Soon the same official returned and looked sorrowfully at the despondent losers. "Mr Barfield has been offered the lectureship and has accepted it. Many thanks for coming, and if you have any expenses, do let me know". I returned to Birmingham railway station with lead in my shoes, and during the stopover at Coventry, I rang Polly to tell her of my

Lawrence Barfield and I sat in a waiting room for our interviews at Birmingham University. Years later, he told me that I should have been appointed. I replied, thank God I wasn't.

failure. It took some time before she realised that I wasn't joking. It was all too real. Our lives were being turned upside down. Exactly 30 years later, at a conference in Italy, I met Lawrence Barfield again. We exchanged pleasantries, during which he confided in me, "Charlie, you should have got the job in Birmingham". I responded from the heart: "Lawrence, thank God I didn't". Four years later, the *Birmingham Mail* reported that "A renowned archaeologist died from exposure to asbestos after working for years at Birmingham University where the lethal material was found." Apparently Lawrence had been exposed to asbestos in his office, and died of mesothelioma.

Polly faced up to the impending upheaval with stoic support and never a word of recrimination at my failure to land the Birmingham lectureship. All I knew of remote New Zealand was contained in my school geography notes – an awful lot of sheep and the best rugby players in the world. I looked at a map of Dunedin, our future home, in *The Times Atlas* and found that there was a motorway leading north out of the city, so I thought, it can't be that provincial. I only found out on arrival that it had two lanes and a cattle grid at both ends. I returned to my desk at the University Press reticent to announce my departure after only a few months in the post, until a senior editor, Anthony Parker, stopped me in the corridor and asked "when are you going to tell us that you are going to New Zealand?" Chastened, I went straight to Dick David's office and informed him. He was magnificent, looking at me with saddened understanding, and wished me well.

There was much to be done. I wrote to Otago accepting the lectureship. Returning correspondence booked the family on the *Rangitane*, departing Tilbury docks on December 10th. Our house was put on the market and I left the Press after the statutory notice to join the ranks of the unemployed. In the event, we couldn't find a buyer for our house, so it was let for just enough to pay the mortgage. Polly and Tom went to stay with her parents, while Augustus Caesar let me stay in his rooms in college. We selected our few items to be shipped to Otago, including our Ford Escort car, an antique desk and a rocking chair. Time ticked away until a cold winter day dawned, and my brother Richard drove us to Tilbury. A cabin on the *Rangitane* awaited us and we had a restless sleep until in the morning, we made steam and progressed down the Thames to an unknown future on the other side of the world.

At last, our first view of Aotearoa, the land of the long white cloud, New Zealand. This is the east coast of the North Island. We soon rounded Cape Palliser to dock at the Pipitea wharf in Wellington.

Five | New Zealand and Introduction to Thailand

I signed a contract with the Cambridge University Press to write a little topic book for schools on the Old Stone Age, so my days on board *Rangitane* were partially filled on my portable typewriter. We reached Curaçao in the Dutch Antilles on Christmas Day before transiting the Panama Canal. Polly had spent time on deck knitting me a jersey. She put it down when we both went to the ship's rail as the Galapagos Islands hove into view, when a capricious wind uplifted it and deposited it in the Pacific Ocean. On New Year's Day we were summoned to the radio room to take a radio telephone call from our respective parents back in snowy Hertfordshire. Our final stop was Tahiti, where we spent an afternoon on the beach. Then it was all ocean until one morning, we sighted Aotearoa, the land of the long white cloud, New Zealand. We docked at the Pipitea Wharf in Wellington. Peter Gathercole had arranged for Professor Jan Pouwer to meet and take us to the airport for our flight south. There we were greeted by Peter Gathercole and his colleague in the Anthropology Department, John Harré, and we were driven to a flat rented on our behalf by the University in Cumberland Street. It was on the first floor of a wooden house and the carpets were dirty. Everything was strange. It was the 14th

Rangitane berthed at Curacao. We spent Christmas day there.

January 1967, mid summer and Dunedin seemed empty of people. We went to bed feeling wretchedly remote from our entire world. The following morning we felt, if possible, even worse. I walked down to the main street looking for a travel agent to find out how much it would cost to fly home. It cost £3 a minute to ring home and we had no telephone.

I went into the Anthropology Department. It was a little brick house and I had a small office on the first floor with no view. Peter Gathercole had graduated from Cambridge and went on to undertake a postgraduate diploma at the Institute of Archaeology under Gordon Childe. He was a dedicated communist who had much annoyed right-wing Grahame Clark by selling the *Daily Worker* outside Peterhouse, the most conservative college in Cambridge. His most recent fieldwork had taken him to remote Pitcairn Island, where he had excavated a prehistoric adze quarry. John Harré was a social anthropologist who had just published a book on race relations in New Zealand entitled Maori and Pakeha. Robert Hamilton (Ham) Parker was appointed as a special assistant. He had no University qualifications, but had been a regular volunteer on Jack Golson's excavations in the North Island. Panchu Gopal Ganguly was an MA from Lucknow, but came to Otago with a failed PhD from the Australian National University. Linden Cowell was the Department technician and Brigitte Hubrich was the secretary. Apart from the house, there was a metal shed-like structure that served as a laboratory.

The flat was so depressing that we looked for a house to rent. We found a student rental property near the University. It was marginally preferable, having an overgrown garden at the back for Tom to play in, but without any insulation and as it turned out, bitterly cold in winter. Peter Gathercole had organised for me to join some students in a survey for archaeological sites about 80 km north of Dunedin in our first February, so we spent a week in a camping ground seeking out

prehistoric Maori rock art. I returned as the new academic year was looming, and was asked to give an introductory course on Palaeolithic Europe, and a second year paper on prehistoric Melanesia. I knew a little about the former, and nothing of the latter. As the term progressed, I set myself two objectives, publishing as many papers as possible from my PhD dissertation and building up a comparative collection of bones from the birds and

During our voyage, Tom helped me type my little school book on the Old Stone Age. A harbinger of a lot more help to come.

mammals most likely to be found in prehistoric New Zealand sites. This included seals, dolphins, moa and lots of other birds. I was also encouraged to apply to the University for funding to undertake my own site survey and excavations and I chose Southland as a possible location.

Peter Gathercole had arrived in Dunedin in 1958 for a half-time post at the Otago Museum, and a half-time lecturer in Anthropology. He spent the next eight years painstakingly persuading and cajoling the Arts Faculty to expand into and create a full Department. By the time that I arrived, he

John Harré and Peter Gathercole met us on our arrival at Momona Airport in Dunedin, and drove us to our flat in Cumberland Street. We were overcome with homesickness.

consistently pushed in Faculty meetings for the creation of the Foundation Chair. By the end of the 1967, a committee was formed to explore this possibility and report back to Faculty. By early 1968, our lives took on a more settled look. We had moved into a lovely house vacated by a colleague on sabbatical leave. I had completed a small excavation on the south coast, and in February James, our second son, was born. In the Department, I came to know a graduate student from the University of Hawaii called Donn Bayard. He had excavated a site in Thailand called Non Nok Tha. In 1966, Ham Parker had joined him there, and they were working on some of their finds.

He returned alone for a second season in January 1968, and having learned of my interest in economic prehistory based in part on faunal remains, he asked if I would be interested in analysing and reporting on the bones from Non Nok Tha. I found out in departmental seminars given by Donn and Ham Parker that this was a site of huge potential. They had found multiple human burials over a lengthy timespan, with a sequence that suggested a transition from an initial Neolithic settlement into burials interred with socketed bronze axes and casting moulds. In 1968, Donn Bayard's supervisor Wilhelm (Bill) Solheim published a paper that reported on the initial radiocarbon dates, with the conclusion that the bronzes dated to the 4th millennium BC (Solheim 1968). This implied that they were far earlier than in China. A socketed axe was nicknamed WOST, the world's oldest socketed tool. The faunal remains when they arrived were right up my street. Domestic cattle bones and pig bones were regularly placed with the dead as mortuary offerings. I published these in an internally produced departmental monograph (Higham 1975).

Donn must have mentioned my analysis to another of Bill Solheim's graduate students, Chester (Chet) Gorman. Both Chet and Donn imbibed from Solheim the mantra that everything in Southeast Asia predated and was more significant in terms of world prehistory than anything in China. Chet's doctoral fieldwork had taken him into the remote forests of Mae Hongson Province in Northeast Thailand where he had excavated a rock shelter called Spirit Cave. He had screened all the cultural deposits and recovered a sample of plant remains. The grape vine was hinting that Douglas Yen had identified some domestic plants and this was taken up by Bill Solheim (1972) when suggesting that Spirit Cave provided evidence for the earliest Neolithic Revolution known. I became involved when a box of Spirit Cave bones arrived for me to analyse. This was quite different from Non Nok Tha, for the bones were small, fragmented, often charred and came from species about which I was unfamiliar. However, in my interpretation, the assemblage came from a forested habitat with access to a stream. There were squirrels, macaques, crab and fish remains. I was, of course, completely ignorant of Southeast Asian prehistory. Bill Solheim was the acknowledged master of the subject, and I was swept along on the wave of excitement that something truly dramatic was emerging from this pioneer fieldwork.

My first excavation in New Zealand took place on the shore of Foveaux Strait, the far south of the country. It was Tom's first dig, and here he is with his trowel.

The Foundation Professor

By the winter of 1968, the committee recommended to the Arts Faculty that the Foundation Chair in Anthropology be approved and advertised. Our department comprised two archaeologists and two social anthropologists, with Peter Gathercole straddling both disciplines. The advertisement was published and everyone felt certain that Peter would be rewarded for all his efforts by being offered it. However, he then put a cat among the pigeons by resigning and booking travel for his family to return to England without a job to go to. I asked him a few years later why he did this, and he answered that he had always resolved not to stay in the same position for more

On arrival, we lived in a slummy little house that was bitterly cold in winter. How we missed Barrington village.

than ten years. His principles dictated that he leave. This meant that the next in seniority in the Department was John Harré. He and I played squash weekly, and in the shower after he told me of his plans for the Department when he was appointed. This would have involved a sharp reduction in the relevance of prehistory. By this juncture I had struck up a friendship with Jack Golson, head of the prehistory department at the Australian National University, who promised me a position there if I felt the need to leave Otago. It never crossed my mind to apply for the chair myself.

During our long voyage to New Zealand, we had befriended Brian and Judy Robinson. Brian was now a lecturer in Chemistry at Otago, and a month or so before the closing date for applications to the chair, he rang encouraging me to apply. I didn't really take his overture seriously. I was 29 years old and it all seemed a bit premature. This was not his first such call. With a week to go he tried yet again, and a penny dropped. The head of his Department was Hugh Parton, Pro Vice Chancellor and chairman of the appointment committee. He also had a known antipathy towards sociology. Was Brian's messaging emanating from Parton? At the last minute, I sent in an application, with a CV that contained all the journal articles based on my dissertation. Then came another coincidence. Grahame and

Molly Clark visited Dunedin, mainly to see their two sons. The Vice Chancellor expressed a wish to see Grahame, and I dutifully took him over to his office door. I have no doubt that Grahame would have extolled my virtues, he was always very ambitious for his young protégés.

It seems that there were only two shortlisted candidates, Harré and me. Perhaps there were no other applicants at all, we were a small remote University and a virtually unknown department. My interview was much more polite than its predecessor at Birmingham but beyond that I cannot recall any details. When I left, the Registrar caught up with me in the corridor and asked if I would be in my office in case Robin Williams, the Vice Chancellor, might wish to ring me. John Harré and I sat in our adjacent offices and my telephone rang first. The Vice Chancellor's voice came down the line. "I would like to offer you the chair in Anthropology, at the minimum professorial salary". I replied "Since you are doubling my salary, I will accept". I was the first professor of prehistoric archaeology in Australasia.

There were quiet celebrations at home that evening, as there was no family to join us. The following morning I went into my office in the Department to a rather unpleasant welcome. Someone had gained entry with a heavy object and smashed my wooden chair to pieces. It lay all over the floor and I had nowhere to sit. The social anthropology coterie in the Department were in quite a state of mutiny, on the assumption that their resolve to disestablish archaeology was matched by mine to downgrade them. This was far from my policy, and throughout my tenure I did all I could to encourage their sub-discipline, culminating when I was to appoint Peter Wilson, of international repute. It was not long, however, before John Harré resigned for a position in Fiji and I found a new squash partner.

My appointment to the newly-created chair meant that my position as a lecturer in prehistory was vacant. I decided that it would be a good idea to give the Department an international interest, and my thoughts turned to Southeast Asia and the claims for remarkably early agriculture and metallurgy. This seemed to suit my interests more than the relatively brief duration of human settlement in New Zealand because even a cursory reading of the available literature suggested a long period of occupation by hunter gatherers followed by my prime interest from Cambridge, a sequence of Neolithic, Bronze and Iron Age leading to the foundation of early states. The University agreed that I should fly to Hawaii to talk to Bill Solheim about his two doctoral students, Bayard and Gorman, and their suitability to join us.

I flew up to Hawaii in late 1968 to be greeted by Bill Solheim with Donn and Daisy, Chet and his current girlfriend Marcia. They gave me a big Aloha and Daisy put a garland of scented tropical flowers round my neck. I stayed in a ramshackle wooden bungalow rented by Chet, the last such home in a row of spanking new

Bill Solheim at Ban Chiang in 1975.

Chet Gorman in his heyday. We were polar opposites in many ways but the closest of friends and confidantes.

condominiums. I met Roger Green there who took me on a field trip to the Makaha Valley, and got to know Chet and Donn. Chet was a very impressive man – tall, robust, with a large ginger beard and a clear lust for life. He was working on his recent excavation finds from Spirit Cave. Donn was tall, slim and more quietly spoken. Bill himself, almost deified by his two graduate students, was also a large man, with bright blue eyes and a carefully manicured moustache. He was clearly dedicated to promoting the cause of Southeast Asia's past.

I asked him about Chet and Donn as potential lecturers in New Zealand, and he spoke more favourably of Donn as being more likely to knuckle down to the teaching commitments he would meet. He suggested that Chet was a bit wild, a bit too keen on illegal stimulants and less likely to fit in. Bill then sounded me on my interest in undertaking fieldwork myself. He told me that he was applying for a very large research grant from the National Science Foundation to undertake site surveys and test excavations in Thailand ahead of the construction of a string of dams on the tributaries of the Mekong. It was exactly such fieldwork that had led to Chet discovering Non Nok Tha when surveying in land threatened with flooding from the Pa Mong Dam. This seemed to me to be a very exciting prospect and I found myself swept up into Bill's research fold.

On my return to Dunedin, my request to offer Donn a lecturership was approved, and he readily accepted. Chet was not overlooked, for I managed to get him the offer of a post-doctoral fellowship on completion of his dissertation. I then thought it diplomatic, despite the flood of American dollars that Bill Solheim had mentioned, to apply for a research grant of my own, and by mid-1969, I had landed $NZ 3500.00 from the University and was looking at airline schedules. Bill wanted me to include in the field team Mei Mei Burke and Terry Marsh, two of his own students. I added to the team my student Angela Calder and Ham Parker. The long vacation in New Zealand fortunately coincides with the dry season for digging in

Air view of my first fieldwork in Roi et Province, Northeast Thailand. A. The salt flat, B. the moated site incorporating the village of Ban Ta Nen, and C. The mound of Don Taphan.

Thailand, so the family and I flew back to England where I left them back at home while I returned for the fieldwork venture. However, just before setting off, Bill Solheim sent me a telegram with bad news, his application to the National Science Foundation had been turned down. I flew from London to Bangkok to meet my team with a tiny budget and no knowledge of Thai, no experience whatever either in dealing with Thai bureaucracy, nor, more importantly, any background in Southeast Asian prehistory.

On the advice of Ham Parker, we all booked into the Royal Hotel, located about a five minute walk from the head office of the Fine Arts Department (FAD), the government department responsible for overseeing archaeology. It was a hotel of moderate comfort but a price tag that made rapid inroads into my budget. I walked across to the FAD office to be greeted by Khun Noom, the Deputy Director General. Bill Solheim had identified the Lam Dom Noi river valley for my site survey, where the Sirindhorn Dam was being planned. Further bad news landed on my lap. Noom informed me that this was a "sensitive area" and that fieldwork was impossible. The trouble was that the area destined for flooding was a mere 10 km from the Lao border. This was the height of the Vietnam War, and communist insurgents were a nuisance, particularly targeting a massive American airbase at nearby Ubon. I returned to the hotel downhearted and perplexed as to my next move to find Ham Parker relaxing in a comfortable seat by the pool.

A day or two later, Victor Kennedy, an acquaintance of his, passed by and they fell into conversation. Victor had travelled all over the Khorat Plateau by ox cart, and hearing of our impasse, recommended Roi Et Province, where he had come across several mounds that might be of interest. I went over again to see Noom and sought permission to go there and find out. He told me he would cable the Provincial Governor for approval.

In the meantime, funds were dwindling and I had nothing to do. However, during my analysis of the Non Nok Tha cattle bones, I became aware that it was vital to be able to distinguish cattle from water buffalo. This was precisely why I had sought a large comparative sample of modern bones in Denmark. So I found my way by bus to the Bangkok Municipal Abattoir and secured an entrée to sample the distal leg bones. All day in the bowels of a slaughterhouse was not the most salubrious way of spending time in the extreme heat of Bangkok. Each day I took the feet to Chulalongkorn University Veterinary Department where a kind lady allowed my to boil them up and remove the hooves, flesh and tendons, and then I returned to the hotel, laid them on my sunny balcony and let them dry. After that, I jumped into the hotel pool.

As the December days ticked by, I went over to the FAD in the hope that there was a positive reply from Roi Et. On at least half a dozen occasions I was told, no. In despair I called on Chin You-Di in the National Museum for advice. He was the leading archaeologist of the day in Thailand, but could do nothing to help. As Christmas approached, I went yet again to the FAD and this time, demanded of the clerk at the front desk to look at my file. Surprisingly he passed it over to me and I riffled through it. Right at the bottom of the papers there was a telegram. "What does this say?" I asked. His translation revealed that it came from the Governor of Roi Et Province enthusiastically welcoming me. It had lain there for a fortnight.

This square at Don Taphan was my first excavation in Thailand. The labels are taken directly from Sheppard Frere's practice at Verulamium.

Our excavation at Non Nong Chik was not extensive, but it did yield my first prehistoric burial. Here Angela Calder, my student, looks on.

During the 1965 site surveys, Bill Solheim had come into possession of an Austin Gypsy. This was a poor man's landrover, and he had made it available. It was a frightful contraption, but better than nothing. I assembled my team and we set off for Khon Kaen, where Terry Marsh's girlfriend rented a house. The following day I had a lonely boiled egg and toast for Christmas lunch and missed the family more than ever. Then we drove down to Roi Et and the Governor's Office. Khun Prachak Vatchapan welcomed me with open arms. In Thailand status is measured by one's retinue, and he ordered a motorcade to take us to his chosen location for us to begin our research. I sat with him in the honoured seat at the head of the line of vehicles with Terry Marsh driving the old Austin well back. His chosen destination was a village called Ban Ta Nen, where an Angkor-period brick temple dominated the top of a distinct mound, that lay next to what looked like a dried-out lake bed surrounded by mounds where villagers were making salt. We alighted and immediately found the surface liberally covered with what looked to me like prehistoric potsherds. The Governor then took us to a nearby village and arranged for an empty house to be made available to us, along with two village women to shop, cook and wash for us. It was New Year's day 1970. I had bought a pair of stout leather boots to wear in case I encountered a venomous snake. Within an hour of our moving into our house, someone stole them. I reassured myself that encountering snakes was unlikely, but the following morning, as I walked along the edge of the low-lying wetland I came face to face with two.

I set Ham Parker and Angela up to open a test square on one of the mounds on the western side of that low-lying wetland. During the dry season, the villagers scrape up the briny soil and transport it to the edge of the wetland. They put it into a wooden trough and percolate water through it. The brine that emerges from a hole in the base is put into an aluminium tray and boiled until pure salt is left. This leads to a rapid accumulation of soil round the wetland. Our test square proceeded down through many layers in which prehistoric ceramics were used to boil the brine. It finally reached a depth of about four metres. There was abundant charcoal, which we later were able to radiocarbon date back into the Iron Age. Meanwhile I excavated a similar sequence east of the village with the same results. We later moved to the village of Ban Ta Nen itself and opened there a second test square, our budget could not possibly stretch to a larger excavation. Here we found evidence for prehistoric occupation again dating back into the Iron Age with the later layers representing historic settlement corresponding to the state of Angkor. I can be excused, given my complete unfamiliarity with Southeast Asia, for not realising that Ban Ta Nen was one of five separate villages within the moats and banks of a massive Iron Age town, one that must have prospered on its exploitation of the salt flats nearby.

The Governor showed continuing interest in our work, and unscheduled visits from him and his entire entourage came thick and fast. On one occasion he invited our team to a competition involving target practice with the guns he brought. I had never fired a gun in my life, so deferred our effort to Ham Parker, since I was well aware that he had fought in North Africa during the Second World War. He faced up against the Governor's top bodyguard, and I winced when our man's shot went wildly astray, thankfully without injuring anyone. This was my first hint that Ham's eyesight was deficient, to be reinforced soon after when I asked him to drive the Austin Gypsy back to base to collect some equipment needed, only to see him drive straight into a tree. This naturally had an impact on his interpretation of stratigraphy.

Towards the end of January, I judged that we had completed our commitment to Roi Et and sent word to Khun Prachak to that effect. He immediately arranged a farewell party. A team was sent down to our village to arrange for tables and chairs. Food was ordered, and copious quantities of the local whisky. Floodlights illuminated a hastily constructed dance floor and when proceedings got underway, every village in the district sent a troupe of dancers and singers, along with the haunting music, to entertain us. Dawn began to streak the eastern horizon before the party dispersed.

In those days, the tight restrictions imposed on foreign archaeologists by the FAD either did not exist or were ignored. I simply decided that it would be a good idea to move from Roi Et to the area centred on Non Nok Tha, so I sent my team ahead to find somewhere to stay, and cleared up the final odds and ends before embarking on Terry Marsh's little motor bike, not much different from my NSU Quickly, for the new area. We found a suitable house to rent in the town of Phu Wiang, and after studying a map, I decided to begin with a site survey within the Phu Wiang monadnock, an extensive geological feature resembling the interior of a large extinct volcano. The skies were full of American jets routinely flying off to bomb Laos and Vietnam. Many would break the sound barrier and the resultant bang would echo round and round the hill ringing our study area.

Non Nok Tha was located on its northeastern exterior flank. We found several low mounds, and I chose one for test squares, known as Non Nong Chik. Unfortunately, the Austin Gypsy ran over a hidden tree stump during this survey and it severed the hydraulic lead governing the gears, so we stumbled back in first gear and thereafter walked a long way into the site and back. Once again I laid out two little test squares near each other on the mound, and left Ham Parker and Angela in one while I worked in the other. I also hired two local villagers to assist, only to find that one of them, seemingly a very decent chap, had recently been released from jail following the end of his sentence for murder. Both squares matched part of the Non Nok Tha sequence, and I experienced my first prehistoric grave. First hints came with the rims of two large and complete pottery vessels, and then dramatically, the human skeleton.

Over dinner one evening back in Phu Wiang, and perhaps lubricated by Ham Parker's intake of whisky, I was taken aback when he launched into a tirade against me for as he put it, "Removing three layers as if they were one". I have always excavated in the square myself, whereas he would sit at the edge of his square chain smoking and watching. I found this criticism absurd and replied that so far in my square, I had only removed the top layer of ploughed soil. Always certain of his own rectitude, he maintained his attack on my competence, and the conversation became somewhat heated. I learned two important lessons from this. The first is, always strive for harmony during an excavation season for as long as it lasts, there is nowhere to hide after a fracas. The second reflected Ham Parker's vivid imagination. At Non Nok Tha in 1966, he had persuaded the inexperienced Donn Bayard that a site little over a metre deep involved about 22 layers and that there were mounds raised over some of the graves. No such mounds have ever been encountered elsewhere in Southeast Asia and I am quite sure that there were none at Non Nok Tha either.

The tiny grant from the University of Otago was now running dry and after

I found a stone grave marker, and then the rim of a large pot. This was my first human burial, and well over 1,000 followed over the years.

we reached the natural substrate at Non Nong Chik, I returned rather relieved to Bangkok to meet Polly, Tom and James at the airport for our flight home to Dunedin. A lesson drummed into me at the Institute of Archaeology was the importance of publishing excavation results. Failure to do so made one little different from a casual looter, I was told. I was able to arrange for our finds to be shipped over in crates and began pondering what I had found and how best to publish my results. One of my graduate students, Rosemary Buchan, analysed the finds from Non Nong Chik and I worked on and finally published a report on the Roi Et sites in 1977 (Higham 1977). This season of fieldwork did not ignite any great interest and no controversy. No claims were made for the earliest of this or that. It set down the main ceramic sequence for the lower Mun Valley during the Iron Age and added a mite to our knowledge of the Bronze Age in the vicinity of Non Nok Tha. For me, it had excited my interest in Southeast Asia. I felt more at home there than on the shore of the Foveaux Strait in New Zealand. But I did not have access to the research resources necessary for further endeavours on my own, and Bill Solheim's relationship with the National Science Foundation was quiescent.

Chet and I spent a lot of time at Ban Chiang trying to make sense of
the disturbed stratigraphic sequence.

Six | With Gorman in Northern Thailand and Ban Chiang

Following Chet Gorman's second season at Spirit Cave in 1971, he came to Otago for a few months as a Postdoctoral Fellow. He had identified further cave sites in the remote forests of Mae Hongson Province, Northern Thailand, and his small test excavations at one of these, Banyan Valley Cave (BVC), had yielded some carbonised rice grains in a cultural context best described as the Hoabinhian. Named after the Vietnamese province of the same name, the Hoabinhian was the classic hunter-gatherer culture of mainland Southeast Asia. To find rice grains at Banyan Valley lent support to the claims of Bill Solheim that here was evidence for a remarkably early Neolithic revolution in the forested hills of northern Thailand. Chet was applying to the NSF for a big grant to pursue this possibility, and he invited me to join him, tasked with assembling a collection of modern bone samples and exploring thereby the Hoabinhian subsistence base.

We walked all day through a forested Shangri-la, until at dusk we saw the overhang of Banyan Valley cave beyond a field of opium poppies.

The good news came through that his application had been successful, and in December 1972, having again taken Polly and by now two sons and a daughter back to England, I flew back to Bangkok, thence to Chiang Mai and finally over the hills to Mae Hongson. There, I was met by Terry Marsh and after a night in Chet's base, we took his landrover over jungle trails to a hill tribe village occupied by a community of Lahu, left it there and then hiked to BVC.

Briefly in the afternoon a shaft of sunlight illuminated us at Banyan Valley Cave. I am excavating in one of our baulks. Soon we would hear mule bells coming to transport out all our finds.

The landscape was almost like Shangri La. The forest was alive with the chatter of macaques, the streams were so clear one could drink from them, the vistas towards Burma seemed endless. It was dusk as we approached the cave complex. It was located next to a rushing mountain stream that disappeared into a limestone sinkhole. Chet welcomed us. There was a raised bamboo platform where we slept, and a roaring fire as the sun set and a mountain chill set in. We ascended some cut steps to the cave being excavated, where half a dozen neat squares had been laid out. Screens were in place, and a generator hummed to provide light, because the sun barely penetrated into the front of the cavern. In addition to Chet, Terry and me, we were accompanied by a handful of Lahu, one of whom, San Wi, was engaged as my hunter to assist in assembling my comparative bone collection.

I spent each day digging. The cultural deposit was not deep, and was rich in the stone tools of the Hoabinhian tradition, along with hearths and living surfaces. In the upper layers, we encountered potsherds decorated with cord impressions, and of great promise, the fine mesh screens retained carbonised rice grains. At Spirit Cave, similar ceramics were found in the upper levels, from which Chet had obtained radiocarbon dates of about 6000 BC. I think we were increasingly exhilarated by the prospect that we were on a new and exciting archaeological frontier. We collected charcoal for radiocarbon dating, confident that this would be confirmed. Might our research break new ground in chasing down the origins of rice domestication, a quest described by Kent Flannery as the $64,000 question of Southeast Asian prehistory?

We were cut off from the rest of the world. Only Chet's short-wave radio brought us outside news. We heard that the North Vietnamese had now in place a ground-to-air missile system and were downing American B52 bombers over Hanoi. Chet celebrated each report by balancing bottles in front of our sleeping platform and using them as target practice. At the end of digging for the day, Chet

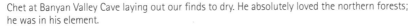

Chet at Banyan Valley Cave laying out our finds to dry. He absolutely loved the northern forests; he was in his element.

Our base at Banyan Valley. We slept on a raised platform, and cooked in front of it. Seated left to right, Terry Marsh and me. Chet stands in front of us, beside San Wi our hunter.

and I bathed in the rushing stream's icy water. One day, he noticed a raised lump on my back, and said that I should have it looked at. I did, and it was nothing of note. But this was a premonition of a much more sinister lump that Chet would one day have on his back.

We then had dinner that was often augmented by what San Wi had managed to shoot. One evening as we ate, he calmly took out his rifle and shot into the tree canopy. About ten minutes later a civet came crashing down through the foliage at our feet. It had taken that time to die, but he knew he had hit it. He would affix a powerful torch onto his head and go out hunting by night, often returning with a deer. Once he returned early, looking ashen. He explained how he had heard a rustling ahead of him, turned on his torch looking up at the stars and lowered his head to blind the animal while readying his rifle only to sight a tiger. We usually heard wild elephants trumpeting away by night. Just before Christmas, a couple of Lahu turned up and told us that they had shot an animal and would I be interested. I accompanied them to the base of a limestone bluff where there lay a black animal looking rather like a large goat. It was a goral, a Himalayan goat antelope. We cut it up, took it back to camp to be skeletonised, and enjoyed a goral fillet steak for Christmas lunch.

As January came to a close, so did the excavation. We reached bedrock and began packing all our precious finds. Early one morning before the mist had cleared, I heard the sound of bells, and soon we were joined by Lahu men leading their mules. We packed everything onto their sturdy backs, and began the long walk back to the waiting landrover. It grew hotter and hotter and I quenched my thirst with a wild pomelo. That night we slept in the Lahu village, and the following day retraced our way along the trails back to Chet's house in Mae Hongson. There was a telegram awaiting Chet that was to change his life and mine. It came from Froelich Rainey, the director of the University Museum in Philadelphia, inviting Chet to an urgent meeting in Bangkok. I stayed in Mae Hongson sorting our finds, while Chet flew down to see Rainey.

He returned with major news. Rainey had been persuaded that the site of Ban Chiang in the far northeast of the Khorat Plateau was of the greatest world significance. This is what had happened. For years, the inhabitants of this remote little village had turned up pottery vessels with painted designs when digging foundations or wells. The son of the American ambassador, Stephen Young, had spent some time there on an unrelated research endeavour when he tripped and found himself looking at the rims of some of these pots. They found their way to the FAD, and excavations ensued. Human burials were found, in association with pots and bronzes. Some of these pots were dated by the thermoluminescence technique and incredibly early dates back in the 5th millennium BC resulted. Elizabeth Lyons, attached as a cultural consultant to the Ford Foundation in Bangkok heard of this and informed the Penn Museum. Hard on the heels of Bill Solheim's claims for the earliest bronze in the world, this seemed an opportunity not to be missed for an ambitious museum director. He looked for an American to take charge of a new excavation programme and his eyes alighted on Chet Gorman.

Chet returned to describe his meeting. He had been offered an academic position at the Penn Museum and funding to excavate Ban Chiang. What should he do? We were now very close friends and we thought through all the ramifications. On the positive side, here was a faculty offer in one of the world's top universities, and built-in funds for extended fieldwork in a site of world potential. It seemed a no brainer. But on the negative side, Chet was a Californian with an inbuilt dislike for East Coast Ivy League elites. He was totally committed to his current interest in the Hoabinhian. He loved the hills of northern Thailand and its people. He simply didn't want to move to Penn. I cannot recall the details of our conversations but do retain a hazy memory that he met my eyes and said "Charles, if you join me at Ban Chiang, I will do it." Whether apocryphal or not, we agreed that we would work there together and he replied positively to Rainey. Steps were then taken to seek the permits from the FAD, and their leading archaeologist, Pisit Charoenwongsa, was appointed co-director. Chet than asked the Ford Foundation for the funds to

Amphan Kijngam joined us at Ban Chiang and worked with me on the faunal remains. He has been a wonderful friend and extra member of our family ever since.

turn this initiative into a training programme for young Thai archaeologists. The Foundation readily agreed and I was one of three specialists to be supported in the field. The others were Mike Pietrusewsky to teach human anatomy and Garry Carriveau to cover metallurgy.

Chet and I realised that dating the sequence at Banyan Valley was our immediate priority. He returned to America with charcoal for radiocarbon dating, and I flew back to England with potsherds to be dated by thermoluminescence. I contacted Martin Aitken, last seen by me at Verulamium 15 years previously when I helped with his proton magnetometer. Now a leading scientist at the Oxford University Research Laboratory for Archaeology and the History of Art, his laboratory was a leading centre for the thermoluminescence dating of prehistoric pottery. He agreed to date our samples from Banyan Valley Cave. I predicted a result in the general vicinity of 8000 years ago, to conform to the dates advanced by Chet from Spirit Cave. When Martin's results came to me by letter, I was stunned. They dated the potsherds to about AD 900. I sent on this information to Chet with a heavy heart knowing how disappointed he would be. Our letters crossed. Chet's letter to me gave the results of the radiocarbon dates from the layers containing the ceramics. They matched mine. Meanwhile, the precious rice grains had been sent to Douglas Yen, the leading palaeobotanist of the region. He reported back a third item of dispiriting news, that they came from a wild variety. A batsqueak of doubt about Bill Solheim's earlier Neolithic Revolution sounded.

The modern comparative faunal remains and the prehistoric sample from BVC in due course arrived in Dunedin and I found them to represent hunting and foraging in a forested habitat. But by now my mind was centred on the upcoming major research endeavour at Ban Chiang. If the evidence for that early Neolithic revolution in the remote hills of northern Thailand was evaporating, surely this would not be repeated for the early bronzes at Non Nok Tha. After all this region is

At Ban Chiang in June 1974. I spent a lot of time down in the square, excavating the human burials.

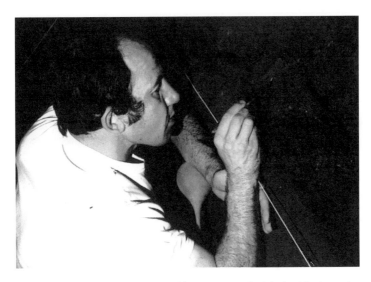

I uncovered a human skull, and on working my way to the left shoulder, began to uncover a socketed bronze axe, the only one found during our 1974-5 seasons at Ban Chiang.

A Thai excavation in 1973 at Ban Chiang had opened an area within a narrow unlooted village lane. In 1975, we extended this under a thatched roof.

so rich in the deposits of copper and tin ore, and why should I doubt Bill Solheim, the acknowledged master of Southeast Asian prehistory?

Chet planned a long excavation season that did not fit with my administrative and teaching commitments, but I was able to join the excavations for a month during the University vacation in 1974. When I arrived, I found that Chet had laid our his excavation in the back yard of a family house, where the owner had assured him that no looting had taken place. The problem he faced was that Ban Chiang was being systematically looted by the villagers, to dig out pots, ornaments and bronzes for sale. There was a ready market. The Udorn airbase was not half an hour's drive away, and busloads of off-duty American military personnel were regular visitors. Even as I walked daily to the excavation from our rented house I would be secretively invited into looters' homes to view what was on offer.

My principal role was to excavate, assemble and analyse the faunal remains. Chet had found a willing young Thai student called Amphan Kijngam to work with me. He had a very sharp eye, and soon became quite an expert in identifying bones to their anatomical name and species. The prehistoric inhabitants of Ban Chiang regularly placed animal remains in graves. Sometimes it might be a single pig or cow bone, but occasionally we came across a complete dog skeleton. Many animal bones also turned up in the occupation layers. Amphan and I would therefore be down in the square revealing burials, and when animal bones were involved, we would go to our lab to sort, identify and prepare them for shipment to New Zealand. My time in 1974 coincided with the Iron and Bronze Age layers. It was my first real experience of excavating human graves.

Early in my time there, I explored a superb painted pottery vessel. As we progressed down into earlier contexts, I found myself revealing a human skull. I worked down towards the left shoulder and my probing encountered a tinge of green. As I went further, it gradually formed into a socketed bronze axe, the only one found in two seasons of excavations there, for bronzes were very rare indeed as mortuary offerings. Amphan worked with me as we continued to open this grave, and as we made our way down the left arm, we found bronze bracelets. We really felt we were working on a new and exciting frontier of knowledge. This male burial we nicknamed Vulcan. Another located nearby became Nimrod, because of the evidence from his mortuary offerings that he was a hunter.

The Ford Foundation supported the excavations as a training programme, and there were regular evening lectures to the Thai students. They absorbed Chet's excavation technique. Within each defined layer, we excavated down in 10 cm spits. We scraped clean each newly revealed surface, and recorded on graph paper, each feature. These could be a grave cut, pit, pothole, or indeed any definable entity. Each was given an individual number. Every artefact was assigned a catalogue number and recorded as to its provenance. We had a site notebook and this could be added to by any one of the excavators.

As we dug down deeper, so a problem surfaced. The site had suffered severely not only from disturbance during the prehistoric period, but also from bioturbation. It was riddled with hard round balls of soil, the nests of some sort of land crab. We often went down into the square to try and nut out the cultural sequence. Naturally, we were also very keen to date this site properly, and this involved collecting charcoal. Here we faced another problem. There were very few concentrations of charcoal in an undisturbed context, such as a hearth or clay furnace. The majority of the samples we collected were fragments collected from the fill of graves until there was sufficient for a radiocarbon date to be determined.

I left for home very satisfied with my time there. I had assembled a fine collection of faunal material, and begun a learning curve on excavating prehistoric sites like Ban Chiang. It was also a very enjoyable team to be with socially. Chet rented a comfortable house near the excavation site. His girlfriend Debbie Paul Kramer and Mike Pietrusewsky shared it with us. About ten Thai students had their own house nearby and Pisit Charoenwongsa and his family likewise. Chet had a thatched roof over the excavation. We were excavating during the rainy season, and the downpours would have made digging virtually impossible without protection. When it wasn't raining, we were protected from the sun, with its propensity to dry out subtle differences in cultural deposits and render them a uniform grey. All excavated cultural material was screened to extract the small artefacts that missed identification in the square. Water flotation for plant remains we did not do, applying this technique was for the future. I looked forward to the second season there.

I returned to Ban Chiang in May 1975. In 1972, Thai archaeologist Nikhom Suthiragsa had excavated a small area within a village lane. This was the only undisturbed place he was able to track down. He had left every skeleton in situ, and they presented a stratified charnel house when I arrived and looked down into his square. Chet and I climbed down into it, and managed to reach right down to bedrock as we gingerly clambered over the skeletons. Right down on the natural substrate, we came across a person wearing bronze bangles. We had every reason to be confident that bronze was here very early in the site's cultural sequence. Chet had decided to excavate right next door. This gave us a very narrow area in which to operate, divided lengthwise into three squares each measuring 4 by 3.5 m and one of 3 by 2 m. The nearby houses and thatched roof necessitated electric lighting. I was very happy to have Amphan with me again as well as several other keen young Thai students one of whom, Rachanie Thosarat, I noted immediately as having an inborn aptitude for the delicate side of excavating.

News of this most surprising and exciting early Bronze Age in Northeast Thailand had spread along the scientific community grapevine. We were visited by Bill Solheim to see what we were up to, and by Theodore Wertime and Rip Rapp. They were there to see us expose what looked like a bronze casting facility, comprising large lumps of fired clay that were probably a casting hearth, ringed by green copper stains and one or two fragments of crucible. There were also some hearths but once again, the majority of our charcoal for dating was accumulated

Rachanie Thosarat joined us at Ban Chiang in 1975 and I recognised at once her excavation skill. We have worked together ever since.

Chet Gorman with Pisit Charoenwongsa on his left led the excavations at Ban Chiang.
I am on the left. We were visiting another site that had been badly looted.

as fragments from grave fill. Amphan and I excavated a complete dog skeleton overlying the bones of an Iron Age child. We found burials of this period with glass beads and curious circular clay rollers pierced with a hole down the long axis and excised on the exterior to form patterns. As we progressed down, we found that bronzes were hardly ever employed as mortuary offerings.

After a day's digging, I teamed up with Rachanie to play badminton against Pisit and Amphan. I then returned to our house to join Chet, Debbie and Jean Kennedy for a drink before dinner. Chet had a superb powerful sound system, and it was there that I got to know of Cat Stephens, Carole King and Gordon Lightfoot. One evening, Garry Carriveau arrived to join the research team. He sat down and said to Chet that he felt stressed and had he any grass. Chet reached for a jar containing some herbaceous-looking stuff and rolled it into a cigarette paper. He called it Sakhon Nakhon crippler. It was then passed round and when it came to my turn, I took a puff and it went on its way. Two or three rounds later, I began to feel very odd indeed, the room began to circle like a windmill round my head and I had the worst night's sleep ever as I entered a sort of kaleidoscope world. Chet more than once disappeared for a long weekend's rest and recreation in Vientiane, returning somewhat frayed, and laden with French cheeses and wine. On another evening he took us all into Udorn to the Wolverine Club, one of many strip joints that had sprung up to attract the United States troops stationed nearby in the airbase. I had never before or since experienced a lifestyle like that. I spoke to several American pilots when they came out to Ban Chiang. One told me that he could start a morning cup of coffee and then fly over Laos, deliver his bombs and finish his coffee on his return while it was still hot. I suspect that several of his fellow pilots did not return at all.

During my time at Ban Chiang I exchanged letters with Victoria Giddens, one of my graduate students now a Professor of Anthropology at Canterbury University. I flew back to New Zealand on a flight already delayed, to arrive in the late evening at Christchurch airport. The heavens had opened: there was a heavy downpour with no connecting flight home and nowhere to stay. What a surprise and relief it was to find her waiting for me in the arrivals hall. She drove me to her home where I met her hospitable parents. She took me to her room and introduced me there to Leonard Cohen and Suzanne as we chatted into the small hours before a deep sleep took over. After her father awoke me with a welcome cup of tea in the morning, I winged my way down to Dunedin and a marvelous reunion with the family. It had been a remarkable experience at Ban Chiang and to this day, the music of Carole King and Leonard Cohen transport me back.

All animal bones followed by sea. It was so easy in those days to get permission to export our finds for analysis. The Ford Foundation provided funding for some of our Thai students to proceed to the University of Pennsylvania to study the Ban Chiang finds for graduate degrees. Amphan was funded to undertake research for his Master's degree with me. This coincided with a sabbatical leave. After my return home I arranged for Amphan to collect the skulls of about 20 village dogs, because I could see a need to be sure that the prehistoric canids were themselves domestic dogs and not from other candidates, the golden jackal or the cuon. When he reached New Zealand, he and I sorted the bones into those we could readily identify to species, such as cattle, pigs and deer. The more difficult specimens were almost entirely the bones from small species, and these we parcelled up to take to England, our sabbatical base.

We returned to our home in Barrington and Amphan and I regularly took the train down to London, where we spent days in the British Museum of Natural History. There we had access to a superb comparative collection of bones from Southeast Asia. There was one vast room with the articulating skeletons of elephants and rhinos. Another had drawers containing labelled boxes of the skeletons from the entire range of civets, squirrels, hares and even the little slow loris. Then there were the bones of the Chinese wolf, the cuon and jackal. We had numerous carapace and plastron fragments, and fish bones, that we took to the resident specialists for their input. Bit by bit, we were able to make the precise identifications that are so vital to track down the environment in which the prehistoric people of Ban Chiang lived, and how it changed over time. Amphan's Master's Thesis remains the most comprehensive such analysis there has ever been for a site like Ban Chiang. We looked forward to publishing it in full in the report series on this site that Chet was already planning.

I kept up to date with Chet via airmail letters. He told me that after I had left Ban Chiang, in the earliest layer, he had found a flexed male skeleton associated with a socketed bronze spearhead. It seemed that our expectations were on the brink of being confirmed. Then, in 1976, came a bombshell paper. *Expedition* is the in-house journal of the Penn Museum. Chet and Pisit that year published "Ban Chiang: A mosaic of impressions from the first two years" (Gorman and Charoenwongsa 1976). They reported 18 radiocarbon determinations from the basal levels of the 1974 season dating back to 3600 BC, that attested to "the presence of bronze metallurgy during the initial Phase 1/Phase 2 occupation of the mound". They went on to anticipate finding evidence for bronze metallurgy well back in the fourth millennium BC, perhaps in the uplands abutting the Khorat Plateau. They then revealed further radiocarbon dates that placed the initial presence of bimetallic iron and bronze spearheads between 1600-1200 BC, centuries before such bimetallic artefacts appeared in the late contexts of the Chinese Shang Dynasty. These were seismic claims. It meant that both bronze and iron metallurgy, two of the most significant technical innovations of the human story, began in Northeast Thailand. This we felt was not totally surprising given the abundance of copper, tin and iron ores. Moreover, the presence of rice chaff as a ceramic temper in the earliest layers suggested a very early onset of rice farming.

In 1978, I arranged to pay a visit to Philadelphia to stay with Chet and find out how his laboratory analyses were progressing. He told me that he was in negotiations with the Smithsonian Institution to mount a travelling exhibition of the finds from our excavations, to spread the word of the world importance of these discoveries. I looked at some of our artefacts now that they were cleaned and stored. There were quite a few cattle figurines that I thought relevant to Amphan and my research and I suggested that I might do the analysis of these for publication, but Chet demurred. During my visit I gave lectures at Harvard, Yale and Temple universities on the new discoveries at Ban Chiang and Non Nok Tha.

The road to Ban Na Di, a gem of a site.

Seven | Ban Na Di and its Aftermath

Amphan completed his MA with distinction, and on his return to Thailand in 1980, was offered a government position in the Fine Arts Department. By a stroke of remarkable good fortune, he was posted to the regional office in Khon Kaen, which was responsible for all matters archaeological in the northern provinces of the Khorat Plateau, including Ban Chiang. He wrote to me seeking my advice. He had inbuilt government funding for fieldwork of his choice. Where did I recommend that he start? I pored over a map, with the aim of finding an area near Ban Chiang where we might be able to identify similar sites, and then choose one to excavate. My eyes alighted on Lake Kumphawapi, about 25 km south of Ban Chiang that was surrounded by flat low terrace land crossed by a myriad of streams that emptied into the lake. I suggested that this would be an ideal area to examine and Amphan agreed. He assembled a team of four Silpakon University students, and in January 1980, I flew over to Thailand and joined him in our rented house in Kumphawapi township. It was so easy for me, we had an FAD landrover and driver, an enthusiastic team and as part of a government initiative, no red tape or paper work. I simply turned up and began work.

We criss-crossed our chosen area, stopping at each village to question the villagers. Had they ever found human graves when they dug their wells or house foundations? How about old pottery vessels or stone axes? I had learnt in Greece under similar circumstances with Eric Higgs that the local people know their area best. We found many sites, and when we identified one we combed the surface for prehistoric artefacts, nearly all of which were broken potsherds. As we drove through the countryside, we also looked out for raised mounds that might be promising. I found one village, Ban Na Di, of particular interest based on what the headman told us, and earmarked it for a future test square. Then we moved south to Mahasarakham Province, and a second potential area, flanking the Chi River. Here we repeated our systematic survey method. There were, again, many sites, but one of these stood out. Ban Chiang Hian is a very large site surrounded by banks, moats, a dam and a reservoir. The surface was littered with prehistoric sherds, and this site too was earmarked for future investigation.

I returned to New Zealand brimming with anticipation that Amphan and I now had the key to confirming the Ban Chiang chronology and assessing its implications in more detail. Amphan returned to Ban Na Di and put in a 2

My 14-year-old son Tom joined us at Ban Na Di. He was great company and a real contributor.
He took the lid off one of the mortuary jars and uncovered the skeleton of an infant associated
with an iron knife and blue glass beads.

by 2 metre test square to see what lay below, and reported to me that he had
encountered some prehistoric human burials. This was a portent for the future. We
decided on this village and so on November 22nd 1980 I returned to excavate. The
same team that had worked on the site survey returned. Warrachai Wiriyaromp,
Metha Wichakana and Suphot Phommanoch went on to have distinguished
professional careers, and each of them was charged with the daily supervision and
recording of their assigned excavation square. We hired a house in nearby Nong
Han, and drove daily to the village, where we had laid out an area of 77 m2 near
the centre of the mound.

During one of my trips back to Cambridge, Eric Higgs had shown me his mark
1 flotation machine. Resembling a large dustbin, water was pumped into the base
to fill the container and as frothy bubbles rose to the surface, so they adhered to the
plant and other light organic remains from the excavation. They were then trapped
in a mesh sieve for detailed analysis. I decided to apply this for the first time in
Southeast Asia, so took with me from New Zealand an appropriate pump powered
by petrol, for the village had no electricity supply.

On arrival, we assembled all the necessary components from local sources and
activated the pump on a trial run. It wouldn't start. My Thai team disarticulated the
pump with every indication of expertise in such matters until it lay in several pieces
on the ground. When they turned to reassemble it, they hit a brick wall. There was

Unlike Ban Chiang, the stratigraphy at Ban Na Di was crystal clear. Here, a row of Bronze Age graves has been cut through a light coloured lens of sand laid down by floodwater.

The dead were interred with articulating limbs of bovids, here a bronze bangle, and remarkable animal figurines: cattle, deer and elephant, even humans as well.

Below: Marble bangles must have been highly valued. This one was repaired three times with bronze wire-like ties.

no way I could reveal any irritation, one never dares to cause a loss of face in Thailand, so I cheerfully thanked them for their efforts, and turned to plan B, to sieve a sample of cultural material manually and look for the organics that were trapped. We recovered a good sample of carbonised rice grains. I also welcomed my New Zealand colleague Brian Vincent, who was fast becoming an expert on ceramics for his doctoral dissertation and Tom, my 14-year-old son.

Ban Na Di was a little gem of a site. After a fortnight digging down through historic material, we struck a soil change heralding a new layer. There is nothing quite like finding what you are seeking, and in my case it was a combination of occupation deposits and human burials. In one of our squares, we found ourselves uncovering the lids that covered large jars, each containing the skeleton of an infant, interred with glass beads and iron knives. Similar clay rollers to those we had found at Ban Chiang also turned up, allowing a layer correlation between the sites. As we progressed downward, there was further excitement as we traced rows of Bronze Age graves. The dead were interred with complete pottery vessels, and the articulating limb bones of domestic cattle. On the 14th January the dig was going so well that we decided to open another area about 30 m metres away. Here we were soon into another set of Bronze Age graves that transitioned into into burials containing the earliest iron. Those buried in this part of the site were wealthier, in terms of grave goods. We found more bronze bangles and shell beads. Exotic marble and slate bangles were worn, and one of these, when broken, had been repaired by boring holes into both sides of the break and inserting bronze wire-like ties. One infant was interred under a crocodile skin shroud, an adjacent woman, perhaps the mother, wore a large pendant carved from a crocodile skull. We also teased away the grave fill to reveal superb clay figurines of cattle, deer, elephants and humans.

On the same January day that we opened the new square, Dell King arrived to make a documentary film of our excavation. This was timely, for she could film not only the burials, but also concentrations of fired clay that turned out to be the hearths used to bring copper and tin to melting point prior to casting. They were surrounded by bronze casting spillage, some complete and many broken crucibles and the moulds that had been used to cast axes and bangles. Naturally, these hearths also contained charcoal, which we retained for radiocarbon dating. As these important finds were being revealed, we were visited on the 24th January by Joyce White. She was based in Ban Chiang where she was undertaking her doctoral fieldwork. Tom, Brian and I had also enjoyed her company for Christmas, when she had served up a sumptuous roast duck. Joyce was a most welcome visitor, she told me how she was studying the soils of the region and their suitability for rice cultivation. She was accompanied by Lung Lee, a village savant who placed at her disposal his many years of accumulated wisdom on the environment. I invited her to include the terrain round Ban Na Di as part of her study.

She passed by the site again on the 14th February, but this time, she brought the worst possible news. I was appalled when she told me that Chet had been diagnosed with a melanoma so advanced that the cancer was terminal. I found this ghastly news almost impossible to believe. I wound down the excavation with a heavy heart

We uncovered the clay furnaces used to bring copper to melting point before casting. The charcoal was an excellent source for radiocarbon dates.

We found sandstone moulds for casting axes and arrowheads, and clay moulds for the lost-wax casting of bangles.

Below: Joyce White was working on her doctoral fieldwork while we excavated at Ban Na Di. Lung Lee, a Ban Chiang *savant*, shared his unrivalled knowledge of the environment with her.

and much foreboding, and left for home on the 22nd February. Amphan packed up all our finds, and they were shipped to Dunedin for analysis. I took the precious charcoal samples for dating with me and sent them to the laboratory in Wellington. The cultural sequence we identified was not as long as at Ban Chiang and the pottery vessels were in the main, quite different. But there were sufficient precise parallels to be quite sure that our radiocarbon dates would confirm or otherwise the published claims for the Bronze and Iron Ages in Northeast Thailand, if not for the initial Neolithic settlement phase. The samples were sent away on the 16th March, and I awaited the results with bated breath.

Events then moved fast. On the 20th March I received a letter from Lisa Lyons about the dilemma being faced in the Penn Museum following news of Chet's illness. What would now happen to their Ban Chiang programme? Then Chet wrote to me a letter I shall never forget. He described his illness in detail. He had visited Hanoi to meet Vietnamese colleagues, and went out to a dinner party. On his return to his hotel room, he took off his shirt and noticed a blood stain on the back. He looked in the mirror and saw the source of that blood, a raised dark spot. He visited a Vietnamese doctor, who took one look and told him to return at once to America for urgent treatment. It was a malignant melanoma. My memory returned to our evening in the rushing mountain stream at Banyan Valley and the spot on my back he had warned me about. Mine was benign. Chet then asked me to take on the responsibility of analysing and publishing our two seasons at Ban Chiang.

A vital key to interpreting Ban Na Di was the clarity of the stratigraphy. Here, you can see multiple sand lenses reflecting periodic flooding of the site, through which graves and pits have been dug.

All this took on the trappings of a nightmare. I replied at once, confirming that I would do all I could to fulfill his request. He replied to say that he planned now to return to Ban Chiang to die there. But he only got as far as his native California, where he was taken so ill that he could travel no further. There he married Martha, on old flame, and she cared for him, taking him to hospital for treatment. On March 23rd, I received a letter from Ward Goodenough at the Penn department, inviting me to travel there to consult with them on how to proceed with my analysis. By the 10th April, Martha was writing to me with news of the sharp downward spiral in Chet's health. The

Martin Biddle was Director of the Penn Museum. I gave him my proposal to analyse and publish the Ban Chiang excavations and he agreed.

cancer had spread to his head. His time was now measured in weeks. I secured permission from my University to travel to Philadelphia and the Penn Museum sent me a return air ticket. On May 7th I received my radiocarbon dates back from the Wellington laboratory. They were in excellent harmony with the cultural sequence, and far later than the equivalent contexts at Ban Chiang. Two days later, I boarded my flight for San Francisco and then the short hop to Sacramento, to Martha's, to stay and talk about the future of Ban Chiang with Chet.

It is too painful, even now, to recall the devastating impact that the cancer had on my dear friend. I found him lying on a day bed in Martha's living room. At Banyan Valley and Ban Chiang he had been on top of the world, bursting with vigour and energy. Now he lay supine, a husk of his former self. We reminisced, but for the most part, concentrated on getting Ban Chiang done. This was his greatest concern. He briefed me on the deep undercurrent of politics that permeated the Penn Museum. I was surprised when, on our last evening Chet summoned the strength to take my arm and give me his final warning: "Don't let those bastards in Penn screw you".

I flew the following morning to Philadelphia, where I stayed as a guest of Betty Starr Cummin. She was a great supporter of the museum, and in particular of the Ban Chiang project. She lived in a sumptuous house in swanky Society Hill. Getting into it was rather like trying to enter Fort Knox, with its defensive rays and secret codes. I was provided with an office in the museum, and access to all Chet's site records and the laboratory where all the data were stored. I met John Hastings, who was putting everything onto a computer data base, and Bob Dyson, one of the senior archaeologists there. Martin Biddle, my old Cambridge friend and now the Director of the Penn Museum, briefed me on their plans for my visit. They wanted

I gave a lecture at Penn on our finds from Ban Na Di, including the remarkable clay figurines. The new radiocarbon dates I presented appear to have surprised the lecture audience at the Penn Museum.

me to find out the progress made so far in analysing everything and how long it would take to produce a full and final report. I set to work straight away. The 1976 report in *Expedition* had described how 18 tons of finds had been transported to Penn for analysis, and this seemed on the face of it, like a veritable Everest to climb. But my investigations soon revealed that the overwhelming majority of that weight comprised broken potsherds that usually attract little attention other than from a specialist ceramicist. In fact, the number of other artefacts was manageable, about the same as we excavated at Ban Na Di. Already too, the human and animal bones were taken care of, the former in Hawaii with Mike Pietrusewsky and the latter in my own lab and by now fully analysed.

I soon listed some important tasks. I concluded that organising a travelling exhibition before we had the chronology properly bolted down and the artefacts fully studied was premature. I took the Amtrak train down to Washington to meet the people with whom Chet had been liaising to discuss this, and left them in no doubt that any thought of an exhibition be put on hold until the right time. I detected a hint of frost as the meeting ended and felt sure that the phone line to the Penn Museum would be running hot with complaints about this intrusive English guy as I took the return train to Philadelphia. My second wish was that the Thai input to the research programme be acknowledged and acted on. Pisit Charoenwongsa was the co-director of the excavations and I felt that he and the FAD should be involved in all decisions. I made an appointment with the Ford Foundation Southeast Asia section and took the Amtrak train to New York. My pitch was that they consider funding Pisit to join in the analysis and publication and that, if he were interested, he should consider combining this with doctoral studies at Penn or with me at Otago. Having already sponsored several Thai graduate students at Penn, all left high and dry now without Chet's supervision, they were interested in helping further, particularly as I had first-hand experience of the fieldwork at Ban Chiang.

My meetings with members of the professional staff, including Robert Dyson, Greg Possehl and Ward Goodenough, revealed their view that the Penn Museum had scored a major international triumph in securing their hold on the Ban Chiang site. So it was challenging when they asked me to give a public lecture on my excavations at the second site in the Ban Chiang tradition at Ban Na Di. I gave a packed house a summary of what we had found, detailing the correspondences between the sequences at both sites. I showed them images of our burials, our figurines and the evidence for bronze casting on site. I did not mention my set of radiocarbon dates, because I wanted to get them completely bolted down. However, the first question came from Greg Possehl, an expert on the Indus Civilization, and he asked if I had yet any radiocarbon dates. I had no option but to set out the new dates and then explain their implications. The audience, until then receptive and keen, seemed to freeze. Could it possibly be that things were not quite as they had been led to believe?

I began to prepare a report on my findings. It had four major bullet points. A final and definitive publication on our two seasons at Ban Chiang would take about three years to prepare. Some of the finds would need to be sent overseas for detailed specialist analysis, I would need to spend extended time in Penn, and it would cost about $27,000. I typed it and on the 10th May, had lunch with Martin. We went over it line by line and he agreed that we would follow Chet's wish, and I would do it. The die was cast. I spent my last day in America sailing with Bill

Amphan, Somsuda and I visited Khok Phanom Di. I climbed down into the inky depths, and marvelled at the stratigraphy, resolving on the spot that one day, I would take on this site in the challenge of a lifetime.

Davenport and Rachanie on Chesapeake Bay before flying to London.

I was anxious to meet Bill Watson and Grahame Clark to keep them up to date with events and plans. Bill was one of the world's leading specialists on early China. He had also directed excavations at the Thai Neolithic site of Khok Charoen, and had the material in London for me to view. Grahame always offered his unique insight into any prehistoric development. I had not realised the depth of their scepticism about the claims for the early dates for the Neolithic and initial Bronze Age in Southeast Asia until I told them of my results from Ban Na Di. Both were relieved and delighted, and congratulated me. Both were also senior fellows of the august British Academy, and without telling me, they set in train a proposal to invite me to London to deliver the prestigious Mortimer Wheeler lecture. My odyssey then took me to Thailand, where I prepared our bronze and iron artefacts for shipment to New Zealand, and caught up in Bangkok with Joyce White to brief her on what had eventuated in Philadelphia.

The rest of 1981 was spent between my laboratory and the analysis of Ban Na Di and teaching commitments. The Ford Foundation confirmed my application for scholarships to allow three of my students who had worked at that site to come over for postgraduate degrees, and I gave thought to how best to balance my responsibilities for both sites. Chet had provided me with copies of all our site plans and records, which allowed me to make some preliminary moves on Ban Chiang. During the course of the year, I heard that Martin had chosen to return to England, and that Bob Dyson had been appointed the new director of the Penn Museum. I got in touch, to arrange my return to Penn and start on my new venture, to analyse and report on Ban Chiang. I spoke on the telephone to Greg Possehl, whom as I learnt later, had been appointed the director of the Ban Chiang project. He said "Charles, come at your leisure".

I did just that, booking a ticket that first took me to Thailand because I wanted to catch up with Pisit and find out more of his intentions, and be sure that the FAD was aware of and approved of my responsibilities for a project that they were so closely involved in. He told me of a newly discovered prehistoric site just an hour's drive from Bangkok, called Khok Phanom Di. Always intrigued by news such as this, I asked if I could visit. He arranged an FAD vehicle and on the 2nd April, Amphan, Somsuda Leyavanija and I went out to inspect. We turned off the main road from Chachoengsao to Phanat Nikhom and headed for a large mound set on the floodplain of the Bang Pakong River. We drove up a narrow track to the top, and parked next to the Buddhist temple that surmounted the mound. A local schoolteacher had excavated a small square to investigate and the ladder was still in place. I descended fully 8 metres into the inky depths, noting more than one human skull looking out from the exposed section. We tracked down

Robert Dyson, who succeeded Martin Biddle as Director of the Penn Museum. Here he is not waving me goodbye, but celebrating the discovery of the Hasanlu gold bowl.

Damrongkiadt, the excavator. He told us that he had found some carbonised rice grains near the base of his square. This site really stunned me. I made an immediate resolution, that when I had completed my commitments to Ban Na Di and Ban Chiang, I would return to this amazing site.

I then visited Ban Chiang before flying to England for a week, and then, on the 15th April, left Heathrow for Philadelphia. I was booked into the Hilton Hotel, and I arrived tired and jet lagged by taxi from the airport. There was a note awaiting me in my room, inviting me to have breakfast with Greg Possehl in the hotel the following morning. After the initial pleasantries, I turned to my immediate plans, and said that I was all set to begin without delay. Greg replied thus: "Charles, nothing is leaving Philadelphia". This simple sentence was a coded message that I was not wanted. Chet's final words to me echoed in my ears. Rather than immediately getting to grips with my responsibilities, I found myself over the weekend in the hotel rather surprised that the Penn museum had flown me round the world only to dispense with my services. Rachanie called on me. She was then living in the home of Gloria Bouilland and family, and arranged for me to join her there. Getting out of the hotel into a welcome family environment was much appreciated. First thing on Monday, I booked the next flight home and departed the following day.

Back to Ban Na Di

It was possible in 1982 to ship all the finds from an excavation in Thailand overseas for analysis. My department now occupied a new building with a laboratory large enough to lay out all our finds. I was lucky enough to have a splendid supporting team of graduate students and colleagues. Warrachai Wiriyaromp had supervised one of the squares at Ban Na Di, and under the supervision of Philip Houghton of our Anatomy Department, he studied the human skeletons. Brian Vincent was working on the ceramic vessels for his PhD. Amphan Kijngam's doctoral research brought together many strands of data to place the site in its full chronological

On arriving in Philadelphia to start work on the Ban Chiang report, I was invited to a breakfast meeting with Greg Possehl. He told me that my services were not needed.

and cultural context. Mehta Wichakana, destined one day to be the Deputy Director General of the FAD, was looking at the pottery rim forms from some of the sites near Ban Na Di where we had opened test squares. I had input from colleagues on the bronze and iron artefacts, and Jacqui Pilditch was charged with reporting on all the jewellery and other ornaments. During a visit to Otago, Bob Maddin, a leading archaeometallurgist from Penn, showed intense interest in the tie wires of bronze that had been used to repair broken marble and slate bangles. He took these away for detailed scrutiny. The precious samples of carbonised rice went to the Philippines to be looked at. Most importantly, I had my illustrations unit working hard on drawing the burials and many key artefacts. Things were going with a swing.

Philadelphia was now silent. I had no news, no explanation for their volte face and certainly no apology. But I did hear that they had appointed Joyce White to take responsibility for analysing and publishing the 1974-5 excavations. She then moved from her research on the palaeoenvironment, that had looked so promising, to investigate the cultural sequence and the chronology of Ban Chiang. The Smithsonian Institution had continued to prepare a travelling exhibition and Joyce wrote the catalogue along with a resume of the site sequence and its wider significance.

My invitation to deliver the Mortimer Wheeler lecture had come through and I spent the first couple of months of 1983 preparing it. This was my opportunity to present as accurate an assessment as possible of the chronology and cultural significance of a prehistoric society that was being promoted through the publicity channels of the Smithsonian Institution and Penn Museum as being of world significance. I took with me the newly published catalogue written by Joyce White (1982) to accompany the exhibition, which was then traversing major American museums.

In February I had presided as Secretary General over the Pacific Science Congress in Dunedin. There I met Pham Minh Huyen and Hoang Xuan Chinh. I expressed my hope one day to be able to visit Vietnam, and they arranged for an official invitation. I broke my journey to London and on the 29th of April, I left a boiling hot Bangkok for Hanoi. It was chilly with a light drizzle when I found myself in

In May 1983, I paid my first of many visits to Vietnam. Vu The Long, back row far right, helped me with translations. He constantly asked me why New Zealand had bombed his country. I had to explain that we hadn't.

a little hotel near the Archaeology Institute. Hanoi had all the characteristics of a provincial French city. The streets were lined with plane trees, there were few vehicles, most people rode bicycles. There were hardly any foreigners, and those I met came from either Russia or East Germany. I was so delighted to be able to meet more Vietnamese colleagues hitherto only known to me by name. Vu The Long was my translator and he organised visits to all the sites that I had listed. When leaving Hanoi, a pass was required for the officials at sentry points located on all the main roads out of the city. We drove down to Thanh Hoa and visited Dong Son, a long-term ambition of mine. I was taken by Pham Huy Thong to Co Loa, Phung Nguyen and Lang Ca, all key sites. At Dong Dau, I explored a site with close chronological and cultural parallels with Ban Chiang and Ban Na Di. I went to the National Museum and admired the collection of Dong Son drums and the boat burials from Viet Khe and Chau Can. Ha Van Tan hosted a couple of seminars I delivered. Each afternoon at 5.00 pm sharp, I was taken back to my hotel, and when there was electricity on, which was intermittent, I read Joyce White's exhibition catalogue in order to write a review for the journal *Antiquity*. Generally favourable, I did raise one or two chronological issues.

I was then stricken down with a very unpleasant bout of food poisoning in Hanoi, whose cause was explained when I came to leave for the airport. It was about 4.00 am when the car came to collect me from my hotel, and all the doors into the street were locked. I had to explore to find someone with a key, and in so doing, passed the kitchens. The area was infested with well-fed rats. I flew to Saigon and then on to London, taking my illness with me. This necessitated an early visit to hospital where I was diagnosed and given appropriate medication. On the 26th May, I took the train down to London and the British Academy to deliver my lecture to a packed auditorium (Higham 1984). The principal thrust of my presentation centred on the chronology. This involved a detailed outline of the contexts from which the dated charcoal at Ban Chiang and Ban Na Da derived. I pointed out what I regarded then, and still do, as essential, namely a secure context is the basic key to successful radiocarbon dating. Prior to AMS dating, that can now date a rice grain, it was necessary to submit a decently large sample of charcoal. I knew that the majority of the Non Nok Tha and Ban Chiang determinations came from fragments of charcoal assembled from different locations until there was sufficient to obtain a C14 determination. I have a movie film I took of Jean Kennedy collecting bits of charcoal from grave fill. I collected some myself. Only very rarely did the dated sample come from a single fixed source, such as a hearth, because so few were encountered.

I pointed out that there was no consistent relationship between a date from Ban Chiang and the layer it came from. In a word, the results were all over the place, and

Top of my list during my first visit to Vietnam was to go to Dong Son. It lies on the bank of the Ma River, a strategic location.

it was just as possible to suggest a long, or a short, chronology depending on which dates were chosen for emphasis. I was not alone in this conclusion. Helmut Loofs-Wissowa, excavator of Khok Charoen, was far more forthright than I when he wrote that the Penn Museum was responsible for "a remarkably successful exercise in public opinion-forming by the media, manipulated – or at least condoned – by a handful of archaeologists and being based on very questionable evidence" (Loofs-Wissowa 1986). I then showed images of the hearths that provided the radiocarbon determinations from the equivalent layers at Ban Na Di, concluding that the claims for the very early origins of bronze technology in Northeast Thailand, and the uptake of iron forging, should be set aside. As far as I was concerned, I had nothing further to add. How wrong I was.

On my return to New Zealand, and for the remaining months of 1983, I devoted myself to completing the analysis of Ban Na Di. This involved four or five graduate student dissertations to be distilled into chapters, working on the settlement patterns on our surveyed areas and learning a program called prose in order to format what ended up as three volumes, about 1000 pages and many illustrations and tables. I contacted Anthony Hands, the founder of British Archaeological Reports (International Series) in Oxford and he invited me to stay as a house guest. We agreed that I would deliver the completed manuscript, and he published it (Higham and Kijngam 1984). I was determined to see this to completion in order to give me the opportunity to turn to the promise I had made myself, to excavate Khok Phanom Di.

We began our campaign at Khok Phanom Di with a site survey, a lot of walking and many sites.

Eight | Khok Phanom Di, my Personal Everest

On New Year's day 1984, I flew up to Bangkok to undertake a search for archaeological sites in a study area centred on this great settlement of Khok Phanom Di (KPD). On the 3rd January, I called on Pisit in the FAD, and he told me that the Ford Foundation representative for Southeast Asia, Tom Kessinger, was staying in my hotel, the Imperial, on Wireless Road. The Foundation had been a great supporter of my participation at Ban Chiang, and I rang him with thanks and greetings. He invited me to dinner. This turned out to be a stroke of incredible good fortune. I took the opportunity to outline my plan to open a major excavation at KPD, and as the evening progressed and another glass of wine was poured, I boldly asked him for funding. He replied to the point. Without any reference to head office in New York, he could on his own initiative disburse individual grants of up to $25,000. That was a figure that I noted in my diary underlined in red.

I was delighted when Pisit asked Rachanie to join me in the site survey, and with three other former students of mine, we based ourselves in the town of Phanat Nikhom and divided our chosen study area into four sectors. Our methodology involved a lot of walking and talking to the local villagers. In two teams, we would be dropped off at a village with the objective of walking to the next village temple, often visible on the skyline, looking for every sign of prehistoric occupation. On some days this yielded four or five sites and on others, none. The most promising site was called Khok Karieng. It was about the same size as KPD, and the surface was covered with prehistoric potsherds. What we lacked, as we were to discover eight years later, was a professional geomorphologist to study the nature of the subsurface deposits, because we were working on a broad river flood plain that had, four millennia ago, been covered by a shallow sea. Many of the sites that we sought were covered over and invisible.

Before the end of the field season, we visited KPD to talk to the abbot of the temple that owns it. The first priority when planning to dig is to secure the permission and goodwill of the landowners. The abbot could easily have said no, and that would have been that. He invited us into his meeting room and after the traditional pleasantries, I outlined our proposal as I anxiously studied his face for signs of agreement. It was a model of inscrutability. When I finished, he rose and signalled us to follow him. We strolled across to the very centre of the mound, and he said that this was where we could dig, because at this spot, we would not need

Tom Kessinger. Without his support, I could never have taken on the challenge of Khok Phanom Di.

to cut down any of his trees.

I returned home on the 6th February with every hope that I would be excavating KPD in the foreseeable future, but with hurdles to cross. The first was securing the necessary FAD permit, the second was to find the money. To achieve both, I had to formulate a convincing case for the need to excavate. In 1983, there was one outstanding problem that needed resolution: where, when and how did rice come to be domesticated? Bill Solheim had claimed an earlier Neolithic revolution in the northern Thai caves, but this had foundered for lack of evidence. There was then no convincing case for an origin in China. But this needed to be addressed because domestic rice was clearly the bedrock on which later Southeast Asian prehistoric societies, as well as early states, were founded. I recalled that Damrongkiadt had recovered carbonised rice grains in the basal layers at KPD, so I generated a model in my mind, that rice domestication had its origins in the coastal habitats of Southeast Asia, where complex maritime hunter gatherers were faced with the need to adapt to environmental changes consequent upon sea level fluctuations. In other words, as the sea level fell, they began to experiment with harvesting rice, the indigenous marsh grass that would have colonised newly formed freshwater habitats in the orbit of their settlements.

Excavating KPD was going to be expensive. It was not a site to take on lightly because of its great depth. The mound has an unusual surface contour. It does not rise to a summit in its centre, but is more like a saucer as it dips down from elevated banks round its margin. Damrongkiadt's excavation reached a depth of 9 metres, I calculated that to dig through the site edge would involve at least 12 metres. A week after my return, I sent off two proposals to Tom Kessinger in Jakarta. The first of these set out my investigative model and asked for a grant of $24,950 to pay for the excavation. The second also for $24,950, was to pay for four Thai students to come to New Zealand to study for their postgraduate research degrees on what we found. Three days later, I sent a request to the National Geographic Society for further financial support. Then a remarkable coincidence occurred. On March 15th came a letter from an organisation called Earthwatch. It was headed "Would you like a research grant?" It came from Brian Rosborough, and I read what was involved. Apparently, Earthwatch advertised field projects worthy of support and then sought volunteers to spend a fortnight in the field as members of the team, and at the same time, contributing to the budget. I replied with a description of my project, and Earthwatch showed interest. In due course, I was added to their brochure and I awaited to hear if any volunteers would come forward. Each would contribute about $1,300, some of which would pay for their keep, leaving a decent margin to cover fieldwork costs. I also had the good luck to be in contact with Precha Phonprasert, an executive with the Shell Company of Thailand. I had met him in Bangkok earlier in the year, and we met with Mom Ratchawong Sarisdiguna Kitiyakara, the Queen's cousin, who was a senior director. Sarisdiguna had been at Magdalene College Cambridge and we were contemporaries, so we had a lot in common. He promised to provide us with either a vehicle, or subsidy for our budget.

The Ford Foundation held the key to KPD. I waited and waited for Tom Kessinger's decision until on the 17th September, I could wait no longer. I rang him and asked for his verdict. It seemed to me that he had either forgotten about me, or had overlooked it. "Ah, let me get your file, hold on," his voice came down the line. My heart raced. There was then one of those pregnant pauses, I could almost hear him riffling through the pages. Then he came back to me. "Yes Charles, this is fine, I will approve both the grants, you will be getting confirmation in the mail".

I was ecstatic, and could now lay firm plans. Amphan was then finishing his doctoral dissertation, and we determined that on his return to Bangkok on the 27th September, he would go out to Phanat Nikhom and organise the construction of a roof over an excavation square measuring 10 by 10 metres. I was determined not to have any intervening baulks between smaller areas because then one would spend most of the time up or down a ladder. I rang Pisit and set in train the

Khok Phanom Di, the mound sits like a stranded whale on the ancient flood plain of the Bang Pakong River.

Amphan had overseen the construction of a splendid roof over our excavation. This is our team as we began in January 1985. I am standing at the far left. Brian Vincent wears a white hat in the back row. Jill Thompson stands tall in the middle of the back row, and Rachanie is kneeling in front of her to her left. Warrachai stands at the far right next to Amphan and Bernard Maloney.

application for the permit to dig. I asked him if he could second Rachanie to be my co-director, and listed the names of my former students, now employed by the FAD, to join me in the field. In the event all were approved – Metha Wichakana, Warrachai Wiriyaromp, Praphid Choosiri and Pirapon Pisnupong. I was also due a sabbatical leave, and knowing that it would take much longer than the two months available between University terms to complete this excavation, I applied for and was granted a year away. I then received Bob Maddin's contribution to the Ban Na Di report, and was able to complete formatting the 960 pages, printing the text and sending it off to Oxford for publication. My promise to finish Ban Na Di before beginning KPD was honoured. It was finally posted away on the 12th December. Six days later, I left for Bangkok and the supreme challenge of tackling KPD.

I drove out to our base in Phanat Nikhom on the 22nd December, and went with Amphan to the site. I was amazed by the roof that he had engineered. Stout timbers from a disused temple building had been employed in the walls to support a metal roof. The entire area to be excavated was surrounded by a low brick wall to keep out the temple chickens, dogs and by night the snakes that abounded. We then bought our own vehicle with the generous help of the Shell Company and welcomed Jill Thompson to the team. I was adamant that we must recover all the organic material and micro-fauna and Jill was to spend the entire excavation season working the flotation machine, furnishing unparalleled results. Bernard Maloney from Queen's University Belfast joined us to core round the site to explore the changing palaeoenvironment. Brian Vincent, fresh from his PhD on the pots from Ban Na Di, was project ceramicist and Jacqui Pilditch came to work on any jewellery we might encounter. My workforce was to change as the season progressed. We employed local villagers throughout. During the first few weeks, about 12 of my Otago students joined us, and subsequently a team of Thai students led by Damrongkiadt took over from them. There were also three groups of Earthwatch volunteers. Happily, son Tom was also with me for the earlier months. Amphan also invited his friend Anat Bamrungwongse, known to us all as Chuay, into the team. Chuay was a phenomenon, who could, it seemed do just about anything. He devised and constructed a tough steel wire precisely over each side of our square, hanging from which was a thin sheet of steel that could be lowered. As we dug down, so Chuay would move the sheet down and along as a guide to ensure that the sides of the excavation were perfectly vertical. Later, with increasing depth, he constructed a sturdy hardwood ladder.

We all stayed in the Yenchit Hotel, a small hostelry in Phanat Nikhom about 20 minutes drive from the site. This is a notably affluent, well-run town with the advantage of an excellent public swimming pool. We hired two cooks who doubled up to do the laundry. Tom, Rachanie and I shared a house, Amphan and his team another. Students and volunteers shared rooms. The FAD made available a minibus to take us out to the site.

We began excavating on the 28th December. The top metre comprised a dark occupation layer with copious evidence for fashioning pottery vessels. There were deposits of clay and the anvils that had been used to shape pots. The faunal remains suggested a woodland habitat. Geoff Wyvill, a colleague in Otago, had programmed

Jill Thompson organised a flotation chamber, and I provided her with willing assistants.

a sophisticated hand-held calculator. We inserted concrete posts into each corner of our square, each having a hook to anchor a tape measure. By measuring the distance from three of these tapes to every artefact find spot, and punching these into the calculator, we quickly recorded precise locations. Pirapon Pisnupong sat at a desk above the square recording these details, giving each artefact a unique catalogue number. We had villagers working the screens to sift through every sample coming out of the square, and a further sample was sent to Jill Thompson for drying and then processing through her flotation tank.

Saturday January 26th was a bad day. I had an appointment in Bangkok on the Friday night and on driving back in the morning, I followed

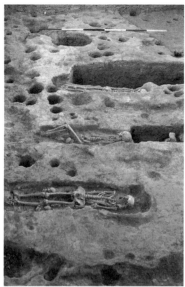

We traced a row of burials, Mortuary Phase 6, interred in a wooden chamber.

Chuay, at the left, constructed a ladder to allow an element of safety as we descended down to a depth of seven metres.

an ominous and unseasonal black cloud. I headed straight to the site, and by the time I arrived, the heavens had opened. Water rapidly rose up round the square, gushing off the roof into a pit that Chuay had dug to link into a channel that everyone was frantically digging to take the water away and over the edge of the mound. I dashed up to inspect the carnage, slipped into the pit and steadying my fall, grabbed the sharp edge of the metal roof and cut my fingers to the bone. Heavily bandaged, I did my bit and in the nick of time, Chuay's newly dug channel reached the edge of the mound and the rainwater cascaded over.

When we recovered our poise, we found our way into a new layer of much lighter colour with much ash and many pits. There were many marine shellfish and from February 19th, we began finding the first human burials, the skeletal remains being in excellent, almost fossilised, condition. The graves we were later to ascribe to our 6th mortuary phase were laid out in a row, within a disposition of post holes that suggested that they had been contained within a wooden structure. These lay in front of a second structure raised up on a platform. It comprised a square room with clay wall foundations and a clay floor that had been severed by three graves.

We were all taken aback by the wealth of the graves in this clay room. One, a child who died when aged about nine years, wore over 18,000 shell beads and a large shell disc. There were also some fine pottery vessels with the dead, bearing complex incised and impressed designs and usually brightly burnished. What surprised me, as I looked from time to time at the accumulating number of biological finds, was the lack of any signs of domestic pigs or cattle. Indeed, most remains came from marine or mangrove species: crabs, fish and turtles.

The excavation was going very well I thought. At the end of each day's digging, we returned to base and drove round to the pool for a refreshing swim. There was a small cinema in town and my students would often wander round for a drink and a movie. After dinner, Rachanie and I usually jousted with each other over a game of chess, and we were equally matched. In early March, we were down over 2 metres deep, into our 7th layer. The stratigraphy was clear as crystal. Many hearths supplied us with abundant charcoal for our radiocarbon determinations. The next few days were to prove amazing. It began with a newly cleaned surface that revealed a circular pit. On exploring further, we uncovered two superb pottery vessels containing an infant skeleton. Then Amphan and I traced a sharp dividing line between ash and darker mixed fill. It continued for about three metres, and then turned a right angle until finally, we had a perfect rectangle. On removing the contents, we found pottery vessels balanced on top of a pile of clay cylinders, preforms for making pots. Then there was a hint of blood red, it was the ochre covering the skull. In one of the most remarkable days of excavation I have experienced, we finally revealed a female skeleton, our burial 15, weighed down with over 120,000 shell beads, two horned

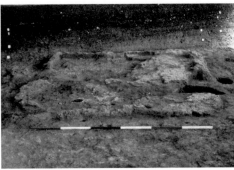

We were pretty surprised when we encountered a room raised on a platform with clay walls and floor. Rich burials had been cut through the floor.

We found an incredibly rich female potter wearing over 120,000 shell beads, next to a poor headless man.

shell discs on the chest, shell ear ornaments, a shell bangle and covered by fine decorated pottery vessels. She must have been a master potter, judging from the strength of her wrist musculature, the shell beside her ankles containing her two stones used to burnish pots, and her clay anvil for shaping them. This was not all in this layer. Next door lay the grave of infant covered in red ochre, who died when about 18 months of age, also endowed with thousands of beads, a shell bangle and a minute clay anvil by the right ankle. An equally wealthy male completed this remarkable group of individuals.

On the 26th March, we were paid a visit by the Director General of the FAD, and his extensive entourage. He brought a television camera news team with him. I covered Burial 15 and after entertaining him over lunch in the temple, we went over to the square and I asked one of my team to unveil the grave. He was very impressed indeed, and descending into the square for a closer look, summoned the camera team and invited me to describe the burial for the benefit of Thai viewers of the evening news. I strung together my few sentences and hoped that what I said was generally understandable. He seemed satisfied with my effort, and making him welcome paid dividends later in the season.

As we progressed downward, so we uncovered more superbly complete inhumation graves, set out in discrete clusters. Men were now interred with deliberately fractured turtle carapace ornaments that had been cut into decorative forms. The females were accompanied by their clay anvils, but there were very few items of jewellery. Now down to a depth of three metres and into our fourth month of excavating, the temperature was rising and the rainy season was looming. Rachanie and I were planning to end for the season and cover the exposed area hoping that the monsoon rains would not flood the square, ahead of returning later in the year to continue on down. We also planned for a brief halt to allow us to accept an invitation to the opening of the British Academy's new Institute for Archaeological Research in Bangkok, and the lectures to follow. On April 7th I booked into my hotel the night before the opening and with son Tom and some of my students, we crammed into my hotel suite. The meeting went with a swing, and the following Saturday, many friends and colleagues came out to visit our excavations following the end of the colloquy in Bangkok. A bus load arrived and were duly impressed, I think, by what they saw. I recall in particular showing Vince Pigott and Ben Bronson round as we discussed the provenance of our radiocarbon samples.

We now faced a serious dilemma. The rainy season was imminent, and we had to decide whether to bed the excavation down for several months, or to soldier on despite the monsoon. To exacerbate the situation, we were fast running out of money and Tom Kessinger, my potential saviour, was far off on a visit to New York. On the 2nd May with little left in the bank and a decision beckoning, I called on the Bangkok Office of the Ford Foundation and spoke to Bill Klausner, the senior representative. Bill was steeped in the traditional customs of Northeast Thailand, as seen in his book *Reflections in a Log Pond*. I explained my plight and he told me that he would let me know what, if anything, would be possible. Five days later my bank account was credited with $12,000. We were cruising again.

The rainy season was now upon us. Chuay had devised and constructed a drainage culvert with brick-lined sediment traps every few paces to take away the monsoon rains. We were now down a dizzying depth of 4.75 metres, so Chuay constructed a hardwood ladder to give relatively safe access to the excavation square. We strung up electric leads over each of the four quadrants to illuminate our working surfaces. Vegetation began to grow out of the upper edges of our perfectly vertical sections. When it poured, as it did often, little water spouts found they way into the square and we feared a wall collapse. I had no intention of continuing for so long, and family commitments during my sabbatical leave now necessitated a brief visit to England. Tom and I left as we reached the 60th burial, and Rachanie and the team carried on without me. In my absence, they continued to reveal the superimposed burial clusters. Jill Thompson had battled with the problem of drying her samples before they could be floated for organic remains with admirable resolve. Only the local villagers remained to work in the square and up above, screening and packing. I was soon back from England. One of my students, Glenn Standring, had joined me and we spent hours recording the sections. I collected charcoal from the many

It was great to have Tom with me at Khok Phanom Di. He later worked on the shell knives for his B.A. honours dissertation.

hearths that we uncovered for our dating programme. Early in July, we were 5.80 metres below the surface of the mound and with an eye again on funds and time, I dug down in a corner of the square and was finding cultural material down to a depth of 6.70 metres. Still some way to go.

We were finding some remarkable and, in my experience, unique surviving contexts. Fossilised wood survived in one posthole. We found leaf impressions and rice chaff, a group of adzes as if they had been placed there yesterday, and concentrations of burnishing stones with clay anvils. Even the ash from pot firings survived intact. There were thick shell middens, numerous hearths, and still burials but now more scattered. One, as with the indigenous hunter gatherers of Southeast Asia, we found in a flexed position. On the 12th July, Jill left after continuously working the flotation chamber for 6.5 months. The day before I flew to Heathrow on the 18th July, we uncovered burial 152. We were down to the natural substrate. I noted at the time, "Nirvana, we have done it!" I had reached the summit of my personal Everest at a depth of about 7 metres. Without the total dedication of Rachanie and Amphan, not to mention the entire team, this would have been impossible. If I learned one lesson from KPD, it was my admiration for the skill of Rachanie as an excavator. I knew that if I were to continue with more excavations, it would have to be with her as my co-director. Her patience was the perfect foil to my enthusiasm, and she had the priceless skill of sharing her skills in training our Thai workforce.

After spending the rest of my sabbatical leave in Cambridge, I returned to New Zealand on the 10th January 1986. Twelve days later, a shipping container with all

We found some remarkable structures like this wall foundation abutting a row of hearths. Perfect for radiocarbon dating.

Below: The first people to live at Khok Phanom Di 4,000 years ago left a cache of burnishing stones, a clay anvil for shaping pots and a brand new stone adze.

our finds except for the mountains of potsherds arrived, and we brought everything into our layout laboratory. Now we could get down to work. Writing a report on KPD was only possible with the input from a team of many players. With the second Ford Foundation grant, Rachanie, Amphan and Pirapon came to Dunedin. Rachanie's doctoral dissertation was a general synthesis of the site's chronology and cultural affiliations. Amphan studied all the fish bones, and Pirapon's M.A. thesis addressed the stone adzes and granite hoes. Alan Grant was one of the students who had joined us in the field, and he studied the mammalian bones. Barbara West of the British Museum was sent all the bird bones and microfauna. Jill Thompson secured a PhD scholarship from Jack Golson at the Australian National University to take on the monumental task of analysing all the plant remains.

The human bones were crucial. Nancy Tayles came to my Department having had a successful early career as an accountant, and sought my advice on a possible PhD topic. I suggested that she take on the analysis of the skeletal remains from KPD, under the supervision of Philip Houghton in the Medical School. After a few days exploring this possibility, she confirmed that this was on, and I was naturally relieved and delighted. Bernard Maloney in Belfast had all his sediment cores and pollen samples to pore over. Rachanie's sharp eye had noted that some of the bivalve shells had been used as tools. My son Tom used an electron microscope to define the minute use wear scratches and compare these with modern experimental wear. We asked Chuay to harvest rice with modern replicas, and Tom incised clay, cut skins, scraped wood, and found that his closest match was rice harvesting.

Jill's flotation samples were found to contain minute shellfish, forams and diatoms. Graeme Mason had been for some years our chief laboratory technician. A remarkable polymath, he also suffered from alcoholism, and in 1985 he had a relapse and we had the difficult task of discussing his last warning before dismissal. It had been agreed that he should go, but I persuaded my colleagues to give him one last chance. He should take on the study of all our shellfish, big and small. I suggested that he report to me every morning to plan the day, and again each afternoon to report on his daily findings. This eventuated. He came to my office at 4.00 pm every day with his clipboard and notes and dictated what he had found as I typed. Over the months, we assembled two detailed chapters, one on the large and the other on the micro-shellfish that illuminated the changing environment throughout the occupation of this site. I also tracked down Ken McKenzie in Australia, an expert on forams, whose results confirmed those from Graeme.

Finding the remains of partially digested food, or faeces, in a grave is uncommon. One of our burials contained a lump of organic material in the pelvic area that on examination, contained fish scales and rice chaff. The former were sent to the British Museum and found to come from the freshwater climbing perch. I was examining the faeces from another grave and under the microscope, found myself looking at a tiny pair of eyes. I took the remains to Anthony Harris in the Otago Museum who ascribed them to a beetle, *Oryzaphilus surinamensis*, that today infests rice stores. I also extracted hairs from this coprolite and found Lynley Moore, a medical student looking for an elective topic of research. Barbara West in the British Museum sent us a sample of hair from all the Southeast Asian species in their archive. These were analysed under an electron microscope, and it was determined that our sample came from mice. It seems that beetles and mice invaded the rice stored by the people of KPD. Further input came from David Morseth, who identified a helminth egg in the human faeces, a serious impediment to good health.

After dispersing these items far and wide for scrutiny, I was left with a massive mountain to climb: the thousands of artefacts now lying on the tables in our layout laboratory. These were dominated by the pottery vessels from the burials, virtually all of which were broken in antiquity and had to be re-assembled. Then there were the stone adzes and flakes, ceramic anvils, bone tools by the hundred if not thousand, turtle carapace ornaments and shell beads. Analysing and preparing illustrations of all these was going to take years if not decades. Then a miracle occurred. The New Zealand Government, at a time of high unemployment, established the Project Employment Programme. This invited applications for workers to join an approved project for up to six months, all wages to be paid by the Government.

I applied for workers to break the back of the basic analyses. It was soon approved, and I was able to employ students of Anthropology to start piecing together all the pottery vessels, clean the stone and bone artefacts, and lay out all the shell ornaments. My daughters Emma and Caroline counted all the shell beads from each burial. It took weeks. I also asked for four professional illustrators to start drawing everything that needed to published. This ranged from each burial to each pot and every adze down to all the bone tools. One of the four, Les O'Neill, turned

We did it, or as Sir Edmund Hillary said descending from Mt Everest, "We knocked the bastard off". This was certainly my personal Everest, after seven months, we reached the natural substrate. Me, Rachanie, Amphan and Chuay.

It was with quite a sense of achievement that we completed our excavation at Khok Phanom Di.

out to be the positive Michelangelo of archaeological drawing, and I was able to secure for him a permanent post in our illustrations unit, where he remains to this day. As if this wasn't enough, I also took several phone calls from the Ministry asking if I would like more workers and in the end the layout laboratory hummed like a beehive with over 30 in our team.

My role was coordinator in the same way that a conductor tries to keep an orchestra playing to the same score. I began this programme of research to a background of radiocarbon dates obtained by Damrongiadt that suggested occupation during the 5th millennium BC, and that rice domestication began in coastal sites such as KPD. I have invariably found, in all my excavations, that the chronology must be secured before any valid interpretations can be pondered. We had opened an occupation sequence that had a minimum depth of 7 metres with a reasonable expectation that this would span a considerable time, particularly given the comparatively shallow accumulation at Ban Chiang and Ban Na Di. Non Nok Tha was just over a metre deep and Solheim had proposed that it was occupied for at least 3,000 years. The anticipated early date and long occupation span evaporated the moment the dates arrived from the laboratory of the Australian National University. The earliest context was dated between 2130-1700 BC, and the latest, from 1930-1310 BC. In those days the standard error was much wider than it is today. I came to the conclusion that the site had been occupied for about 500 years and when I considered the nature of the stratigraphy, this made sense. Much of the build up of cultural deposits comprised shell middens, and these can accumulate very rapidly.

The next objective was to construct a valid cultural sequence. This was relatively straightforward if based on the mortuary data, because the superposition of clusters of graves made separation into seven phases clear. I worked in close conjunction with Les O'Neill and his colleague in the illustration unit, Martin Fisher. I did not then incorporate many photographs into my reports, it was years before digital images, dpi's, tiffs and jpegs let alone photoshop, came on stream, so it was very much a matter of illustrating with drawings. There was then the question of where to publish what was clearly going to be a series of volumes reporting on various aspects of the site. I discussed this with Grahame Clark, who recommended that I approach the Society of Antiquaries of London. The oldest such society in the world, it publishes a series of Reports of their Research Committee. I was then a Fellow, and sounded the Society out to see if they would be receptive. The answer was positive save for two caveats. The first was the expense and the second was where would the volumes be printed.

The first of these was resolved when the Shell Company of Thailand provided a generous subsidy. The volumes would need to conform to the Society's style. This involved very high quality paper, hard binding, a dust jacket, their page size and preferred font. There was nowhere to turn to format the first report, so I went to the University Computer Advisory and spoke to Graeme McKinstry, an expert on the formatting program known as Latex. He taught me how to accomplish this and was always on hand with necessary advice when I ran into a problem. I couldn't print anything in my department and was a constant visitor to the computing centre printer to see if my latex formatting was up to scratch. Finally, I found that the University Printery could take my final page paste ups and convert them into a volume that satisfied the Society of Antiquaries. The first in the KPD series, edited and written by Rachanie and me, was published in 1990 (Higham and Bannanurag 1990). It set out the chronology, the detailed cultural sequence and a description of each burial. The dust jacket had an illustration of my chosen logo, the magnificently decorated pottery vessel from our burial 11.

As I worked on volume 1, so reports were coming in that covered many aspects of the biological remains that we had uncovered. No site that I have excavated has produced such a variety. Bernard Maloney joined us from Queen's University Belfast, bringing his expertise in pollen analysis to bear on several cores that he sank in the vicinity of the site. His chapter began with the totally reasonable statement that his pollen diagrams are "not only the most detailed associated with any South-East Asian archaeological site but they also stand in their own right as the most thorough from a mangrove area of the mainland" (Maloney 1991:7). He reconstructed the mangrove

I returned from a visit to Bangkok to find that Metha had revealed this woman's last meal, lying in her pelvic area: domestic rice and fish bones and scales.

Les O'Neill, the Michelangelo of archaeological illustrations, drew all our shellfish species.

habitat prior to the occupation of KPD, and then the human impact when the first settlers arrived next to the estuary of the Bang Pakong River. Importantly, he found that if rice were cultivated or collected from wild stands, then it must have been some distance inland, because the site was then in the intertidal zone and rice is not adapted to salinity. Nor did he find any evidence for rice cultivation in his pollen cores prior to the occupation span of KPD.

We took samples of the cultural deposits from sections through the site as we progressed downward, and I was lucky enough to find that Ken McKenzie in Australia was willing to look at these for the surviving microscopic ostracodes and forams. His results were fascinating. The initial occupation was next to the sea, but over time the sea level fell, and the water became brackish before briefly, there were freshwater ostracodes present. This coincided with the presence of granite hoes, harvesting knives and domestic rice in human stomach contents and faeces.

Alan Grant had joined the excavation as a volunteer student, and he and I analysed the large mammalian bones. There were far fewer than at any of the inland sites I have been involved with. During the period of mangrove dominance, pigs, deer and monkeys were prominent, but always in very small numbers. Cattle and water buffalo were virtually absent. Only in the top metre, after the final mortuary phase, did the number of mammal bones increase. I was very lucky to have the cooperation of Barbara West of the British Museum of Natural History, and I packed off the really difficult large and the smaller mammal and bird bones to her, where she had access to one of the finest comparative collections in the world. She identified crocodiles, the Javan rhinoceros, tigers, small cats and civets, otters and bandicoots. Rats infested the site. The birds were also very interesting. There were seabirds such as cormorants, herons, storks and spoonbills, that gave way when the sea level fell to forest species such as crows, broadbills and jungle fowl.

I was fortunate to find experts to identify some of the rare and minute biological remains. Anthony Harris identified two species of beetle in human faeces, one of which is adapted to life in rice stores. P.H. Greenwood from the British Museum reported on the scales of the climbing perch found in the partially digested food of burial 56, along with fragments of rice chaff and the tooth of a stingray. The hair in faeces from burial 67 came from mice. This unhygienic diet is also reflected in a helminth egg probably from an intestinal fluke ingested as a rule from eating raw plants.

The last contribution destined for our second volume came from Graeme Mason. It listed 120 species of the larger species of shellfish that he identified, most illustrated by the anatomical drawings of Les O'Neill. The principal purpose of this exercise, was to reconstruct the environment over the occupation span of the site. Each species of shellfish was assigned to its preferred habitat, ranging from marine mudflats to freshwater, and passing through the seaward, landward and estuarine mangroves. A fascinating picture emerged of the decline over time in the seaward mangrove habitat in favour of the species from freshwater rivers and lakes, and then a rise in landward mangroves as freshwater species declined. Thus we traced the rise and fall of the sea level, and noted that the presence of the granite hoes and shell harvesting knives coincided with fresh water conditions. This stands as the most incisive and detailed examination of shellfish anywhere in East or Southeast Asia. The most abundant species, the cockle *Anadara granosa*, was represented by over 650,000 specimens. The second volume was published in 1991. I was very pleased with it (Higham and Bannanurag 1991).

Volume 3

During 1987-90, I was supervising students who had been assigned artefacts. When I ran out of students or colleagues, I did my best myself. Being a coastal and estuarine site, fishing was of considerable importance, and I wrote a descriptive chapter on the fishhooks, clay net sinkers and harpoons. I also was confronted with a large assemblage of bone awls and what I called bobbins, which my colleague Brian Vincent later suggested were in fact, scribers to incise designs on pottery vessels before they were fired, and I think he was right. There were also bone burnishers to polish pots. We found worked stingray spines that were probably used in hunting. I reported on the antler tools and the worked turtle carapaces. The people of KPD had a very wide expertise and introduced into this part of the world a totally different technology from the hunter gatherers who had lived there for at least the previous 50,000 years. Fish must have abounded in the estuary and along the mangrove shore and Amphan Kijngam identified them all, dominant being the barramundi. He also counted hundreds of turtle remains and thousands of mangrove crab chelae.

Virtually all the stone was imported. Pirapon Pisnupong undertook a detailed examination of the stone tools for his Master's thesis and we worked on a synthesis of the results for his contribution to the final report. This centred on the geological sourcing of the stone, and the forms of the adzes and the manner in which they were used, sharpened with the whetstones we found, ultimately worn down to stubs before being recycled as chisels. Stone was obviously highly valued. During a brief period within the sequence, granite was also imported and made into what look like hoes.

Michelle Moore, one of my students, gave me a report on the burnishing stones, each of which had smooth facets from constant use. These were interred only with women, and are still being used for the same purpose today. They are so treasured that potters do not willingly part with them. Jacqui Pilditch was with us at KPD for several months with the brief to identify and report on all personal ornaments. Shell beads were the most abundant, coming in the tens of thousands, but there were many other items of jewellery as well. Although rarely found worn in burials, there were numerous ivory, shell and stone bangles from marble, slate, andesite and slaty shale in occupation contexts. Bangles were also made from fish vertebrae and found worn by the dead. Pendants were fashioned from shark, crocodile, dog, cat, pig, muntjak and small mammal teeth, all bored for suspension. Among the most remarkable ornaments were those carved from large sea turtle carapaces, and worn only by men in the later part of the cultural sequence.

We found over 400 large bivalve shells that had been used in some way, having a concave depression with tiny scratch marks on the working edge. My son Tom rose to the challenge to find out what they might have been used for. He experimented with modern replicas on a wide range of potential activities, and concluded that the use wear was most likely the result of harvesting rice. Interestingly, these shell knives were found at the same time in the cultural sequence as the granite hoes. My niece Dinah also contributed a chapter on the worked shells of the genus *Placuna*. Diane Hall had joined us in the field, and for her dissertation, she pored over and described every single decorative motif incised and impressed onto pottery vessels. There was an immense variety. She then tracked their changes throughout the cultural sequence, finding that some endured in significant numbers throughout, whereas others were time specific. One was very rare at the beginning but grew in popularity, others had the opposite distribution. I formatted all these chapters and with the agreement of the Society of Antiquaries, it was published in 1993 (Higham and Thosarat 1993).

Publishing KPD was a continuing commitment and as the specialist reports came in, I found myself learning a great deal and constantly developing my mind-model of what was going on there and how it fits into a broader picture.

The logo for the dust jacket of our seven volumes reporting on Khok Phanom Di. It looks down into a pot decorated with a human motif widely found in Neolithic Southeast Asia.

Volume 4

Jill Thompson performed heroically in the field, processing the cultural material sent her way in her corner of the mound month after month, right into the heart of the monsoon rains. She was rewarded with a PhD scholarship at the Australian National University to draw all her data together and, after completion, came as a Postdoctoral member of our Department in Otago to write it all up for our fourth volume. In it, she presented identifications of trees, mainly mangroves, that were found as charcoal and mineralised wood, finding supporting evidence for the transition from the near-shore mangroves when the site was first occupied to back swamp and then more open habitats. Much charcoal in the earlier layers came from ash spreads that we think resulted from firing pottery vessels. Her research on the rice remains was truly ground breaking. The survival of spikelet bases enabled her to be specific in identifying domesticated rice, including the exceptionally well-preserved specimens from human faeces. Rice was present as temper in pottery vessels, in faeces, adhering to clay attached to the exterior of potsherds and as husk impressions and silica skeletons on the clay daub of buildings. Not all could be labelled domestic on surviving fragments, but where this was possible, it was always domestic. This does present a conundrum in that the salt water habitat for much of the occupancy of the site would have militated against local cultivation. It is not impossible that rice was traded in to the settlement. Moreover, as Jill pointed out, there are salt tolerant varieties that can be grown successfully in slightly brackish conditions.

Jill generously shared her volume with Lisa Kealhofer and Dolores Piperno, who wrote on the phytoliths from Bernard Maloney's sediment cores, and Graeme Mason, who reported on the micromolluscs that she had retrieved through flotation. How these tiny shells found their way into the site remains a mystery,

but it might well have been fortuitously in the fish guts brought in as an economic catch. Fifty-one species were identified. To this day how Graeme achieved this is beyond my comprehension, but he did collect a lot of comparative specimens, often wading knee high through the mangroves to do it. His conclusions confirmed other sources of information, that tidal estuarine conditions prevailed until fresh water habitats briefly formed.

Graeme Mason identified all our shellfish, large and small. He contributed mightily to our understanding of environmental changes.

Close coastal conditions then returned until, in the uppermost layers, land snails made an appearance. This volume was published by the Society of Antiquaries in 1996 (Thompson 1996).

Volume 5

Three years later, Nancy Tayles's report on the human remains was published (Tayles 1999). There are sites with an acidic environment where no human bones have survived, others where the condition of bones is marginal for the sort of information that prehistorians seek. For KPD, the bones are in an outstanding state, virtually semi-fossilized. Nancy's findings are crucial to assessing this prehistoric community. There was a very high incidence of infant mortality, that was probably the result of a pathological gene for thalassaemia. This condition gives protection against malaria, but is debilitating if one parent suffers from it and lethal of both confer it on the newly born. All sorts of fascinating information emerges from the pages of her contribution. In early phases of the mortuary sequence, men had powerful upper body musculature, but this was to fall away later. Could it be that the earlier men habitually took to their boats to trade the pots made by the women and bring back the marine shell for ornaments, and doubtless other valuables? A detailed inspection of genetically determined cranial and dental abnormalities suggested that the successive clusters of graves contained related people. Bones revealed an excellent diet, and as in other Neolithic sites in Southeast Asia, particular teeth were extracted, probably to mark rites of passage. Nancy was to obtain a post in the University Anatomy Department and found a long and successful tradition of bioarchaeology that continues to this day. I was so fortunate that she took up my offer of studying our human skeletons from KPD.

Volume 6

Brian Vincent's early career was as a builder. He successfully accumulated a portfolio of commercial properties in Dunedin that provided him with a substantial income. In about 1970, he decided to embark on studying for a University degree that included my first year paper in archaeology. He was a zealous student who often approached me after a lecture with questions. When he graduated, he expressed an interest in post-graduate research, and I told him that pottery vessels and broken potsherds were easily the most abundant artefacts found in Southeast Asia and that they contained a wealth of potential information. He funded himself to go to Southampton University to learn from the master ceramicist, David Peacock, and then joined me at Ban Na Di as project ceramicist. Our pottery vessels formed the basis of his PhD dissertation in which he stressed the importance of fabric analysis to source clays and evaluate exchange patterns. Just having graduated, it was natural that he came to KPD, one of the greatest pottery-making sites known in Southeast Asia. He came with his wife Margaret and two young sons for months at the site. We provided him with tables and as many villager assistants as he wished, and he processed every one of hundreds of thousands of potsherds with a hand lens as they emerged from the excavation square. In those days we enjoyed the luxury of securing permission to transport all our finds to our laboratory in Otago, and this included every complete pot, not to mention the numerous clay anvils that had been used to form them, and a handsome sample of the sherds.

Brian died suddenly in March 2016, and at his funeral I said that his volume on the ceramics from KPD would never be bettered and very rarely if ever matched. Running to 896 pages, it presents in almost excruciatingly exhaustive detail the prehistory of a community for which pottery making was, in many ways, the raison d'etre. We have seen how the infant buried alongside burial 15 was accompanied by a miniature anvil. Even a little girl barely 18 months old was already sitting beside her mother learning to shape and manipulate clay. Brian took clay samples from the surrounding terrain and was able thereby to identify local wares, and tease out the few sherds that were imported from elsewhere. He traced the evolution of preferred forms, and it was he who pinpointed the shift in sources and decorative forms that led to our mortuary phase 3 being subdivided. It was much later that we learned from the isotopes in teeth that this was also a period when some women entered the community from elsewhere. Brian was almost certainly correct in pointing out that what I had described as a weaving implement had actually been used to incise designs on pots before they were fired (Vincent 2004). His report, the sixth volume in our series, was published in 2004 and Rachanie and I then had the challenge of composing the final synthesis of the site.

Volume 7

Distilling such a wealth of information from 32 contributors was a taxing responsibility. Bryan Manly joined us in undertaking a statistical analyses of the burials based on the degree of mortuary wealth and Alex Bentley showed us that while the majority of the dead were raised locally, based on the strontium isotopes in their teeth, the initial settlers and women during the third mortuary phase came from a different environment. On the basis of the superpositions of the burials, we also constructed likely lineages of related individuals over about 17-20 generations, and then traced the temporal changes in artefact styles, wealth and burial rituals. The pottery forms and decoration were also deployed to seek relationships with other settlements. All these and many other sources of information related to the key issue. Who were the people of KPD? Were they descended from marine hunter-gatherers whose ancestors lived in Sundaland, that vast tract the size of India submerged by the rising sea during the Holocene? Moving progressively inland as the sea rose, were they already adapted to life on an estuary? Or did the first settlers come to KPD as part of the diaspora of rice farmers, whose ultimate origins lay in the pioneers of rice farming located in the Yangtze River habitat far to the north? A model straddling both would have KPD occupied by marine hunter gatherers, people of Australo-Papuan stock, who melded with incoming farmers into a community of mixed origins.

Brian Vincent's volume on the ceramics from Khok Phanom Di will never be matched for any other Southeast Asian site.

I was struck throughout the excavation and subsequent analyses by the sheer quantity of marine shellfish, crabs and fish remains, and the rarity of domestic cattle, pigs and dogs. This made me veer towards thinking of the inhabitants as essentially rich and in some phases socially ranked, coastal hunter-gatherers. On the other hand, it was also quite clear that domestic rice was part of the diet, whether imported from inland communities such as have been well documented in the Khao Wong Prachan Valley and at Ban Kao, or locally grown during phases of lower sea level. We also in our conclusions, were aware of the linguistic evidence for a spread of rice farmers who probably introduced proto-Austroasiatic languages.

Since our final report was published in 2004 (Higham and Thosarat 2004), the situation has greatly clarified. Excavations in contemporary coastal settlements in Vietnam have shown beyond reasonable doubt that rice farmers who expanded south from the Yangtze River lowlands into northern Vietnam encountered and mixed with the Australo-Papuan indigenous hunter gatherers. This is based on several lines of enquiry including cranial and dental morphology and DNA. In 1991, I made a first attempt with Erica Hagelberg to extract DNA from the KPD bones but with no success. Then, in 2015, Hirofumi Matsumura came to Phimai and I watched as he began to take dimensions from the KPD human skulls. He then added these to his database, ran multivariate statistical tests, and showed that the population of our site was virtually identical with not only other Neolithic farmers in Southeast Asia, but also the rice farmers of Weidun in the lower Yangtze Valley (Matsumura et al. 2017, 2019). Hence, I published a revision of my interpretation of KPD, that saw the site settled by a group of expansive rice farmers who chose to settle on the shore of a sub-tropical estuary, brought with them their preferred adze forms, fishing technology, pottery forms and associated decoration, expertise in manufacturing shell and stone ornaments, and who survived despite debilitating thalassaemia, for five centuries, about 20 generations (Higham 2017).

The excavation of Nong Nor. Nancy Tayles front right is dealing
with a very rich burial with bronze and tin ornaments.

Nine | Ban Bon Noen and Nong Nor

I did not contemplate any further excavations between 1985 and 1989 as I was fully involved in the analysis of Khok Phanom Di. I really thought after all the commitment to Khok Phanom Di that my digging days were over. During 1989, however, my trowel hand began to itch and I thought of returning. Rachanie was based in Bangkok and we knew of a site near Khok Phanom Di called Ban Bon Noen, where our earlier site survey had turned up glass and gold beads and prehistoric potsherds. I secured some funding from my University, and Earthwatch accepted my proposal for their participation. As the number of volunteers increased, so I had sufficient for a modest excavation.

Two of my former students, Jacqui Pilditch and Lee Aitken joined us and we lived in the village just a few metres from the excavation square. I was only in Thailand for three weeks, and the excavation itself is the only one I have directed in Thailand that was disappointing. We found little of interest, and what we did find was ultimately written up by one of my students for a Master's dissertation. For me, there was a serious positive when a villager called on us with the news that he had found something of interest when he was digging in his rice field. We drove to his find spot and found that, a metre or so below the ground surface, he had come across concentrated marine shells. We expanded his pit and found cord-marked prehistoric potsherds in among the shells. I concluded that this could be an interesting site and marked it down for future investigation. The site was called Nong Nor.

Once again, it was necessary to seek funding. Henry Wright from the University of Michigan was on the Research Committee of the National Geographic Society, and in 1987, I heard that he was visiting New Zealand. I contacted him and invited him to stay with us. During his visit he asked what I was up to, and I gave him a quick summary of Khok Phanom Di along with some colour slides. He was very impressed. I told him that the National Geographic was the only institution that had declined

I am a great admirer of Henry Wright, who provided continual support from the National Geographic Research Committee.

133

Between seasons at Nong Nor, I lived in sumptuous rooms in the Tudor second court of St John's College, Cambridge, seen here on the first floor to the left of the Salisbury Tower. There I wrote my book, *The Bronze Age of Southeast Asia*.

my application for funding to work there. However, my next approach was successful, for they provided us with a most welcome grant to work at Nong Nor. Further financial support came from the British Academy, the University of Otago and Southern Cross University in Australia. This, together with the ever faithful Earthwatch, made it possible. On the 13th January 1991, I left for Bangkok and a week in the seaside resort of Hua Hin, for a small meeting on later complex societies in Southeast Asia. We stayed in the sumptuous Railway Hotel in rooms bedecked with teak and marble, right on the sea front. Rachanie and I then drove to Ban Bon Noen, our village base for the excavation of Nong Nor. Our funds had just about allowed us to buy a new Toyota pickup, that was to serve us loyally for the next 20 years.

The first Earthwatch team arrived the following day and we billeted them with family homes in the village, while my team occupied our own house. Bill Boyd is a geomorphologist, who had contacted me to ask if he could join us, and I willingly agreed. He arrived as we began, and set to work trying to figure out the environmental history of what to me looked like a monotonous plain of rice fields. Graeme Mason came too, and he took charge of sorting the shellfish. Nancy Tayles was with me for her first of many seasons excavating the human burials. Three of my students added to the team, one of whom, Nigel Chang, was to play a prominent role in my research for the next thirty years, and still does.

Our first excavation area was disappointing. A very thin layer of shell midden, incorporating burials most of which had been looted. Ownership of the land was divided between two villagers, one of whom gave us permission to excavate, while the woman heading the other family adamantly refused. Even after soliciting help from the abbot of her temple, she stood firm. And it was her two sons who had looted the neighbour's property but not it seems, their own. Socially the dig went well. Rachanie and I played an evening game of chess, while a nearby swimming hole was visited after each day in the field. The initial disappointment was alleviated when we extended the excavated area and found the shell midden thickening, and a good number of complete graves. The dead were interred with pottery vessels unlike any at Khok Phanom Di, and wore bronze bangles, shell beads and shell neck pendants. Quite a few were also interred with dog's skulls. One stratigraphically taxing issue was sorting out the relationship between the shell midden and the burials, since the graves were found within and apparently sealed by the shells, of which there were literally thousands. By my departure date, the 23rd February, we had uncovered 41 burials, some of which were complete and impressive in terms of mortuary offerings. I arrived home to news of a military coup in Bangkok. Rachanie continued for a few days after my departure and by the 1st March she reported 50 burials. The presence of so much bronze clearly placed them later than KPD, but there was also a complete absence of iron. It seemed prima facie to be a Bronze Age site.

In 1991-2, I had a sabbatical year, and successfully applied to St John's College Cambridge for the Benians Fellowship, given to honour a previous Master. I took this up in October of that year, and was given a sumptuous set of rooms in the same Tudor court that Barry Cunliffe had enjoyed 31 years previously. I threw myself into college life, playing squash, tasting wine, attending numerous seminars and lectures and delivering my own on Nong Nor so far. I listened to Bach's St John's Passion in the chapel and met the Archbishop of Canterbury – it was quite a time! In December I returned briefly to Dunedin to be at son Tom's wedding and daughter Emma's 21st birthday. Then on the 11th January I left home for Bangkok and another season at Nong Nor. This season we were lucky enough to be joined by Chuay and Jong, our foreman at Khok Phanom Di, Nancy, Bill Boyd and Graeme Mason. As we explored the site further, we found that the shell midden grew increasingly deep and stratigraphically complex, including animal bones, potsherds and clay anvils, hearths and stone adzes. There were also many burials and in this our second season, we uncovered a further 65, most of which were intact. We found infants interred in mortuary pots, and adults in an extended, supine position associated with pottery vessels, marble,

One day, all the shell bangles were stolen by looters. We did recover them thanks to the local police.

Burial 105 was a beauty, 4 metres long for a rich male who wore a bronze bangle and a tin earring. Nigel Chang wears the yellow hat.

Our excavation at Nong Nor. Graeme Mason in the yellow hat, Bill Boyd also in a hat.

serpentine and bronze bangles and bone neck pendants. The distribution of the graves increasingly suggested two groups.

One grave contained a cache of thin socketed bronze implements resembling little chisels, a type known to us at sites in the Khao Wong Prachan Valley, 240 km to the north. The site of Non Pa Wai was then under excavation led by Vince Pigott, and on their down day a team including Andy Weiss, Roberto Ciarla and Miriam Stark arrived, just in time to view our remarkable burial 105. This male lay in a grave nearly 4 m long, and wore a splendid bronze bangle. When we removed the skull, we found a tin earring. One of our village excavators, Suwanna, I recall as just about the best excavator I had encountered up to this point. Left handed, she had a eagle eye and I was lost in admiration when I watched her deftly trace and uncover tin bangles in another grave, bangles so fragile and similar in colour to the surrounding matrix that they were virtually invisible to the ordinary eye.

One morning we arrived to commence digging when to our horror, we found that looters had descended on us overnight and ripped all the shell and marble bangles off the arm bones. Rachanie called the Phanat Nikhom police to investigate and we convinced ourselves that we would never see our precious finds again. The police moved swiftly, following some local leads to a temple in the neighbouring town of Chachoengsao. The thieves must have taken fright, given the ornaments to the abbot, and by evening all were safely returned. We celebrated that evening, and the regular game of chess with Rachanie was deferred.

While digging away in the main square, Bill Boyd was out and about with a hand-picked team of what we called "the moles", because we could see the mounds of earth accumulate where they were burrowing down into the natural substrate. He was evaluating the sections and the accumulation of different layers, mapping where there was sand here, or riverine deposition there, and gradually a picture began to emerge of where Nong Nor had once been situated. During the midden occupation phase, they had chosen the shore of a marine embayment, with access to the open sea by boat. We had surveyed round the Nong Nor site, and lo and behold, the other shell midden sites were also dotted along the same ancient shore.

I left Bangkok to return to Cambridge on the 18th February, arriving at St John's in snow flurries and a freezing temperature. My sabbatical had been approved on the basis that I would compose a book for the Cambridge University Press on the Bronze Age of Southeast Asia, and this occupied my working hours throughout the rest of the year. I was fortunate to be where I was with access to the University library and a lot of Chinese sources, because I began the book in northwest China and the arrival there of stimuli from the Steppe practitioners of copper smelting and casting. Noel Barnard had written on those Chinese sites and the limited range of simple artefacts cast. I then traced the spread of metallurgy south, and ultimately into Southeast Asia, citing for chronology my results from Ban Na Di and my personal views on the dating of Ban Chiang and Non Nok Tha. On chronology, I find that on re-reading what I was saying nearly 30 years ago, I was not far off more recent findings. I said then that knowledge of alloying and casting and the exchange of ingots were rapidly disseminated from southern China into Southeast Asia between 1500-1000 BC. However, I was not adamant, adding that "I am not prepared to reject an alternative hypothesis, that were quite independent local origins for the southern bronze tradition, because it is still possible that acceptable assemblages of dates before 1800-2000 BC for bronze casting will one day be obtained." (Higham 1996:338). I also concluded that there was no evidence for rapid social change involving the presence of marked social inequality. This was self evident on the basis of the available evidence from the few Bronze Age sites examined, including Nong Nor.

I arranged in September to present a paper on Nong Nor at the European Association of Southeast Asian Archaeologists in Rome. We drove down first to Bagnac-sur-Célé in Quercy, where I had arranged to stay in Jack Goody's old stone farmhouse. Jack and Esther lived just up the road, and we had a wonderful sojourn, exploring this part of France that included visits to the caves at Pech Merle, to admire

Dating Nong Nor was not easy. We found some hearths below the shell midden, however, that placed initial settlement in about 2500 BC.

the Palaeolithic cave art, and the Romanesque church of Conques. We then drove south through the Tarn Gorges to Arles, where we admired the Roman amphitheatre. We then moved on to Lucca, Florence and Siena before checking in to our hostelry in Via Cesare Balbo in the heart of Rome.

It was a memorable meeting, in which I gave a summary of our findings at Nong Nor to date. I do not have a copy of my paper, and my publication in the conference proceedings came after the third season. My memory tells me that I was still undecided on the relationship between the midden phase at Nong Nor and the

It was quite uncomfortable digging at Nong Nor, the carpet of *Meretrix* shells was sharp and hard.

Left: We were incredibly lucky to have Chuay with us again, and he did all the recording of the burials.

Right: Initially, we had difficulty as to whether the burials and the shell midden were contemporary, but this grave shows how the shells in grave fill were dispersed, meaning that the burials were later.

burials containing bronze mortuary offerings, but no iron. I had no radiocarbon dates as yet. It was thus a work in progress, and I recollect raising the possibility that the first bronze metallurgy might have been earlier than my suggested span of 1500-1000 BC that I was putting into my book draft. Vince Pigott gave his paper on the copper mining sites in the Khao Wong Prachan Valley, noting that they could possibly go back to 1500 BC. On our way home, we left our two daughters near Aix-en-Provence to join a Cambridge University excavation, and drove on to visit once again, Arcy-sur-Cure where we met up with the excavation team still with some of our friends from 1956, including André Leroi-Gourhan.

I spent the rest of the year in Cambridge, hearing from the National Geographic Society that they approved a further grant for our third season at Nong Nor. After returning to Dunedin for Christmas, I set off once again for Bangkok on the 9th January. Our third season went very well. There were many more burials, including one male interred with bull's horns placed round his skull. Two more teams of Earthwatch volunteers came and went, meaning that over the three seasons we had assistance from a total of 50. Nigel Chang was a huge help in organising their accommodation in the village and keeping them informed of what was needed of them. By the end of this season, they helped us reach a grand total of 167 burials and a massive sample of biological and artefactual data from the thick shell midden that we dealt with. Amphan was a great help with logistics, and by my departure for home on the 22nd February, he had secured permission for us to ship all these finds to Dunedin in a container for the long commitment to analysis and publication. Rachanie and I had already plans for a fourth season to try and trace the entire perimeter of the site in the part of it for which we had permission to excavate. But on the 18th March, I received a letter from her that was to change dramatically my future in archaeological fieldwork. The Fine Arts Department was moving her from head office in Bangkok to the regional office in Phimai. This ruled out a return to Nong Nor and focused my attention on an entirely new venture on the Khorat Plateau.

Dating Nong Nor has not been entirely straightforward. By minutely examining the stratigraphy where a grave was cut into the deep shell midden, we decided that they were later and intrusive. While the grave fill contained many shellfish, they were more diffuse than in the tightly packed midden itself. Only one burial was clearly contemporary with the midden, that of an old female found in a flexed, seated posture under four pottery vessels. This is the typical mortuary ritual of the indigenous hunter-gatherers of Southeast Asia. In our final report, my son Tom and his colleague Alan Hogg at the University of Waikato dated the initial settlement of phase 1, the occupation represented by the midden, on the basis of charcoal taken from in situ hearths. All indicate settlement in the vicinity of 2500 BC, comfortably earlier than the arrival of the first occupants of Khok Phanom Di. However, no in situ charcoal was found in the second, or cemetery use of the site, for which there was no hint of the site being occupied, save for some fragments of charcoal from an infant jar burial. We therefore turned to the possibility of dating fragments of rice chaff temper taken from pots placed with the dead. This is not a technique that is currently recommended for a variety of possible sources of contamination. For what they are worth, they suggest that the cemetery was in use between about 1000-500 BC. No iron was found at this site. But one burial contained a handful of carnelian beads that are typically thought to date to the Iron Age. There are two groups of graves, and I think that one of these is earlier and belongs in the Bronze Age, while the other probable takes the site into the early years of the Iron Age, that is beyond about 500 BC.

Once all our finds arrived in Dunedin, my students, colleagues and I set to work. The broken pots were stuck together and sent to Martin Fisher and Les

An abiding memory of Nong Nor was the millions of shellfish, all studied in the field and lab by Graeme Mason.

O'Neill to prepare illustrations, and the human bones were laid out for Nancy Tayles to examine. Bill Boyd worked on his field observations and sent me three chapters in which he detailed the environment that the first settlers encountered. He found that there were three palaeogeographic phases beginning with the middle to late Pleistocene, when the site lay on an undulating plain at least 100 km from the coast. The second saw the sea rise and form a marine embayment, the rich natural resources of which attracted the phase 1 settlement. These included the shellfish of the sandy shore, marine mammals, and the fish of the embayment and the open sea. This reconstruction drew on Christine Pailles's identification of estuarine and coastal diatoms from one of our sections.

Dougald O'Reilly came to the Otago Department from Canada, keen to pursue his interest in Southeast Asian prehistory. I suggested that for his Master's degree, he take on the analysis of the artefacts from the midden representing phase 1 of the occupation. He found that there are a number of similarities between the bone, ceramic and stone artefacts we found in the midden, and those from basal Khok Phanom Di. Some of the pottery vessels and sherds, for example, were embellished with incised and impressed patterns. The fish hooks are very similar. Clay anvils had been used to shape pottery vessels. There were similar bone points that might have been used to incise designs on the pottery vessels before they were fired. Stone adzes, grinders and whetstones were also a good match between the two sites. Were the inhabitants of this site in the mid-third millennium BC incoming rice farmers, indigenous hunter-gatherers who also used polished stone adzes, one-piece barbed fishhooks and incised and impressed pottery vessels, or perhaps, a mixed population of both? The single human burial points markedly towards a community that certainly practised the mortuary traditions of the indigenous hunter-gatherers. What was the subsistence base of these people?

Here again, we turned to the mammalian bones and the shellfish and fish. Large deer and bovid bones, including water buffalo were found, many having been worked into artefacts. We felt that bones were collected for industrial purposes rather than systematically hunted. Not one bone came from a domestic animal, and that included a complete absence of dogs. This is significant, prehistoric dogs were descended from the wolf, and there are no indigenous wolves in Southeast Asia. Hence, any dog must have been introduced, as by immigrant farmers. The inhabitants hunted dolphins and we found a crocodile tooth. Graeme Mason achieved a second monumental contribution on the shellfish. Our sample was dominated by the bivalve *Meretrix*, that is adapted to sandy ground just below low tide. He counted 2,520,445 specimens, 99.7% of the entire assemblage of 50 different species. Just four of these prefer a freshwater habitat, and another four are today found on dry land. The vast majority prefer marine or mangrove conditions. He concluded that the site was surrounded by mangroves and within a short distance of an open sea coast. Crabs were also collected, while his report on the fish identified deep sea fishing for weasel, tiger and oceanic white-tipped sharks. While out at sea, they caught eagle and shovel-nosed rays and, as at Khok Phanom Di, they also fished for barramundi.

I am still left with an element of indecision. I can envisage a situation in which early farming groups, perhaps following a coastal route, settled along or behind the coast of the Gulf of Siam. Dougald O'Reilly concluded that the midden phase might not have lasted for more than a season. Perhaps a subset of a farming community occupied the shore of this rich marine embayment for the dry season, having already met with and integrated with local hunter-gatherers. We found not one particle of evidence for rice, either as a ceramic temper or in the midden itself. Again, it is conceivable that this community decamped inland for the duration of the wet season when rice cultivation would have been undertaken. As they say, only future research will tell.

I let two of my students loose on the phase 2 mortuary offerings. Joss Debreceny looked at the pottery vessels, finding a distinct tradition quite different from Khok Phanom Di, with the pots often red slipped and generously tempered with rice chaff. Nigel Chang described the ornaments. These numerically were dominated by marine shell, marble and bronze bangles, shell beads and so far in Thailand, unique shell pendants worn at the neck. We also found rare serpentine, talc, nephrite and carnelian ornaments in the eastern group of burials. A couple of glass beads turned up, neither securely linked to a human burial. It is the carnelian in particular that makes us think that burials continued into the early Iron Age despite the complete absence of any iron. I asked my geologist colleague Tony Reay, together with Nigel Chang, to look at the metal artefacts. They found that the bangles were cast from a tin bronze, but the little socketed implements found in a cache with one of the burials were unalloyed copper. Our field estimate that some bangles and earrings were made of tin was confirmed. I looked at the mammalian remains placed in the graves. These were, most unusually, dominated by dog bones, particularly the skull, followed by the foot bones of young pigs.

Nancy Tayles was joined by another promising student, Kate Domett, to report on the human skeletons, all of which had been drawn for publication by Les O'Neill. These were nowhere near as well preserved as at KPD, and no complete skulls survived to be measured. However they did present a similar form to the people of KPD. The cemetery incorporated males and females in equal proportions and only 20% of the graves contained infants or children, a very low figure compared with KPD. People were in general healthier than their Neolithic predecessors, perhaps because they no longer lived in a mangrove habitat.

With 55 different artefact types distributed across 49 complete and undisturbed burials, I decided that it would be best to ask Bryan Manly to join with me to undertake statistical analyses. He subjected our data to various programs including principal component analysis and multidimensional scaling. We found that in the western group a male and row of four females stood out for rather more mortuary wealth than the norm. The eastern group contained all the exotic stone ornaments, but not in sufficient numbers to make an impact on the results of our analyses. Overall, we did not find any convincing evidence for different wealth based on gender or age. Only grinding stones were favoured with male interments. There was no relationship between bronzes and tin offerings and other sources of wealth, but one pottery form was specific to eastern group graves, probably due to change over time.

Rachanie and I then had to summarise and try and locate Nong Nor in a broader pattern of adaptations and changes. This was not easy. We had to wrestle with the similarities in material culture between early KPD and Nong Nor, against when and how the first rice farming was established. There were at least four different models, varying from a wave of advance that brought farmers into the coastal tracts by the mid-third millennium BC, a local transition into farming, or a situation in which intrusive rice farmers interacted with long-established coastal hunter-gatherers. Nong Nor phase 1 remains unique for Central Thailand, as there is no comparative site for the mid-third millennium BC. We wrote 30 years ago, and can reiterate it today, that if only we could extract DNA from the human bones, we would be a long way to resolving the status of this site. We then favoured an interaction model, but this, again, needs more comparative information.

When turning to the Bronze Age cemetery, we also faced some difficult issues. Uniquely, the second occupation phase of Nong Nor contained no occupation evidence. The people must have lived somewhere else and chose this area for burying their dead. We still have no satisfactory radiocarbon-based chronology. In our report, we had a date range of 1000-500 BC, but noted that the dating of rice-chaff temper was experimental. We have since learned that there are too many sources of potential contamination to rely on such evidence. I think that the correct span for the cemetery lies between 600-400 BC. Our conclusion with regard to the social organisation reflected on my published findings for Ban Na Di and other available sites, that Bronze Age communities were autonomous, small and expressed individual status through ownership of exotic valuables.

I turned to Les O'Neill to format the 23 chapters, that included 243 figures and 66 tables from 23 authors, using the program Aldus Pagemaker. Our report was published in 1998 as a monograph by the Otago Anthropology Department, handsomely printed and bound by the University Printing Facility (Higham and Thosarat 1998). One great plus of our Nong Nor campaign is that it was where a group of young contributors, in the field and laboratory, laid the foundations for their future in Southeast Asia, including Dougald O'Reilly, Nigel Chang, Kate Domett and Hallie Buckley.

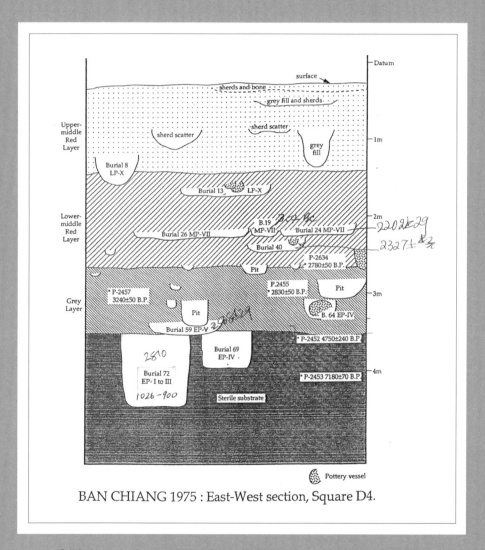

BAN CHIANG 1975 : East-West section, Square D4.

This is the section I devised for Ban Chiang from the site level plans Chet had given me, with my handwritten notes. I showed it at the Chiang Mai conference.

Ten | Back to the Northeast and Ban Lum Khao

In January 1994, the Indo-Pacific Archaeological Association held its four-yearly conference in Chiang Mai. I thought that the time was right to give my views on the chronology of the Bronze Age with particular reference to Non Nok Tha and Ban Chiang. Twenty years had elapsed since we began our excavations there, and I had already in 1983 shown that the dates published by Chet Gorman and Pisit Charoenwongsa were derived in the main from disturbed and therefore unreliable contexts, particularly when compared with those from the in-situ hearths we had uncovered and dated at Ban Na Di. In 1988, I had also presented a critique of the dating of Non Nok Tha, at a meeting in Kioloa, Australia, again mentioning the unreliable contexts from which the charcoal for dating had been collected. I began my paper with this statement: "The potent influence of radiocarbon dating upon archaeology was recognized from its earliest availability. But it is a double-edged sword. Handled judiciously, it opens new horizons for understanding the prehistoric past. Used incautiously, it will confuse and distort the images we seek".

My stance was to adopt what colleagues Atholl Anderson and Matthew Spriggs (Spriggs 1989, Spriggs and Anderson 1993) had described as "chronometric hygiene", along with a review of the contexts from which the charcoal samples had come from, and the layout of the early Bronze Age cemetery at Ban Chiang. Chet Gorman had long since provided me with xeroxed copies of all our level plans from the 1975 excavation. There was no difficulty by using these, to prepare a section through the site. Onto this, I projected the location of the burials in the square D4, and the location from which the very few in situ radiocarbon determinations were found. These included a hearth that had furnished 800 grams of charcoal, located within the lowest stratigraphic layer from which early Bronze Age graves were cut. This determination I cited as 1118-891 cal. BC, a date in agreement with the corresponding layers from Ban Na Di. It was a detailed and, I thought, convincing re-assessment of the chronology for the Bronze Age as then documented. Several people congratulated me after I had finished. Andrew Weiss came up and said that he now saw more clearly the stratigraphic issues at Non Nok Tha.

The meeting ended and on the 12th January, I drove for 12 hours to Phimai, to join Rachanie in the first of our surveys to determine a site for our next excavation

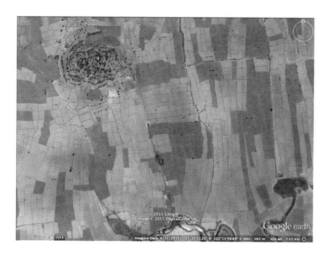

Noen U-Loke, surrounded by five moats and with a probable canal running down to the south, easily spotted now with Google Earth.

campaign. She was now on the staff of the Phimai Office of the FAD, living in a very attractive house in the compound there, with a garden that sloped down to the Nam Khem stream. There was a gazebo on the river bank where we could dine *al fresco* and watch out for kingfishers. I felt that we could not start seeking out sites in the immediate area round Phimai, because David Welch and Judith McNeill had made it their own. So I consulted with them both and agreed that we would work to the west of the area that they had already surveyed. When she was not committed to meetings or desk duties, Rachanie and I drove out to identify prehistoric sites in our chosen area. It is much easier now, with access to Google Earth, to pinpoint moated sites. We managed to obtain air photos from the Non Sung regional government office, and our first port of call was a site already known and excavated by Metha Wichakana called Noen U-Loke. I had this one underlined in my notebook for its potential. A large mound ringed by five moats, it lay in the rice fields with no modern occupation to obstruct excavation. Metha had found both Bronze and Iron Age occupation and burials, the latter including a male wearing an interesting bronze headband.

Field walking also revealed small, steep-sided mounds covered in industrial-looking pottery that we felt were probably the result of processing salt. January 29th was a special day, we visited Ban Non Wat to inspect this village surrounded by two moats and banks, spotting as we walked over the site a beautiful bird we identified as a chestnut-fronted bee eater. I wonder if it ever found as much nectar at this site as we did a decade later. Two days on, we tracked down another fine moated settlement, Non Ban Jak, near the village of Ban Nong Khrua Chut. Like Noen U-Loke, it was out among the rice fields with no modern settlement on it, but we were informed that a looting gang had recently crawled all over it with their metal detectors. It was a very useful month in the field, and I returned home on the 8th February my head buzzing with anticipation of a return to the field sooner rather than later.

On the 13th September, a really important event took place. I went to a meeting at which Sir Ian Axford described the foundation of a new government basic science research fund. Christened the Marsden Fund, it was to prove the breakthrough I badly needed to fund my ambitions in the Phimai area fieldwork. This programme continued in November of 1994, when I obtained University funds to attend a conference in New Delhi. I used this grant to travel via Bangkok in order to continue my site surveys. This venture took an unexpected turn when Rachanie drove me to the airport in Bangkok for my late evening flight to Delhi. I checked in my suitcase and awaited my boarding pass, but the check-in clerk spent a long time looking through the pages of my passport. Finally she asked after my India visa. I had none. I lamely asked if I needed a visa on my other passport, which was British. Yes was the reply. My suitcase was returned and I took a taxi back to Rachanie's house, and surprised her by throwing some stones against her bedroom window pane. I learned later that the Delhi meeting was an utter shambles, marred by riots between Muslim and Hindu delegates over the Ayutthaya temple. Colin Renfrew had to borrow a slide projector from the British Embassy, and I would have arrived at about 3.00 am with no hotel booked.

Rachanie and I drove straight up to Phimai, and we continued our site survey. This included a visit to the newly constructed museum at the site of Ban Prasat, a very impressive moated site just off the main road from Bangkok to Khon Kaen. Most attractive ceramic vessels had suddenly shown up in the Bangkok weekend market for sale, and the FAD traced them back to Ban Prasat, scene of Ban Chiang-style looting. They arranged for an excavation in the centre of the site. After an upper layer of Iron Age graves, they uncovered rows of Bronze Age burials endowed with an unprecedented number of fine pots identical with those that had been seen in the weekend market in Bangkok. One male burial in particular stood out for its extreme wealth, that included a bronze, socketed axe. These burials were all left in place. I asked for access and clambered down a very long ladder to examine these interments close up. I was very impressed, it seemed that perhaps the initial Bronze Age was more socially effervescent than seen at Ban Na Di and Ban Chiang.

I was back in Phimai the following February, to complete surveying our study area, this time equipped with an early version of a GPS gadget to record the precise location of any identified sites. On the 3rd March, we visited a village called Ban Lum Khao. It too had been looted, but the owners of a property towards the edge of the mound took us to where a stream had eroded into a bank, and there in section, we saw a human skull and the same style of trumpet-rimmed red Bronze Age pots as we had seen at Ban Prasat. Knowing that we would find at least a Bronze Age occupation here, I earmarked the site for potential excavation. Two days later, we

We visited the open museum at Ban Prasat and gazed down into a remarkable scene of super rich Bronze Age burials.

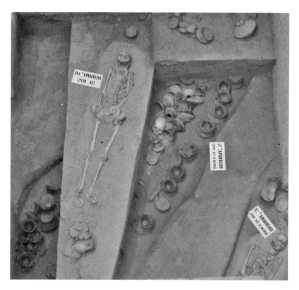

This burial at Ban Prasat attracted my attention: a very wealthy male with multiple pots and a bronze socketed axe. The grave above was left undisturbed.

turned a corner on a remote track to see ahead a high mound. We drove up onto it and alighted. The surface was covered in prehistoric potsherds, and as we wandered over it, we began to realise its extent, it was a very large and impressive prehistoric settlement. A passing villager told us that it was called Non Muang Kao, "Ancient City Mound". Air photographs revealed two moats and linear earthworks radiating out beyond them. This site was also added to the list for future excavation.

We turned a corner, and saw a low mound. Driving up onto it we found many prehistoric potsherds. It was Non Muang Kao, "Mound of the Ancient City".

A fortnight later, I was back in Dunedin and preparing my first application to the Marsden Fund. If successful, the amount awarded was spectacularly more than I could ever have dreamed of. Over the three years of funding, I would be able to fulfill my ambition to open up a far more extensive area than had been possible under earlier campaigns. To hedge my bets, I also put in for further support from the National Geographic Society, and had useful feedback from Henry Wright on my draft. On the 5th May I had some hopeful news, my application to the Marsden Fund had made it through to the final round. This meant I had a 50-50 chance of success. I now had to work on the greatly expanded application papers. There was further good news on the 26th July, both my referees gave the application the top grade. The wait seemed interminable, but finally came through on the 5th September: $95,871.00. I was elated, and planning could now go ahead. Further good news came through a month later, $15,000 from the National Geographic Society. On November 22nd I departed for Bangkok and the excavation of Ban Lum Khao.

Ban Lum Khao

Rachanie had arranged for a roof to be constructed over our excavation square, and on arrival, we immediately began removing the top 20 cm of disturbed garden soil. As I had predicted from the exposed river bank, we were soon finding human burials, the first on just the second day of fieldwork. The next came a day later, when I wrote "couldn't believe it, just put in a 10 by 10 inch hole and there were pots". On the 1st December, I decided to excavate a small reconnaissance in the corner of the square, and to my surprise, began tracing round a very large and complete pottery vessel. No human bones were found outside it, but when we took off the lid and explored the interior, we came across two miniature pots of the same form and finish as those from Bronze Age Ban Prasat and a large bivalve shell, next to the skeleton of a newly born infant. The mortuary vessel was an impressive sight, red slipped in the upper part of the body and cord marked below, with an appliqué band rather like a snake running round the circumference at the shoulder. We were to find many more of these. Indeed, over the next few days, we continued to uncover more human graves and infant jar burials. I was by now joined by Nigel Chang and another student, Renée Flockton. As we continued down, we realised that we had sufficient time in hand to extend our excavation square. I had arranged to return home for Christmas, and by the time I left on the 20th December, we had recorded 30 burials.

I returned on the 1st January 1996 to find that Rachanie and Nigel had continued on down in my absence. Not satisfied with just the one site being excavated, I had a roof constructed on the top of Non Muang Kao, and began opening a 5 by 5 m square there too. Initially I worked there myself with a small team of villagers, but after a day or two I asked Dougald O'Reilly to take over, since so much was happening at Ban Lum Khao. My colleagues from Nong Nor also began to arrive, Nancy Tayles was going to be kept very busy as the number of graves accumulated at Ban Lum Khao, aided by a new recruit, Hallie Buckley.

The excavation square at Ban Lum Khao. The sacks are protecting burials.

I couldn't resist opening up an excavation at Non Muang Kao, and gave it over to Dougald O'Reilly to handle. He did a brilliant job.

Graeme Mason processed samples to retrieve all the shellfish and small faunal remains, and Jill Thompson had a new flotation chamber constructed to do the same for the flora. Bill Boyd joined us, and I asked him specifically to put his geomorphological expertise to the matter of the moats.

Non Muang Kao was proving to be very interesting. The cultural deposits were at times concrete hard, but this had the advantage of preserving intact clay wall foundations and floors. All sorts of new information flowed. The Iron Age occupants of this site had often cut circular pits in their floors, and placed lidded bowls within them. The pots were shiny from burnishing and fall into the category known from Bill Solheim's early work at Ban Suai in Phimai as "Phimai Black" ware. We also found that graves had been cut through the clay floors, giving us our first glimpse of genuine burials in what we took to be the rooms of domestic houses. The dead were interred with bronze and iron ornaments, fine ceramic vessels and beads of glass, exotic carnelian and agate. Some graves also contained masses of carbonised rice. My real regret about this remarkable site is that we only opened such a small area, and never found an opportunity to return and greatly expand further. If I had the opportunity, this would be very high on my list for a major assault through a mega excavation.

I had long puzzled over the broad moats that surround the Iron Age settlements of the Mun River valley. Were they constructed for defence, or to store water? Were they excavated deep into the substrate, were they associated with palisades, and when were they constructed? When there are multiple moats, were they all contemporary or were they progressively added to? It was at Non Muang Kao that Bill Boyd and I decided that the only way to solve these riddles was to hire a mechanical digger and cut sections through them. Some long-standing questions were answered within a day or two. They were constructed by building up banks to retain water that flowed into them from the adjacent stream. They had a flat base, and in no instance did we find evidence for a V-shaped cut into the substrate that would suggest a deep

We found rows of Bronze Age burials. Some wore exotic shell and marble bangles, and pots just like those from Ban Prasat.

We found a lot of lidded infant burial jars.

At Non Muang Kao we hired a digger to cut a massive trench through the moats.

defensive purpose. Sediments had built up and the moats always contained only shallow water. Bill collected charcoal from hearths stratified within the banks and sediments for radiocarbon dating.

Three Earthwatch teams joined us, each with eight or nine volunteers to stay for a fortnight. The additional funds were invaluable for all the extras one had to fund, particularly the cost of the roof, local labour and bringing my colleagues and students half way round the world. My task, not easy, was to find each one of them an interesting assignment that did not require previous excavation experience. Nancy Tayles ruled out any involvement of a volunteer in exposing a human skeleton other than on the very rare occasion that she had confidence in their manual dexterity and anatomical knowledge. Fortunately, the Ban Lum Khao dead were associated the pottery vessels often

Graeme Mason was there to study the shells again. But we could not export any to New Zealand for detailed analysis, and they have never been published.

placed away from the skeleton, and I assigned volunteers to uncover the pots, and clean them for photography in situ. If the pot was broken, I could then ask them to remove it, once it had been fully drawn and recorded, and take it up to the field lab to reconstruct it. This proved an invaluable string to our bow.

We continued to accumulate human burials at Ban Lum Khao, and as we progressed, the layout of the Bronze Age cemetery began to clarify. There were rows of graves and, in some cases, burials were also laid out with the head of one person next to the feet of another in straight as it were, vertical lines. We found many fine trumpet-rimmed Bronze Age pots, and marble and marine shell bangles. However, bronzes were virtually absent. We did not encounter any significant evidence for occupation in the form of structural post holes, pits, or middens. That bronze casting had taken place, however, was assured, since we found fragments of moulds and crucibles. Towards the end of our season at Ban Lum Khao, we entered the initial phase of occupation, seen in half a dozen deep pits filled with shellfish, animal bones and broken potsherds some of which were decorated with Neolithic incised and impressed designs. There were also ten burials that were earlier and different from those assigned to the Bronze Age. The pottery vessels associated with these burials were now small globular pots and little footed bowls. One male wore 786 shell beads, but ornaments were otherwise virtually absent.

Our third and last Earthwatch team left on the 16th February. It included three stalwarts with us for many further seasons, Meph Wyeth, Wilbert Yee and Roger Prior. Two days later I wrote that it was my first day off and I collapsed with tiredness. It poured with rain, and we dashed out to the site to cover the remaining baulks with tarpaulins. We found our 110th burial on the 22nd of February, as well as the biggest tridacna shell bangle I had seen to date, and then pronounced the excavation finished. New regulations had been promulgated by the FAD. Due to a general uprising of complaints against the fact that the finds from Ban Chiang were still, over 20 years after we had finished our excavations there, languishing in America, we were now forbidden from exporting our artefacts and other items for in-house analysis. We therefore had to move all our boxes of finds into the regional office of the FAD, with a detailed list of their contents.

I returned to New Zealand in the sure knowledge that the season had been a success. Rachanie was left in charge of reconstructing all the pottery vessels, and curating other artefacts. I did take back all the site plans and photographs and was therefore able to start cataloguing the latter and preparing the former for publication. Within a week of my return, I sent son Tom half a dozen samples for radiocarbon dating. These came from charcoal recovered from the basal pits, and they would reveal the date of the presumed Neolithic occupation. They came back on June 13th and were virtually identical, revealing that the initial Neolithic settlement took place in about 1275 BC, followed later by the initial Bronze Age.

Because we were unable transport any of our finds to Dunedin, I had to transport myself to Phimai, and I left on the 22nd June 1996 for the three-week duration of the University vacation. On arrival I found that Rachanie had done a splendid job in re-assembling the pots, and I took coloured slide images of each, for those were the days before digital images came on stream. We then took images of the adzes and bone artefacts, all of which had been cleaned ahead of my return. The principal objective then was to analyse all the animal bones. Fortunately, most were readily identifiable, and I noted that the Neolithic occupants hunted a lot of deer. There were also very large and probably wild water buffalo bones, but the number of buffalo fell markedly in the Bronze Age layers.

On the 8th July, we visited the headman whose village owned the site of Noen U-Loke. This highly impressive site, ringed by five moats and banks that covered a linear distance of about 200 metres, had long been in my sights, particularly after the promising finds encountered when Metha Wichakana had put in a couple of

We made such good progress at Ban Lum Khao that we extended the excavation twice.

small test squares. The headman was receptive to our overtures for permission to excavate.

While I was working in Rachanie's office at the Phimai Historic Park, I met Paisarn Piemmettawat. He was calling on the sales office with some books published by River Books in Bangkok, where he was the Manager. It struck me that the time was right to compose a book on prehistoric Thailand, and he expressed interest, saying that he would arrange a meeting with the owner, Narisa Chakrabongse.

One evening during my stay, Rachanie asked if I would like a swim. I naturally leapt at the idea, but where? She took me to the Phimai Inn, located on the outskirts of the town, and there to my delight, was an excellent swimming pool. As I cooled off after a long, hot and dusty day, it occurred to me that this Inn might be the perfect base for my colleagues and Earthwatch volunteers to stay. The experience at the Rice Research Institute, where they had stayed hitherto, had not been entirely successful. The provision of breakfast and lunch was difficult, the restaurant food delivered in the evening often arrived cold and I found myself in the evenings driving round delivering drinking water and other essentials to about four houses. We found that the Phimai Inn tariff was within our budget, and the restaurant was of top quality for breakfast and dinner, while they would prepare a picnic lunch to go out to the site daily. In the evenings we had projection facilities for lecture presentations, cold beer and, of course, the swimming pool. The Phimai Inn came to be a huge mainstay of our fieldwork. The details of accommodation sent out to prospective Earthwatch volunteers was a major means of filling our teams, and that meant the funds we needed so badly for all the extras of bringing in my students and specialists. I have always been, like Napoleon, a believer that an excavation team, as for an army, marches on its stomach.

One of the outstanding requirements of the Marsden Fund was the need to attend international conferences to inform on our findings. In August of 1996, I set off for two meetings, the first in Leiden and the second in Italy. My wife Polly came with me, and we stopped over in Bangkok. I took a taxi to meet Narisa, and found that she lived in a palatial compound with gardens tumbling down to the Chao Phraya River, commanding a view of the Wat Arun, Temple of the Dawn. She was directly descended from King Chulalongkorn through his son Prince Chakrabongse, and had a passion for publishing beautiful books on Thailand. We hit it off at once, agreed on the proposed new book, and have remained friends ever since. There were many highlights of the conference in Italy. I coincided with many old friends, had lunch with Paul Mellars and Desmond Clark, a chat with Philip Tobias and caught up with Colin Renfrew. But the most interesting was with Lawrence Barfield, last seen at the Birmingham University interview where I had been rejected. "Charlie" he said, "you should have got the Birmingham job". Reflecting on my life since that day, I replied "Lawrence, thank God I didn't".

What a Christmas present, burial 14, the richest Iron Age man
I have ever found.

Eleven | Noen U-Loke and Cambodia

We invested one season at Ban Lum Khao before turning to Noen U-Loke. The Earthwatch teams began to fill, and the National Geographic sent another cheque. If I had got that job at Birmingham, I would never have begun counting down the days to taking on this massive site, that lies out in the rice fields a couple of kilometres from the nearest village. We could have dug anywhere but I chose to excavate next to where Metha had worked. On my arrival on the 25th November 1996, I found that Rachanie had already organised a fine roof adjacent to the still-open square left by Metha Wichanaka a year or so previously. The following day, my student Paul Rivett and I laid out our own area to be excavated. As at KPD, it covered 10x10 metres, divided into four units, three under the direction of one of my graduate students. This introduced Paul Rivett, Sarah Talbot and Jeremy Habberfield-Short to the team. We began by exposing and cleaning the eroded edge of Metha's area where it abutted ours, and encouragingly came across some complete Phimai Black pots and a bronze bangle. Barbara Anderson also arrived. She had worked with Jill on the flotation programme at Ban Lum Khao, and we set her up by a stream near our site, where there was plenty of water available. As we proceeded down, we came across several complete lidded Phimai Black bowls, often in a small pit, a feature we had grown familiar with at Non Muang Kao where they had been placed in pits cut through room floors.

There was nothing to match the evidence for house structures at Noen U-Loke, but we did encounter pits and evidence for iron smithing. A fortnight into the season, however, and down to a depth of 1.3 m, we began to trace the contour of a large and complete pot that lay on its side. Before long, the human foot bones appeared, and by degrees we revealed a complete male skeleton. The complete pot contained the bones of an infant who died at or very soon after birth. The offerings within included a second, tiny pot, an iron knife, bronze earring and four metal bangles that looked like bronze covered in a thin layer of iron. We called these bimetallic, but years later Oliver Pryce told me that in fact, they were bronze. As we uncovered the male skeleton, I was taken aback by the wealth of grave goods, particularly in the light of the relative scarcity of bronzes I had found at Ban Chiang and Nong Nor. He wore about 55 bronze finger rings and 17 bangles, bronze coils to infill each ear lobe and was also accompanied by three pottery vessels.

For the first time in 17 years, I spent Christmas digging far from home. By now down two metres, we had a very acceptable seasonal present. Jeremy was off sick and I took over running his square. We found some foot bones among a mass of multi-coloured glass beads and rice. There is always the hope that on extending the operation, one will find an undisturbed grave, and this was increasingly likely as we traced up the leg bones. We could not see the finger bones because they were covered by about 70 bronze rings, but the real surprise came when I revealed a hint of green over the pelvis. This continued on and on until I reached where I had begun, there were three bronze belts each with a sophisticated catch at the front to secure them in place. And so this journey continued. There were 75 bronze bangles on each arm, and a silver coil covered in gold on either side of the skull, that had been inserted we think, as ornaments in the distended ear lobes. This one burial, in the space of 48 hours, transformed my perception of social elites during the Iron Age.

The ensuing two months were in retrospect, like a revealing newsreel of Iron Age society. We encountered two sharply-defined groups of graves, each first recognised by a silhouette of white rice chaff. Out of each emerged the skeletons of men, women and infants bedecked with glass, agate and carnelian beads and multiple bronze ornaments. Two contained the complete skeletons of young pigs. When Nancy lifted one skull and turned it over, it had a large bronze spiral attached. Rachanie had tutored our village excavators to uncover glass bead necklaces without disturbing a single bead. We also found the remains of a clay floor through which, it seemed, a grave had been cut. These two tight clusters were clearly earlier than our burial with the bronze belts. A sequence was beginning to emerge. This was expanded upon when we neared the natural substrate at a depth of nearly four metres, for here we found ourselves revealing two crystal clear grave cuttings. Each contained the complete remains of a male. One was clearly a hunter/warrior, he had a massive iron spear beside his head, and two spears of bronze by the feet. He wore four tiger's canine teeth, each pierced for suspension, round his neck, and his ear lobe inserts were made of shell. The fine ceramic vessels placed beside his ankles contained pig bones and fish skeletons. The adjacent male wore two pierced boar's tusks as neck pendants. Again a large pottery vessel contained a fish skeleton. It is notable that these early pottery vessels were quite different from the Phimai Black pots we had found in such profusion in the higher layers.

The season had many high points, but I also remember it for some unusual moments. Overnight, we always left our buckets used to remove excavated material within the square. One morning as we descended the access ladder and set to work, one of our villagers spied a lethally poisonous snake lurking in a bucket. He immediately warned us all, and covered it with another bucket so that it couldn't escape. My daughter Caroline was with us, and I have never seen her move so fast up the ladder and out of the square. The bucket was hoisted aloft, where a

We found that graves were filled with rice and when we removed it, the human skull appeared.

worker awaited with his broad bladed hoe. The snake was tossed onto our spoil heap of screened soil and immediately dispatched. It was a cobra. On the 11th February, I drove over the rice fields to the site, to find that overnight a fire had swept across Noen U-Loke, turning the surface into a blackened cinder. I panicked at the prospect that our finds, stored next to the excavation, would have gone up in smoke and that we had lost our cherished roof. But I need not have feared. The spoil heaps had by now encircled our site and protected it from the flames. We then realised that the mound was home to many families of pythons, their nests being exposed by the fire. Our villagers hauled these out, some many metres long and beautifully coloured. I can't recall what happened to them.

I left for home on the 21st February, leaving Rachanie to backfill the square and start on the huge task of sorting all our finds for once again, there was no way to export them to my lab in New Zealand. It had been a far more successful a season than I could possibly have imagined. We had encountered at least four mortuary phases in over 50 burials, along with domestic remains, floors, pits and iron-smithing facilities. At least I could take with me my site plans, sections and photographs to begin piecing together the sequence and think further on the wider implications of our discoveries. I also always pack my radiocarbon dating samples and sent them to Tom as soon as I returned. These came back in double quick time, and revealed as I suspected, that occupation covered the span of the Iron Age, a millennium from about 450 BC. I could also plan for our third Marsden-funded fieldwork season, which would undoubtedly involve extending our area opened at Noen U-Loke. I was able to decide this on the spot, as mid-year I spent what was necessarily becoming a new regime, flying up to Thailand to photograph and study our finds, and greet Judith Cameron who joined me to look at all our spindle whorls.

As the months ticked by before returning to Noen U-Loke, I had many commitments. I was learning to master the MX Freehand software to make my own

I always admired my Thai excavators who could uncover a necklace without disturbing one bead.

Right down at the bottom of the site we came across this splendid hunter wearing tiger canine pendants, bronze torcs and accompanied by his massive iron spear.

maps and plans for publication, and integrate them with the Pagemaker program for formatting text. Brian Vincent was giving me chapters of his Khok Phanom Di report on the ceramics for comment. I was working on Nancy Tayles's volume on the same site, and putting the finishing touches to the book on Prehistoric Thailand for Narisa. In October, I flew to England at the invitation of the British Academy to present a paper at a day to celebrate the life and contribution of Grahame Clark. I raised a gale of laughter when I recounted a conversation I had with him in 1966. Torn between accepting a position in a provincial museum in England or the lectureship at distant Otago I asked for his advice. His Seraphic response was immediate: "Higham, do you want to be a porter or a station master?"

I was garnering more money as the year progressed, the ASIA2000 Foundation gave $3,000 each to three of my students to join me in the field. The numbers of Earthwatch volunteers grew week by week, and there was another welcome cheque from the National Geographic Society. It would have been inconceivable to miss my daughter Emma's wedding on December 20th, but on the 1st January 1998, I took the well-trodden path to Momona Airport in Dunedin for Bangkok and our second season at Noen U-Loke. The luxury of having Rachanie in Phimai meant that on arrival, we had the roof put up and a 25-strong village labour force readied. We decided to wrap the new area round the old, to end up with a total excavation area of 235 m2. Knowing the stratigraphic intricacies of this site meant that we could proceed briskly through the disturbed upper layer and within a couple of days we were already uncovering an infant jar burial and an adult inhumation grave.

I have always done my best to keep everyone on my excavations relaxed and on good terms. Any disagreements and arguments are best avoided, because digging is team work, and in the confined space of an excavation square, there is nowhere to hide. Graeme Mason arrived on the 7th January to continue his excellent

James Chetwin asked me if these were seeds. I replied that they were gold beads.

fieldwork processing all the shellfish that were so abundant in the middens at this site. Not long after we set to work, my site supervisors Sarah and Paul awoke me in the small hours to say that Graeme had suffered an accident and was in the local hospital. Rachanie joined us and we drove round to see what was going on. Graeme had a nasty injury to his head. We assumed that he had been hit by a vehicle. I was deeply troubled and saddened to see this gifted friend so badly injured, and for his own wellbeing, we arranged for him to return to Dunedin. I missed him greatly.

This was not the only deeply troubling incident that confronted me during this season. Marshall Dudeck was the Mayor of a small town in Minnesota, and joined our second Earthwatch team. Nicknamed "Moppie", he was excellent and cheerful company in the excavation square. I called at the Phimai Inn en route to the site on the morning of the 31st January, to be told by Nigel Chang that Moppie had fallen ill during the night, and had been taken to the local hospital. I went to visit him and found him suffering from a painful leg, but otherwise seemingly well. I asked Bill Boyd to lend him his mobile phone and he rang his wife in icy cold Minnesota, assuring her that he was already on the road to recovery. The

Sarah Talbot was a tower strength, supervising an area full of Iron Age burials. She also awoke me in the early hours with the news that Graeme Mason had been badly injured.

I spent a lot of time taking photographs.

Steve McCurry from the National Geographic came to take photographs of the excavation.

following day he suffered a heart attack and was taken to the big regional hospital in Khorat city. I rang his son and Earthwatch to keep them informed. On February 3rd, the following morning, I rang the hospital from Noen U-Loke and was put through to the specialist heart surgeon. He told me "Mr Dudeck had massive heart infarction in the night, he died". I was completely stunned, and looked around at everyone working away, the only person here to know this. I had no choice but to stop digging and inform everyone. The aftermath was a nightmare. I immediately informed Earthwatch headquarters, completed their report forms to describe by the hour what had happened, and what actions I had taken, liaise with the US Embassy in Bangkok, arrange for Moppie to be identified, and meet with Embassy staff to take his body for transport back to Minnesota.

The show had to go on. I was particularly intrigued by our burial 61, a young male interred face down. As I was uncovering his spinal column, I found myself tracing a reddish pointed object that turned out to be a viciously sharp tanged arrowhead. It had completely severed one of his vertebrae. I recalled my lectures at the Institute, when Sheppard Frere was describing the Roman sack of Maiden Castle, the massive Iron Age hillfort on the outskirts of Dorchester. Mortimer Wheeler had found the burials of the Iron Age defenders, one of whom had an identical wound from a Roman ballista projectile. Here was some pretty convincing evidence for community conflict during the later Iron Age.

James Chetwin was one of my new site supervisors, and on the 20th January he asked me if the round things he had found with burial 68 were seeds. No, I said, quietly, they are gold beads. The last thing one wants is the word to spread into the village and beyond that there is gold. If this happens in Cambodia, the site is promptly scoured by looters and before long, there is little left. The following day another 12 gold beads turned up from the same grave and in the end we counted 53. We were also finding a lot of evidence for burning. There were hints of clay floors and the burnt daub, impregnated with the impressions of the wattle framework for house structures. By the end of the month, we were descending down into a fascinating realisation that the burials we were now finding were laid out, as at Khok Phanom Di, in tight clusters, with gaps between each. The four such groups we were now delineating each comprised about a dozen graves of adult men, women and infants. Again, we found that the graves were filled with rice; even the infants had been interred in pots filled with rice. Barbara was turning up sacks of carbonised rice grains in her flotation chamber.

I spent most of my time moving round the excavation, keeping up to date with what was turning up and recording my thoughts and observations in my site note book. I took all the photographs and recorded each burial, ascribing a unique catalogue number to each mortuary offering, and ensuring that they were all recorded on the accompanying drawing. When I had a spare moment, and something looked really interesting, I joined in excavating. One such opportunity came on the 31st January. We were working in one of the tight clusters of graves when I spotted something jutting out of a pot. I decided to look further, and found myself delineating a large iron object, covered in rice, that looked like a socketed spade with wings. A few years later I found an identical 'spade' and a third more recently. As we shall see, these turned out to be very significant indeed. Another burial in this cluster joined the spectacular list. This man was weighed down with bronze ornaments: well over 120 finger rings, about 40 bronze rings on his toes, a disc for each ear lobe, 20 bangles and four splendid bronze belts.

I had been forewarned that the National Geographic was sending a photographer to take images for a planned article so we left this grave in place awaiting his arrival. This came on the 19th February. At midnight a shower of gravel hit my window pane and awakened me from a deep sleep, I looked down at Steve McCurry and his girlfriend. It was he who took the famous and haunting photograph of the green-eyed Afghan woman. I took him to the Phimai Inn, and the following day he came to the site and with about four cameras, took literally hundreds of photographs of me and burial 69 one of which ended up in the *National Geographic* magazine some months later.

Burial 113 was also a highlight. At the very limits of our excavated area, we came across the edge of what looked as if it might be a very promising grave. Rachanie suggested that we extend our square by a couple of metres to investigate. I readily agreed and away she went. Before long she was revealing the clay cap to a grave filled with rice. One problem with the rice bed burials, as we called them, was that the rice had a deleterious effect on human bones, turning them to what Nancy described as wet Weet-Bix. But at least it is always encouraging to delineate a complete skull as Rachanie was soon doing. However, it was the necklace that really excited, as the gold and agate beads and two agate pendants were gradually exposed. Again I had concern for the presence of gold,

Burial 69 was very special, a man wearing four bronze belts and multiple other bronzes.

so I asked one of our most trusted villagers to stay all night in the square to guard against looting. The female in this grave also wore 64 finger rings, silver finger and toe rings, and at least 38 bronze bangles.

As the distribution of the graves began to crystallize, it became evident that the clusters were very sharply defined. Between two of these, that contained the particularly wealthy individuals just described, we revealed a third that was markedly poorer. The central figure in this set was a female who had died from repeated savage cuts to the head, which was contained in a large pot. She was surrounded by the graves of several infants. Her mortuary offerings included four spindle whorls, so she was evidently a weaver. She wore just 11 bronze bangles and eight key-shaped ear rings.

When we had finished with these clusters, we dug on down to a depth of about five metres, finding more early Iron Age graves. In one of these, an old female, wore four iron bangles and a neck ring. Another young male lay prone, with some most unusual pottery vessels. He had suffered from leprosy. But we did not confine our excavations to the mound itself. Bill Boyd was with us, and we again hired a back hoe to cut a 200 m long trench right down three metres through the moats and banks. Before the section filled with water, he tracked along recording the sequence of depositions and taking radiocarbon samples. He then repeated the exercise at other key sites in our study area. As the excavation in the main square drew to a close, I spent as long as possible taking photographs of our complete pots and jewellery before leaving for home on the 10th March very relieved and satisfied by our second season and looking forward enormously to returning for more.

A break from digging

One of the lessons drummed into me at the Institute was that if you don't publish what you find, you are little different from a looter. I had three seasons of excavations immediately behind me and set to work catching up on my responsibilities. I also realised that to get archaeological reports published, it would greatly expedite matters if I were able to format them myself. I had relied on Les O'Neill to prepare the Nong Nor report for publication, and while valuing his professional input, he had other responsibilities in the Department and the vibrations coming back to me were that it was unfair for me to monopolise him when colleagues also needed his input. I obtained a scanner so that in pre-digital image days, I could convert my slides of artefacts into publishable files. I then had photoshop software loaded, and continued to learn Pagemaker. I juggled a lot of editing, writing and proof reading. The book on prehistoric Thailand was now with River Books in Bangkok. I was delighted to receive numerous requests from Narisa for more and more colour images, and my colleagues were generous in giving me access to theirs. I had to report on my fieldwork findings to the National Research Council of Thailand, Earthwatch and the Marsden Fund. I designed the front cover for the Nong Nor report, and had chapters from Brian Vincent and Nancy Tayles for their volumes on Khok Phanom Di ceramics and human remains.

There were also two conference papers to prepare. In June I flew up to Bangkok for a brief chance to take more images of our newly restored artefacts, and then to Melaka for the conference of the Indo-Pacific Prehistory Association. Three months later, I was away again, this time to Bellagio on Lake Como. I had been invited by

With Ian Glover, we visited the Shwedagon temple in Yangon.

Burial 113, a woman wearing gold and agate beads, silver rings and bronze bangles.

Sarah Nelson to a meeting on gender in prehistory, and I leapt at the chance to attend, given the new information from my excavations on the wealth and high social status of the prehistoric women at Khok Phanom Di and Noen U-Loke. I arrived to find a magnificent palace that commanded gardens tumbling down to the lake shore. Fekri Hassan and I were the only men, and we joked that for the duration there we were honorary women. The meeting was fascinating and was finally published under the title "In Pursuit of Gender" (Nelson and Rosen-Ayalon 2002).

I had a few days in Cambridge after the meeting ended, and on the 19th October, I had dinner with Colin Renfrew, now the Master of Jesus College. He surprised me when he said "Charles, its time we got you into the Academy". He was referring to the British Academy, that most distinguished learned society for the social sciences and humanities in the United Kingdom. I must admit that I was pretty naïve about this proposal, assuming until then that one had to be resident in the British Isles to qualify, but Colin explained that there as a category for foreign scholars who if elected, are known as Corresponding Fellows. I gave him my CV the following day and carried on to my next assignment, the annual meeting of principal investigators with Earthwatch in Boston.

1999 was to be a sabbatical year for me, and my first commitment was a lab season in Phimai with Earthwatch help, with no need to return to New Zealand in February to start teaching. The numbers of volunteers keen to join me came as a welcome surprise. A fax came in from Rachanie on the 29th December with the

Daw Ni Ni Myint was our hostess in Myanmar, and was treated like royalty, even having her parasol held over her in the sun.

In Mandalay, I saw a pathetic caged .hawk for sale I bought and released it. The bird soared up into the sky and alighted on a cross above the nearby church. A good omen?

I was delighted to get to know Lew Binford on our first cruise. Here we visited Borobudur in Java, the magnificent 9th-century Buddhist temple.

welcome news that the permit for our lab season was granted. The following day Polly and I flew up to Bangkok, and then on to Yangon. I had been invited by the Burmese authorities to join a group of Southeast Asian specialists to visit the first Bronze Age site in Myanmar, at Nyaung-gan.

I had always wanted to visit Myanmar. My father had lived there for about five years in the 1920s. Our group met at Bangkok airport on New Year's day 1999 and on arrival in Yangon, we were lodged in a high-rise hotel. Ian Glover joined us to visit the Shwedagon Temple. Early the following morning, we flew up to Bagan and Mandalay and then took the bus to Monywa to check into a comfortable guest house. That afternoon we were taken to Nyaung-gan. It is perched on the edge of an extinct volcano, and the excavation squares were roofed over. Within, the open squares still contained the human skeletons and associated grave goods. The authorities were in favour of a site that attracted tourists, who would require something to see. There were quite a few large pots and my fingers were itching to get inside them to see if they were infant burials. The following day was also spent at this site, and we examined some of the bronze axes, spears and stone bangles. We then returned to Mandalay and visited the reconstructed royal palace and the Mahamuni temple to see the bronze statues from Angkor, seized by the Burmese after they sacked the Thai capital of Ayutthaya in 1564.

All this time we were escorted by Daw Ni Ni Myint, wife of General Ne Win. She was treated like royalty, and indeed we too were royally treated. On our return to Yangon, we gave some lectures, and were then ushered into a large crowded auditorium, taking our seats in the front row. Then, unannounced, in came the

My first visit to Angkor. I stand in front of the southern entrance to the city of Angkor Thom, fortunately before mass tourism took off.

First Secretary of the Junta and six of his ministers to shake our hands and take their seats. Cameras flashed. After speeches, this was billed as the opening ceremony, we were invited to have tea. For some unknown reason, Polly and I were ushered into a private room, and I was seated between First Secretary Khin Nyunt, the future Prime Minister, and the Minister for Education. It was an awkward occasion for me, not wishing to offend my hosts while finding their policies unacceptably distasteful. The following morning, photographs of our group cosying up to the Junta appeared in the official English-language newspaper *New Light of Myanmar*.

On our return to Thailand, we went straight up to Phimai, and I set to organising the lab season. We were allowed access to the store rooms of the Phimai National Museum, where all our finds were now boxed and ready for us. My students began to arrive, Bec Connelly to study our iron artefacts, Morag McCaw the animal bones, Nigel Chang the jewellery and Judy Voelker the pottery vessels. I left Nigel to run the operation on the 15th January, because I had accepted an invitation to be a guest speaker on a Swan discovery cruise.

We joined Minerva, a luxurious vessel with a maximum capacity of about 350 passengers, in the port of Bangkok and after lunch, taxied to River Books for a swim and the good news that they had already sold 2,000 copies of the book on Prehistoric Thailand. One of my fellow guest speakers was none other than Lewis Binford. I had heard many anecdotes about this towering figure, stressing his short temper and lack of empathy for those with whom he disagreed or found tedious. However, we immediately hit it off, he was excellent company and we had numerous hilarious dinner parties on board over the ensuing fortnight.

We cruised along the coast of Cambodia and Vietnam to Saigon, then to Kuching and Singapore. On Java we visited Borobudur, and finished the cruise in Jakarta. Each guest speaker gave about four lectures. Lewis Binford was then very much involved in his fieldwork among the Alaskan Inuit, a very long way from the heat of Southeast Asia. Unfortunately, he showed a steely resolve to talk about the Inuit, and I noticed that the audience in his lectures soon began to droop. His next lecture was sparsely attended, and in advance of his third he asked me to join him at the podium for a joint presentation, an offer I politely declined.

On the 28th January we flew to Bangkok and Polly and I parted company. I returned to Phimai to join the team, now in full swing, cleaning, sorting and recording a myriad of finds from Noen U-Loke. Nancy arrived as I did to start on her assessment of the human bones. The Earthwatch volunteers were a tower of strength in our endeavours, save for two young Japanese sisters who had joined us with the expectation of digging. Bemused, they asked me when the dig would start, and I told them that they could start right away excavating the contents of the complete pots from the human graves. I think that later they received a partial refund of their contribution.

The usually silent vaults of the Phimai Museum were converted into a veritable beehive. Pots were reconstructed and photographed, animal bones laid out, identified and measured, bronzes carefully cleaned and photographed, spindle whorls prepared for Judith Cameron to pore over. Clay anvils were photographed, carnelian and agate ornaments were given over to Bob Theunissen to analyse. Glass beads were counted. All this time I couldn't help looking back at the much more relaxed time we had when it was possible to do all this in my own layout laboratory in Dunedin. The museum closed at 4.00 pm sharp. There was no internet to catch up with world news, so after a jog, I had the *Bangkok Post* delivered and enjoyed a gin and tonic before going round to the Phimai Inn to have dinner with the team. When each Earthwatch team came to its last evening, we hired a boat to cruise the Mun River before dinner at the riverside restaurant. On the 9th March, I flew down to Bangkok for dinner with Adrian Macey, the New Zealand ambassador, before driving to the Siam Society in his limousine with our national flag proudly fluttering, to give a lecture in the company of Princess Galyani Vadhana, the King's sister. We were honoured with an audience after the lecture, during which the Princess showed much interest in our work. The last of four Earthwatch teams departed on the 13th March, and with a massive sense of relief and achievement, Rachanie and I treated ourselves to a holiday that had once seemed impossible, a visit to Angkor.

Phimai itself, a vice-regal centre dominated by its Angkorian temple, is impressive enough, but Angkor is staggering. Our driver took us up the access road that opened up into a view across the moat of Angkor Wat. Our first objective was the city of Angkor Thom, the Bayon mausoleum of Jayavarman VII and the royal palace. The following day we drove out to visit the moated Iron Age site of Lovea, a possible focus of a future excavation, before taking the boat across the Western

Baray to the Western Mebon temple. Naturally we explored Angkor Wat, and took in the temples and the baray-reservoir at Hariharalaya. It was a memorable visit, enjoyed not long before tourist hordes descended. On the 18th March, we flew back to Bangkok and I departed for home with a wealth of data to absorb and work on. I was particularly glad to have visited Angkor, because a publisher had asked me to write a general book on the Civilization of Angkor. In Siem Reap, I had met Michael Vickery, the great authority on the Chenla states that preceded the foundation of Angkor, who had just published his seminal work on the subject (Vickery 1998). He had impressed on me his mantra, that it is essential to go back to the original documents when getting to grips with the history of Angkor, so I embarked on a learning curve by reading Cœdès's French translation of the corpus of Angkorian inscriptions most of which were carved in Sanskrit. Michael was one of the most savage critics of other's efforts when he felt it necessary and I thought it wise to keep on the right side of his potentially acidic pen.

Indeed, I was looking at the possibility of a project in Cambodia, now getting over the nightmare of the Khmer Rouge regime, and showing some promising green shoots of recovery, at least in the Angkor region, for archaeology. I was therefore reading and casting around for likely sites. In June, I flew to Phimai and with Rachanie, we went again to Angkor to explore. We met with Van Molyvann, the head of the Apsara Authority that controlled access to the necessary research permits, and he seemed cooperative to the possibility of our moving there. We then travelled up to Angkor by boat from Phnom Penh and explored. I was interested in a site at the southwestern corner of the great Western Baray, where air photos suggested the square outline of an early city called Banteay Cheou. We walked over the area and I found one or two pieces of cord-marked pottery. Another possible site, said to be in the northeast corner of the Jayatataka baray, did not yield a single clue.

I had met Janos Jelen, a Hungarian diplomat with a keen interest in Angkor, and he was very encouraging. In September he invited me and Elizabeth Moore to Budapest, where he gave me most helpful advice on dealing with the Khmer bureaucracy, and took us to some of the sites that I had been so keen on revising for my finals in 1962 in the Tisza River valley. On November 15th I was again in Phnom Penh, and Van Molyvann with a minimum of fuss, gave us a permit to excavate. Rachanie and I then joined a meeting and field trip that centred on the remarkable fortified Neolithic village sites in far eastern Cambodia. This included a visit to Banteay Prei Nokor, the massive early city site that was reputedly the base from which Jayavarman II set out to establish the kingdom of Angkor.

The last year of the old millennium had its ups and downs. I continued processing and formatting chapters reporting on Ban Lum Khao and Noen U-Loke as they became available in final draft form, and agreed to write a new work for

River Books on the Archaeology of Mainland Southeast Asia. In June, Rachanie and I joined a most interesting meeting in Kunming on the population history of our region based on new results from DNA. En route, I went up to Phimai and we drove out to the village that owned Noen U-Loke to discuss my proposed return to the site to extend our excavated area there. The headman was adamant: he would only agree if we built a road to the site and a site museum on it to attract visitors. Both were totally impossible, so we decided on a back-up plan. Ban Non Wat was also on my list of potential sites, and is only a couple of kilometres from Noen U-Loke, so we went there to look for a possible location to excavate. Ban Non Wat is also a modern village, so it was a question of finding a homeowner with a big enough garden for our needs. Our first request was declined, the owner had plans to build on the area that looked likely. It was all rather depressing.

In July I heard that I had been elected a Corresponding Fellow of the British Academy, which came as a very pleasant surprise, and I flew to London to be inducted and attend the annual dinner. Two months later came the excellent news that I had been successful with another Marsden Fund application. In October I took off once again for Europe, this time to Italy for a meeting of the European Association of Southeast Asian Archaeologists, held in a beautiful restored monastery at Sarteano, with some of the sessions being held in Siena Cathedral. On my way home, I again went up to Phimai to find a villager at Ban Non Wat prepared to let us dig on her land, provided that all other official permits could be landed. I took the chance when in Bangkok to sign a contract for the new book on the Early Cultures of Mainland Southeast Asia. This was timely as I had just finished my book on the Civilization of Angkor.

Then there was a significant development. An anxious email landed on my computer screen from Gerd Albrecht, my German colleague who had been working in eastern Cambodia, to tell me that a splendid Iron Age site near Angkor called Phum Snay was being literally eviscerated by village looters, could I do something about it. Rachanie and I decided that we would leave Thailand, and next season excavate at Baksei Chamkrong in Angkor and try and

At Angkor, we opened a small test square in front of the Baksei Chamkrong temple, and came across an Iron Age settlement.

Our little excavation at Baksei Chamkrong lay in the shadow of the temple of the same name.

At Phum Snay, Dougald O'Reilly, right foreground, white T-shirt, put me in charge of one of the excavation units. I hit a big rock seen under the green bucket.

salvage something from the devastation of Phum Snay. For the latter, I contacted Dougald O'Reilly, then a lecturer at the Fine Arts University in Phnom Penh, and asked him to help at Phum Snay, along with assistance from my team versed in Iron Age excavations at Noen U-Loke. He also enlisted some of his students.

The new year of 2001 began with excellent news. Tom, our son, was offered a post in the Research Laboratory for Archaeology and the History of Art at Oxford University. He was destined to join their radiocarbon dating unit, a move that was to have a decisive impact on my own dating projects to come. He then joined me as my guest on another Swan Hellenic cruise that took us from Bangkok up the coast of Vietnam to Hong Kong before I returned to Phimai. Rachanie had packed our necessary excavation equipment in the back of our vehicle and we drove to Aranyaprathet. We were unable to take the car into Cambodia, so we transferred everything into a hired pickup and Mr Lai, our driver (who had six fingers) drove us eastward towards Angkor. En route we diverted to Phum Snay to assess the question of digging there. I found a shambles – holes everywhere, dumps of human skulls, fractured pots, and villagers wearing superb looted carnelian, glass and agate beads. We drove on deeply saddened to Siem Reap. The car broke down at Puok, near the Western Baray and we had difficulty finding Ashley Thompson's house, where we had arranged to stay while she was away in America.

Baksei Chamkrong is a modestly-sized temple about 100 metres from the access bridge across the moat of Angkor Thom to the southern Gopura entrance to the city. Excavations by Bernard Philippe Groslier in the 1960s in front of the temple, had revealed an Iron Age settlement, but they were never published. One can still see the outline of his excavated squares. Rachanie and I wanted to put in a test square to see what the Iron Age occupation looked like, and the potential for a major campaign one day to match what we had found at Noen U-Loke. We only opened an area of 3 by 3 metres, with six workers seconded to help us by Ang Choulien of the Apsara Authority. The day we began, news came through that my Otago team had arrived in Siem Reap, comprising Dougald and Nigel Chang, James Chetwin, Jacinta Beckwith and Beatrice Hudson. I collected them from the boat and the following day, they set off to begin the rescue excavations at Phum Snay.

The excavation at Baksei Chamkrong was small and over quickly. We soon came across a wall foundation of square clay tiles. We informed Ang Choulien, who asked us not to remove them. This made our excavation even smaller, and we were soon into a thin Iron Age occupation context over the natural substrate. With no prospect of exporting any of our finds to Dunedin, we did our best describing the pottery and the two or three hearths we encountered, prior to putting together a brief report. Then we joined the team at Phum Snay. This involved finding somewhere to stay in Chup. This small town is centred on a dusty main street and its morning market. Electricity was limited to an hour or so each morning. We lived above a little shop, while the students and Dougald crowded into a house opposite. Pigs roamed the town, and after the morning market closed, dogs moved in to scavenge what was left, often jumping up on the butchers' stalls. One plus was being able to buy freshly baked baguettes in the market for breakfast, but the evening meal was uniformly awful.

On the 14th February, we drove up the mile or so to Phum Snay to find that Dougald had identified a field that had not yet been looted. He had laid out a smallish area covered with a makeshift roof. About 15 local villagers, almost without exception sporting looted bead necklaces, were helping. I had rather expected to take on the role of senior statesman, offering advice and encouragement here and there. But this was not the case. Dougald assigned me one of the squares to supervise and record. It was a situation of role reversal that I could feel caused some amusement among my fellow students. On my first day, I found the skull of burial 1 and several features, such as postholes and pits, to record. Two days later we uncovered the complete burial of a child, wearing I think, ivory bangles. But we also found ourselves confronted by a large area of solid stone that suggested that we were already at or close to the bedrock. It was not going to be a deep site like Noen U-Loke. I was out of contact with the world via my mobile phone, I couldn't get any reception, so I borrowed a bike and pedalled up a steep hill until I just got a strike and rang Polly to book me a return flight home for the following week. The next day I completed my square and helped Nigel next door excavating a large pottery vessel. Rachanie and I then decided that this was an excellent opportunity to hire a car and visit Banteay Chhmar.

This is a remote temple site with a massive *baray* reservoir constructed in honour of one of his sons by Jayavarman VII, and I had long wanted to see it. We drove along rutted lanes through several villages, and found the site utterly deserted, just as the first Portuguese might have found Angkor in the 16th century. We were entranced. We walked along the length of an exterior wall, covered with bas reliefs that recorded Jayavarman's war with the invading Chams. By now a handful of village urchins had joined us. They took us through the luxuriant forest cover, and into the heart of the temple that like its contemporary the Bayon at Angkor, was crowned with huge stone heads of the king in the guise of a bodhisattva. Then we asked the boys to take us to the spot where not long previously, a Cambodian general had ordered his men to crowbar out an entire section of wall, and load the stones onto a lorry for dispatch to the antiquities market in Bangkok. Mercifully, Thai police stopped the lorry and curious as to its cargo, had it confined in the Prachinburi compound of the FAD where Amphan, now in charge, identified it as likely looted reliefs from Cambodia. After a legal wrangle, the stones were ultimately returned to Phnom Penh.

The following day we left Chup. My diary records that "I was glad to leave that dusty dirty place". I heard from Dougald years later that he suffered severe gastric problems for months after his experience there. We had stored our car in Aranyaprathet and it was such a relief to drive to Phimai along excellent roads. The following day, with fluey symptoms and creaking joints, I joined in the FAD excavations at Ban Suai, the Iron Age settlement in a Phimai suburb. It was great to be back in a seriously deep excavation, at an iconic site first examined in the 1960s by Ham Parker and Bill Solheim. Rachanie took over directing operations there, and I uncovered a most interesting clay feature associated with complete Phimai Black pots. Unlike Solheim and Parker, she and Amphan published a complete report on their research (Thosarat and Kijngam 2004). Two more days of digging ensued for me before I travelled down to Bangkok to visit River Books and on to the airport for my flight home.

I was asked by Facts on File in early 2001 if I would be prepared to write a 300,000 word Encyclopaedia of Early Asian Civilizations. I had just finished a biography of Somerset Maugham which said that he regularly wrote 1000 words each morning and then enjoyed himself for the rest of the day. I reckoned I could probably do the same so I signed the contract and jumped in at the deep end.

We had left Angkor filled with trippers and here at Banteay Chhmar we were alone, save for some curious village boys.

Banteay Chhmar was an amazing experience. Rachanie and I were the only visitors.

At Banteay Chhmar, some village boys guided us through the jungle-clad ruins to the section of wall looted by a top military man in the Cambodian army.

By June I was half way there and 70% was written by October, covering from Afghanistan to the Philippines and from Japan to Malaysia. In March I was checking the proofs of the book, *The Civilization of Angkor*, and in June, I went up to Phimai and again to Ban Non Wat, where we finally had success when a venerable lady called Mrs Suan gave us permission to excavate on her land in the centre of the village. I was determined to excavate again, if not at Noen U-Loke, then at another site in the upper Mun Valley.

I had a special reason to visit England in December 2001, namely to celebrate the 50th anniversary of our victory in the Varsity rugby match against Oxford. We had a memorable dinner in University College Oxford, and went down to Twickenham the following day, this time to see an Oxford victory. On my way back home, Rachanie and I went out to Ban Non Wat to finalise where to dig and make advanced plans to assemble a workforce drawn from the village. I then flew to Hanoi for a conference before returning home for the Christmas break.

Our first season at Ban Non Wat began with an excavation 20 by 4 metres, the area dictated by the size of our roof.

Twelve | Ban Non Wat, Incredible Surprises

I left for Bangkok on the 6th January to take on Ban Non Wat. I had so hoped that it would have been Noen U-Loke but that was not to be. Rachanie had laid out an area of 4x16 metres, divided into four units. I assigned each unit to one of my graduate students, Nu, Katherine, Beatrice Hudson and Hayden Cawte. Nigel Chang, James Chetwin and Jeremy Habberfield-Short also joined us, and Sian Halcrow came to take charge of any human burials until Nancy Tayles arrived. I also welcomed Rachanie's friend Daeng, who was to prove such a tower of strength. I had expected to find a similar sequence to Noen U-Loke, with deep occupation and mortuary remains covering the duration of the Iron Age. We did encounter a furnace and an infant jar burial, then a disturbed late Iron Age adult grave with some carnelian beads, but during the first week, little to match the Noen U-Loke rice-bed graves in clusters. By the 18th of January, I recorded that it had been "a very frustrating and depressing day all round". I discussed with Rachanie the possibility of moving to another site, with Ban Ko Hong in mind. I had read that excavations there had come across an Iron Age burial with bronze belts, and it sounded more promising than Ban Non Wat so far. Throughout our excavations, I was always the impatient one and she the steadying hand. Whenever I saw her digging in a quiet corner all on her own I knew she was onto something. She told me to relax and carry on.

The very day following, her advice proved correct. I decided to put in a 1x1 metre test probe in the corner of our square A4 to see what was coming up. I scraped clean the newly revealed surface at a depth of 2.7 metres below our datum saying to myself, "what would I give to have a complete pot rim right here". Within two minutes, there it was, the complete red rim of Bronze Age vessel, soon to be followed by two more with a human pelvis and finger bones in perfect condition. I was elated. I stopped the excavation and called everyone to hear my prediction, that within a week, we would have rows of Bronze Age burials across the site. And I was proved right, as more and more complete pots and graves began to pop up.

On the 25th January, Per Sørensen visited us. Per had excavated at Ban Kao in the 1960s, the first Neolithic cemetery in Thailand. As I was showing him over the excavation, almost simultaneously, we spotted some just-revealed black potsherds with incised and impressed designs. They could only be Neolithic. The sherds were soon resolved into a complete pottery vessel associated with a Neolithic burial. This was turning into quite a season.

Things were now going so well that we decided to open two test squares in other parts of the site. The first of these was located where we had first sought permission to dig from the owner, Mr Tu. He had refused, but since joining our workforce, he and I had become good friends, and he changed his mind. I put Jeremy Habberfield-Short in charge. The second I placed on the southern part of the mound, directed by Hayden Cawte. The following day, the 31st January, I received another stunning surprise. Way down nearly four metres, below the level of the growing group of Neolithic graves, Nigel Chang summoned my attention, and showed me a deep pit containing eight uniquely large Bronze Age pots. It must, I thought, be a major burial. By the following day, this had extended to reveal 13 pots and had become our burial 20. Then we found a skull sitting upright and only partially within our excavation area. We decided that we must extend to explore this dramatic find, and I put James Chetwin in charge of a new 4 by 5 m square.

Bridling my impatience as James continued on down, I was drawn to tracing the rim of a pot of unprecedented size in my experience. It was in Beatrice Hudson's square, and I anxiously watched to see if the rim made the complete circuit. It did. Then we found that it was lidded as well. By the 8th February, I was describing a vast lid over a pot with incised and painted designs on the shoulder. After we photographed and removed the lid, we delved inside and called on Nancy Tayles to identify some bone that emerged: the knees of an adult. Over the ensuing days, we gradually revealed the skeleton of a man interred within the pot in seated flexed position, holding a small pot and a bivalve shell. I sampled a piece of charcoal from within the pot for future radiocarbon dating.

We found the huge rim of a lidded pot. When we removed the lid, we found human knee bones emerging. What was going on here, I wondered.

The answer soon came, a male buried in the pot, in a seated position, with a small pot and a bivalve shell as mortuary offerings.

By the 18th February we were tracing the path of burial 20. The complete skull had been placed upright on a relocated set of long bones looking to the rising sun. We excavated along the edge of the grave, and it was fully 5 metres long, with at least 28 pottery vessels so far. This was unprecedented in size for the Bronze Age I was familiar with in Southeast Asia. But we were now nearing the end of our first season. We had so far uncovered 33 burials, one in the last days wearing 38 exotic shell bangles. It was clear that our super rich burial 20 extended further into the unexcavated part of the site and I was already keenly looking forward to returning for a second season. On the 23rd February we hired a tractor to back fill our square and I returned to Bangkok for my homeward flight with an overwhelming sense of achievement.

Burial 20 was our first hint of something extraordinary going on, five metres long and full of marvellous pottery vessels.

On my return home I turned again to the Encyclopaedia commitment that had languished during the excavation season, and I spent some time preparing the Reckitt lecture, due to be delivered in May. I chose to talk about the prehistoric foundations of the civilization of Angkor, as I thought we had some relevant new information. It was a memorable mid-year visit to England because en route we diverted to Angkor, where I featured in my first of several television documentaries. Directed by Phil May, it was entitled "City of the God Kings". We spent several days shooting in the main temples there, and living in the luxurious Angkor Village hotel. I really enjoyed the experience and while in London over the ensuing three months or so, went down to London to help Phil edit the final version.

The lecture at the British Academy was a splendid affair. I went there in the morning to learn how to work the slide projector, because for maximum impact, I had to have a precise harmony between my image and what I was saying. I returned in the early evening for the event itself. The lecture theatre was packed, as was a second room for the late comers. But the lecture got off to a disastrous start. When I pressed the button for the next slide, either nothing happened or the projector went

In square Y, Jeremy did a brilliant job in a real hot spot, with dense clusters of burials and post holes.

haywire and shot through five images before stopping. And there was no immediate help from a technician. I managed to continue albeit very disappointed with the initial impact that had been so carefully prepared. There was a reception after in the grand vestibule of the Academy, that had once been William Gladstone's town house when he was Prime Minister, followed by a dinner for the Academy brass, my family and a handful of close friends.

I spent the next several weeks working on the Encyclopaedia in Cambridge libraries, giving a lecture at Oslo University, attending a conference in Sweden and checking the proofs from River Books for the *Early Cultures of Mainland Southeast Asia* book. The year ended back in New Zealand with the completion of the Encyclopaedia and two chapters for Thames and Hudson's *The Human Past*. Sadly, on the 8th September, Donn Bayard died. He had been one of the most addicted smokers of cigarettes I have ever known. One day I sat beside him at a seminar and he confided in me that he had difficulty swallowing. I knew at once that smoking had caught up with him, he was suffering from cancer of the throat. So my two friends from 1968 on my visit to Hawaii looking for a promising young appointee to a lectureship with us were no more.

On the 6th January 2003, I left for my second season at Ban Non Wat. I could hardly wait, but in all fairness could not expect to replicate the excitement of the previous excavation. I cannot over-emphasise the easy ride I had with Rachanie and Daeng at the helm, I simply arrived to find the roof in place, the top disturbed layer removed and we were back into it. In the separate square Y1, Jeremy was dealing with a real hot spot of Bronze Age burials, with 15 being exposed at once in a square measuring only 4x4 metres. The stratigraphy was crystal clear and Jeremy was doing a magnificent job there. We decided to double the area and I put Hayden Cawte in charge. The new excavation in the main area covered 4x20 metres, the width being determined by the coverage provided by our hired

Rachanie found 14 earrings before tea, and I found 14 more after tea on burial 105. Note the shell beads on the skull, always the sign of wealth.

Some burials were so big I had to risk all to get a good picture.

Some of the over 80 pots with burial 90. I had never seen anything quite like this before. The biggest is 30 cm across.

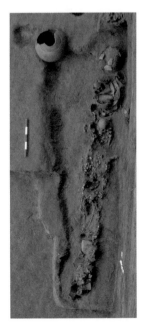

It was really great to find a double super burial containing two females.

Burial 86 was one of the finest Early Neolithic graves we came across.

roof. I keenly anticipated reaching the balance of burial 20, and this took place on the 25th January. What we found confounded even my most sanguine hopes. It turned out to be a double burial, the second, our burial 90, had also been partially exhumed and the bones then carefully replaced. We even saw the cut marks on the leg bones that enabled part of the body to be removed. The grave was 5 m in length, and as each day passed, so we counted more and more pottery vessels, first 42, then 61 and finally over 80. Moreover, the pots were superbly formed and decorated, with four particularly large ones in each corner of the grave. We also came across a socketed bronze axe, and thousands of shell beads.

Meanwhile Jeremy was now down to a dizzying depth of 6.2 metres, where he revealed five early Bronze Age graves cut through hearths full of charcoal. I collected samples for radiocarbon dating. The wooden log coffin survived in one of these, due to the waterlogged conditions, for Jeremy had to cope with the rising water table down there. One of the best of all our early Neolithic burials was turning up in the main square. 3.6 m long, the grave contained a young man with cowrie shell ear ornaments and splendid incised and impressed pottery vessels. The head end of the grave was ringed with about five infant jar burials. And then, on the 8th of February, as I wandered round the excavation checking on what was turning up, I came across one of the workers revealing more huge pots. Sensing another super rich burial, I realised that it would be necessary once again to extend our excavated area slightly by protruding into a village lane. The headman provided permission and before long, we were uncovering the arms of a female covered in magnificent tridacna shell bangles that must have traversed hundreds of kilometres from the warm coral sea to which this shellfish is adapted. Then one morning before tea break, Rachanie traced 14 shell earrings on the right side of the skull. After tea I grabbed a spot and found 14 on the other side. I left uncovering the thousands of shell beads to more skilled hands than mine. This was burial 105. In the same grave we found another adult female, equally wealthy, and in her case, a socketed bronze

Koh Ker was a remarkable visit, land mines everywhere and the ruins of Jayavarman IV's temple in the background.

axe and the skeleton of a rat, carefully laid out by her ankle under a pellet bow pellet, an artefact still used to hunt small game.

Two days later, I received an email telling me that I had been appointed a James Cook Fellow by the Royal Society of New Zealand. This meant two years free of all teaching and administration and inbuilt research funds. My second season at Ban Non Wat had, if possible, exceeded the first, and it ended with another surprise, an emailed invitation to film another television documentary, this time at the remote Angkorian palatial centre of Koh Ker in Cambodia to start in a week. I sensed that the company in question was pretty desperate to get me involved, and I told them in reply that I would do it for a healthy fee and business class travel from Auckland to Siem Reap. I was right, the conditions were immediately agreed. I returned home on March 1st, and a week later I was on my way to Siem Reap.

I arrived to find that my luggage was lost. There was no time to wait for it to catch up with me, Dean Love the director of the shoot was anxious to be off to Koh Ker, a rugged journey on a landrover along jungle trails to our remote destination. We stopped at a roadside stall to buy me a new shirt and that was it. I learned on the way that they had already completed the project, but with such unsatisfactory presenters that the National Geographic had told them to try again, and quickly. We arrived at dusk, at the tented camp of the mine clearers. The magnificent temple mausoleum of King Jayavarman IV towered over a scattered village marked by extreme poverty. The doctor in the unit kindly vacated his tent for me and I slept on a bed of hard wooden boards. Dean and Jason the camera man slept on the ground. Koh Ker had been a stronghold for the Khmer Rouge, and they had littered the area with land mines for their protection. Angkorian temples were easily defended due to their stout stone walls, and there were many at Koh Ker. Why Jayavarman IV chose this remote spot for a new city is not known, but he poured labour and resources into its construction, including a massive *baray* reservoir. The theme of the shoot was that the land mines had protected the site from looting, hence its title, "Guardians of Angkor"

We lived a Spartan existence on noodles and little else. There was no electricity, and I had two tea bags that were recycled with diminishing value. On my first evening, I tracked down a villager up a palm tree and bought a bamboo container of frothy palm wine. We three sat down for a sundowner and taking pity, a woman came with a little tray of nibbles – black dried frogs. Each morning we were up at dawn to follow the mine detectors. This meant strictly adhering to the narrow pathways, as they gingerly criss-crossed the demarcated area under clearance, behind masks and body armour. Once the detector scored a signal, they gently probed until the ugly, lethal green canister surfaced. At 4.00 pm all mines identified that day were detonated. We entered and filmed in numerous temples, and I noticed several inscriptions lying around untended and still to be translated. The programme became an award-winning documentary, and for me, it was an unique experience made all the better when we returned to Siem Reap to find my long-lost suitcase waiting for me.

My appointment as James Cook Fellow came when I was 63. It seemed wrong for me to return to my chair aged 65, although New Zealand has no retirement age, so I tendered my resignation to allow the University to appoint my successor. I also now had freedom to do whatever I was inclined to. In May 2003 we flew to England, where I was appointed for two years a visiting scholar in my college, St Catharine's. We then flew out to Salonika to join a Black Sea cruise with Swan Hellenic. I particularly enjoyed this one. We began by visiting Pella, seat of Philip of Macedon, which I had previously been to in 1961 when digging at Nea Nikomedia. There I had a casual chat with a new friend, Freddie Raphael, over the mosaic floors. On this same day we went to Vergina to see the incredible royal tombs, a site we had driven past on innumerable occasions back in 1961, when we were driving out to Nea Nikomedia without anyone yet knowing what lay beneath those mounds. We moved on to Troy, a site I had long wished to visit, and rounding the Black Sea anticlockwise, to Trabzon, Sochi, Yalta and Sevastopol to view the site of the Charge of the Light Brigade. We visited the Greek colony of Chersonesos, and in Romania we went to Adamklissi, where I drew on my Latin inscription tutorials under Sheppard Frere in a site lecture before disembarking at Istanbul. And all that for just four 50-minute lectures.

From the cruise I flew out to Cambodia for another television documentary shoot, this time involving travel down to the early city of Angkor Borei on the Mekong Delta. There I liaised with Miriam Stark, whose excavations and fieldwork were a feature of the filming. In July we were back in New Zealand. I worked pretty well full time on formatting the volume reporting on our excavations at Ban Lum Khao. But where could it be published? I contacted British Archaeological Reports, that had published Ban Na Di in 1984 and they agreed to take it on. However, Amphan intervened and persuaded the Fine Arts Department to publish it, and ultimately all its successors, in sumptuous volumes with most illustrations in colour. And as the year progressed, so the number of Earthwatch volunteers grew ahead of out third season at Ban Non Wat. Already I was getting a trickle of radiocarbon dates back from Tom, and they were looking exactly as expected, with the initial Neolithic settlement in the early 2nd millennium BC, slightly later than Khok Phanom Di.

Our third season at Ban Non Wat began on the 1st December, when Beatrice Hudson and I laid out an excavation area comprising five 4x4 squares, later extended with three 4x3 squares, the area again determined by the maximum coverage of a

After a long day in the field, and feeling like a gin and tonic and quiet time,
I went round the Phimai Inn for dinner and, often, a lecture.

hired village marquee. I was only there for a few days before flying to Guilin for a
conference and then home to attend our daughter Caroline's wedding. However,
I was back with a vengeance on the 4th January for another memorable season.
We were finding a concentration of clay bronze-casting furnaces in one area while
in another part, we came to recognise a set of late Bronze Age graves, the pottery
vessels showing signs of evolving from their predecessors. Burial 154 also heralded
our recognition of a Bronze Age phase 3A, being later than the superburials 90 and
105, and on a different orientation. However they were still remarkably wealthy,
burial 154 being found with 60 exotic trochus shell and three marble bangles,
not to mention numerous pottery vessels. Burial 93 also turned out to be another
remarkable case of exhumation and later, re-interment, this time of a very wealthy
female.

My work was cut out with five Earthwatch teams, each with up to 15 volunteers.
This meant that at the end of a long day in the field, when I felt like a couple of gin
and tonics before a quiet dinner and early night, I had to drive round to the Phimai
Inn to join the volunteers and often give a lecture. However, they all worked with a
will, and I thanked the spirits guarding over the dig that we had so much of interest
for them to do. I recorded a fabulous day on the 17th February with a very rich
Bronze Age burial 178, and a number of early Neolithic infant jar burials. We also
came across a most unusual grave, that of a dog interred with its paws holding a
pottery vessel. News of this discovery reached the Fine Arts Department, and then
the palace. HM King Bhumibol was a dedicated dog lover, and he sent his secretary,

Sometimes the stratigraphic sequence of burials was clear.

Quite a complex sequence: In the centre, a Neolithic 1 adult is interred in a huge pottery vessel, that underlies a Neolithic 2 grave, that in turn was disturbed by a Bronze Age 3 grave that overlies a Bronze Age 2 infant grave.

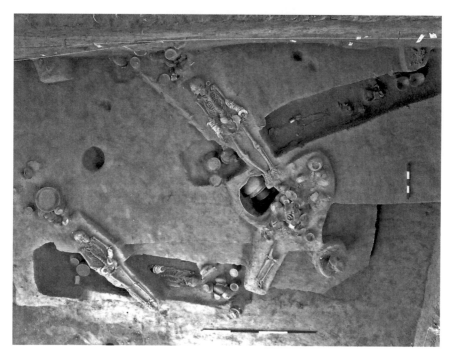

Khunying Amporn Sukonthaman to find out more and take some dog bones back for the King to view. In late February, I was off to Angkor to record a programme for New Zealand national radio, and then back to the dig until we finally laid down our trowels for the season on the 7th March. Then I flew directly to Hong Kong and Changsha in China to participate in a television documentary filming of the world's most remarkable mummy, that of the Han Chinese aristocratic lady Xin Shui of Mawangdui for the National Geographic channel. The programme, *The Diva Mummy*, was widely viewed.

The following year cemented a pattern of writing, research and travel. I kept up the momentum on preparing the final volume on Khok Phanom Di, and the reports on Ban Lum Khao and Noen U-Loke. By May, the Ban Lum Khao book was ready for dispatch to Bangkok for the printer. Given the impossibility of having access in New Zealand to our artefacts and biological remains, I headed in June to Phimai, where I found that Rachanie, Daeng and our village workforce had reconstructed many of our superb Neolithic and Bronze Age pottery vessels for me to photograph, thankfully now digitally. I then went on to Angkor for another television documentary before travelling to England for an extended visit that involved the London conference of the European Association of Southeast Asian Archaeologists. This was held in the British Museum. My friend Magdalena von Dewall had contributed funds to pay for my attendance in order to present the keynote lecture on the links between China and Southeast Asia in later prehistory. My lecture was attended by HRH Princess Sirindhorn. She arrived with a large entourage and took notes throughout my delivery. At the end she approached and asked me a number of penetrating questions, before I escorted her round the Victoria and Albert Museum. We returned to New Zealand in mid-October, and to the encouraging news that the number of Earthwatch volunteers was growing daily. I could count on $47,000 US for the fourth season at Ban Non Wat and so, on November 30th, I set off once again into the field.

We began with five 4x4 squares, extending further our already excavated area, and we soon were expanding our knowledge of the site and its sequence. We came across Iron Age burials, one with a crucible as a mortuary offering, and another with a bivalve mould. A red-letter day occurred on the 23rd December when I heard that the final volume on Khok Phanom Di was published, 20 years and five days since we began there. A few days later the Ban Lum Khao report was sent to the printer. My memories of that season are legion, but two stand out. We thought we were finished in square B7, and were scraping the surface of the natural substrate when Rachanie drew my attention to a large rectangular discolouration, clearly another super burial. We delved carefully into the grave fill and were soon tracing the outline of many pottery vessels. Then on cue we uncovered the complete cranium, and set Nancy to work on the skeleton. More pots were found beyond the feet. As we progressed, so we found that this woman of Bronze Age phase 3 had been interred with 31 pottery vessels, wearing nearly 30,000 shell beads, and 13 bangles, 12 shell and one marble. Moving into the adjacent square, we had a real jigsaw to sort out. In close proximity was another Neolithic lidded jar containing a seated adult. It lay next to a late Neolithic extended burial, and the grave of an extremely rich Bronze Age infant, far larger than necessary to contain the corpse, as well as a rich Bronze Age adult. All four were being excavated at the same time.

Towards the end of the season, a film crew arrived from Earthwatch, involving four young students chosen to visit about ten field programmes throughout a six-month period. They arrived as we were uncovering yet more elite Bronze Age graves so the timing could not have been better. We had by now recorded not only over 300 burials, but also a wealth of evidence for bronze casting and pottery manufacture. There were many broken crucibles and moulds for casting bronze bangles, spears and axes. Clay anvils had been used to shape pots. We found many spindle whorls, and at the base of the sequence, in situ shell middens with Neolithic incised and impressed potsherds, shellfish and animal bones. This was clearly going to take some time to absorb, restore and analyse, and on the 28th February, a golden door of opportunity opened. Rachanie resigned from the Fine Arts Department in order to work full time with Daeng and our team of villagers on our project. This encouraged me to think in terms of returning to Ban Non Wat for yet more.

This, as always, depended on money. Nancy Tayles and I set to preparing another Marsden application, choosing to stress the fact that we had identified Neolithic occupation at Ban Non Wat, and this could be an entrée into documenting the spread of early farmers into Southeast Asia. It was sent away in February, the first hurdle being whether or not it made the cut into the finals. About 6% of applications were funded, but if you made it through to the finals, the chances rose to 50%. I heard that we had passed the first hurdle on April 22nd. In the meantime, I had flown up to Taipei to contribute to a symposium on a new museum to be constructed there, dedicated to Southeast Asia. From there, I took a flight to Beijing to participate in another television documentary, that took us way out into remote Gansu Province to film the Great Wall of China in a region usually barred to foreigners. The wall there had no similarity to the modern concrete reconstruction that tourists are taken to near Beijing. For part of the shoot, we drove up and up to find the tamped earth wall as left by the last defenders, with regularly spaced watch towers. It was freezing cold, and we were interrupted by heavy snow. There was no option but to drive down to shelter, but the track was simply unmade loess and very slippery. The driver turned one corner, lost control and we were left teetering on the edge of a precipice. We all got out of that vehicle and walked the remaining stretch to safety.

It was a most significant move when Rachanie joined our team full time.

I returned to New Zealand unemployed. My James Cook Fellowship had been wonderful but it

Our new roof made it possible to open an area of 10 by 10 metres, making it much more efficient.

We uncovered a row of incredibly rich Bronze Age burials.

ended after just two years. However, the Dean of Social Sciences, Geoff Kearsley, and Alistair Fox, the Deputy Vice Chancellor for Humanities, asked me to a meeting to discuss my situation. I was pleasantly surprised when they asked if I would return to the fold as a Research Professor. This I happily accepted, and it was soon confirmed by the Vice Chancellor and friend, Sir David Skegg. It was for a five-year term, and to add icing to the cake, David said that I was to regard myself as a free agent. And that is exactly what I did. With no teaching commitments, I accepted an invitation from Colin Renfrew to contribute in Cambridge to a meeting on archaeology and languages, in which I identified a relationship between the spread of rice farming into Southeast Asia and the distribution of Austroasiatic languages. Just as I arrived back in Dunedin, on September 7th I heard the wonderful news that Nancy and I had been successful in our Marsden application, to the tune of $NZ 777,000 over three years. My first decision was to ask Rachanie to have a massive roof constructed of canvas and metal scaffolding so that we could, as at

Khok Phanom Di, open a much bigger square. It was a vital investment, for it could be dismantled, stored and moved when necessary.

I seemed to be travelling an awful lot. In late September we were off round the world to Istanbul for another Black Sea cruise with Swan Hellenic, this time taking us to Varna in Bulgaria to visit the amazing Golden Man burial, that son Tom had just radiocarbon dated, and Pergamum in Turkey. In early November, I was off again to Penn State University to give a lecture, followed by the annual meeting of Principal Earthwatch Investigators in Boston. And whenever I had some time, I was using the Pagemaker program to format the chapters on Noen U-Loke as they came to me from the team of collaborators.

I left for the 2006 season on New Year's eve and at once appreciated the scope presented by our large new roof. We opened an area of 12 by 11 metres, under a light white canvas roof. Almost at once we were into the early Iron Age, seen in the remains of clay floors, with graves cut through them. It was the beginning of quite a fortnight, as we explored an early Iron Age cemetery with graves at times covering the entire excavation. As the days slipped by, I became increasingly confident that we were uncovering the best early Iron Age cemetery yet in Thailand, possibly in Southeast Asia. An infant wore a bronze anklet on each foot, each containing tiny clay balls that would have tinkled when it was running and playing. The configuration of broken pots strongly suggested that the dead were interred in hollowed tree trunk coffins. Two men had been interred with bimetallic spears,

Left: The flexed burials were a surprise. Here a mother clasps her baby.

Right: We found a curious clay abject, then many more, they were moulds for casting bronze bangles.

an iron blade on a bronze socket. We found a mortuary offering of thin, socketed bronze implements virtually identical with those found in the copper-smelting sites in the Bangkok Plain. There were very rare ornaments of carnelian, glass and agate. Moreover, these graves coalesced with those I had previously assigned to the late Bronze Age. I began to think it likely that we were tracing the actual transition into the early Iron Age – the pottery vessels in graves before and after the initial presence of iron were virtually identical.

Recording all these graves and occupation floors took an age, but we were then down into the depths, and another very welcome surprise awaited. We found first burial 443, another of our Bronze Age superburials. This in itself caused a stir among our full 15-strong team of volunteers. Then we found ourselves uncovering an entire row of them, including an infant in a superbly painted and lidded mortuary jar and another wearing a bronze anklet with bells attached. One of the key findings in this row, was that one of the rich graves had cut through an earlier burial with quite different forms of pottery vessel, and a socketed bronze axe. It began to dawn on us that we were finding two distinct phases of the early Bronze Age occupation of this remarkable site.

There was much more to come. We uncovered a female in a crouched position, holding an infant in her arms. She wore a necklace of crudely fashioned beads made from *Anadara*, a marine shell the like of which was new to me. Then two more flexed burials, a man and a woman. One wore shell beads that again, I have not seen before or since, as well as having a small pot quite different from those of the Neolithic at this site, and a stone adze. The indigenous hunter-gatherers of Southeast Asia preferred burying their dead in a flexed position, so what was going on here? Was this site also occupied by a different population than the incoming Neolithic rice farmers? So many questions arose as the season drew to a close, but one definite fact emerged as I flew home in early March. It had been the best season ever at Ban Non Wat. However, before departing for Bangkok I faced a pressing issue that needed immediate resolution. I wanted to expand in our sixth season to the north, but a house was in the way, owned by Mr Lop, one of our workers. We negotiated a mutually acceptable settlement, and he agreed to move his house 20 metres to the east.

I was now well able to produce my own plans and sections using Freehand MX to format my illustrations, and returned to Dunedin to try and complete the Noen U-Loke volume, and start on the huge task of working out the cultural sequence and the chronology for Ban Non Wat. In September, I flew to Phimai to catch up with our progress on restoring all the artefacts, and spend days taking images of pots – we were ultimately to have about 5,000 of them restored. My return to Bangkok coincided with yet another military coup and the streets were filled with tanks and soldiery. I then carried on to England, and to deep rural France for the 11th International Conference of the European Association of Southeast Asian Archaeologists at Bougon. I gave a paper summarizing our first five seasons at Ban Non Wat, presenting the cultural sequence as I then understood it, along with our first radiocarbon determinations that suggested that the initial Bronze Age fell between 1150 and 1000 BC. Our burial 197, for example, contained a freshwater bivalve shell that Tom had dated to 1112-914 BC.

On the 31st December, I set off for our 6th season, writing in my diary "Up and away to Bangkok for my last ever dig". I was wrong again. I have been so lucky to have Rachanie as my co-director. On my arrival at the site, the roof was up, square laid out and the disturbed top centimetres removed down to the early Iron Age level. Under the immediate direction of Alison Carter, Nigel Chang and Carmen Sarjeant, we found that the early Iron Age cemetery continued, but the orientation of the graves was reversed. Perhaps there were two social groups. Again we found strong evidence for the use of log coffins, and many of the pottery vessels placed with the dead were filled with complete fish skeletons. There were also intervals when the area we opened had been used for butchering cattle and water buffaloes, for their bones littered the floor in association with iron knives. We had grown accustomed to finding the later Bronze Age burials next, and on cue, there were many including one of the most fascinating of all.

I first noticed a most unusual clay object next to a human tibia. Peter Petchey and I uncovered it and then found another, and then a cluster of them, tightly packed together. It dawned on us that they were moulds for casting bronze bangles. Then we found a second such cluster, and a third. We had the rare grave of a bronze-casting specialist. We tracked up to the head, and beyond it lay two complete sets of bivalve moulds for casting a socketed axe. It was huge, I was delighted. Here lay evidence beyond doubt for local expertise in casting bangles and axes. More was to follow. We examined the bangle moulds as they were lifted, and it became obvious that they were bound together like books on a shelf, for multiple casting. We called them concertina moulds, and to my knowledge nothing like them has been found elsewhere in Southeast Asia.

By February 16th, with the temperature under our roof hovering around 40ºC, we came across more of the enigmatic flexed burials, and then yet more rewards for our endeavours. Burial 569 was first identified as a long grave cut with a pointed end like a boat. Delving deeper, it turned into one of our rare earliest Bronze Age burials, a young female who had indeed been interred in a wooden boat-shaped coffin, wearing belts of shell disc beads and a shell bangle. A socketed bronze axe lay on her left shoulder. Then with her eagle eye, Rachanie spotted and traced another sharp distinction between an ash lens and mixed fill that followed a straight line for

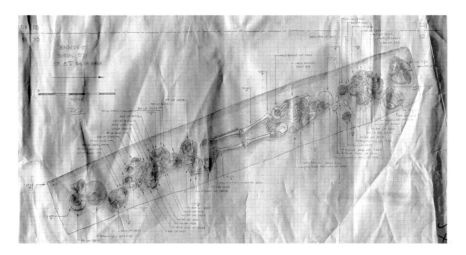

I was particularly fortunate to have Peter Petchey with us, to record and draw each burial with such skill. This is his field drawing of burial 571.

fully five metres, before resolving into a rectangular possible grave cut. Down into it we went and on cue, a mass of complete red pot rims heralded another Bronze Age elite male, in a burial so long that I could not get it all into one camera shot. This was burial 571, interred with 40 pottery vessels, 53 trochus shell bangles, over 1000 shell beads and as expected, a bronze socketed axe. Next door, burial 553, there was another case of a body being exhumed and then replaced ritually at one end of the grave. All these finds were ongoing when we received a large delegation from Bangkok headed by the Director General of the National Research Council. On March 2nd, the square was bare, we were down to the sterile substrate. I felt euphoric and that evening, downed half a bottle of red wine. But the feeling was also bitter sweet; the end of my time as an excavator. I now faced a daunting task of digesting six seasons of unparalleled discoveries at this great site, and bringing them all to publication.

There were other responsibilities on returning home, beginning with the proofs for the report on Noen U-Loke, but in April what was becoming an annual trip to England came along again. It began with another Black Sea cruise with some new destinations, including Santorini, and Istria and a return to Troy. On our return, we paid our regular visit to Sheppard Frere in his lovely rectory home at Marcham, just south of Oxford. I owed him so much for my early journey into archaeology and in his 90s he maintained his insight and impish wit. On this occasion, he gave me one of my most cherished archaeological possessions, his trowel, with F incised on the handle. There is a saga about trowels. The smaller the blade, the greater the mana, because it will have been worn down by use and experience over many years.

In his case it was worn down after decades of digging. The only problem was that I would never now be able to use it myself.

Over the course of May 2007, Tom was emailing me a succession of radiocarbon dates from Ban Non Wat. I always check every area of my excavations for assured in situ contexts for my samples. I was fortunate at Ban Non Wat to find discrete charcoal-rich hearths, and several of these were either stratified above or below burials, or had been cut through when digging a grave. Although even this method has its issues, it is far more reliable than accumulating unrelated fragments of charcoal from grave fill or occupation layers, as at Ban Chiang. It was therefore, coincidental that at this very juncture, Tom drew my attention to one of the most ground-breaking publications I have ever read: it was a special issue of the *Cambridge Archaeological Journal* for 2007 (Bayliss and Whittle 2007).

I had been invited to give two lectures in the Canary Islands and had time to read the articles during the flight south, and in my hotel room. In an article entitled "Bradshaw and Bayes: towards a timetable for the Neolithic", it dawned on me that here was a further radiocarbon revolution that simply had to be invoked for Ban Non Wat and all other sites in Southeast Asia for which there were multiple radiocarbon dates from assured contexts in a stratified sequence. This article was a prelude to six further papers applying OxCal 4.0 Bayesian analyses to the chronologies of British chambered tombs. I had to reflect on these distant days in the South Lecture theatre at Cambridge, when Glyn Daniel would tell us of a new radiocarbon date. How times had changed. On my return from Spain I talked

I took extreme measures to get a good picture of our latest elite male.

I hold Sheppard Frere's trowel as I work with Daeng on the latest Bronze Age super burial.

I really appreciated the opportunity to visit Isanapura, the great capital of a Chenla kingdom.

to Tom about the possibility of dating the freshwater bivalve shells that had been placed as mortuary offerings, and further charcoal samples, from Ban Non Wat. This had to happen.

In early July, back in Dunedin, Amphan Kijngam came to stay with us on one of his fishing holidays. He borrowed my car daily and drove down to the Taieri River, usually returning in the evening with some sea-run trout. On this occasion, he arrived with the printed copy of the report on Noen U-Loke, again published by the Fine Arts Department with many fine colour illustrations. And then, one morning a quite unexpected email arrived from a documentary film company in America asking if they might visit my next excavation season at Ban Non Wat, in order to shoot a progressive excavation of one of our wealthy superburials. I replied explaining that the programme there had now ended, but they were persistent, promising sufficient funding for a season of excavations. I consulted Rachanie, and we concluded, why not? The money was banked and my ticket booked. I knew exactly where I wanted to extend our excavated area. On a previous season, we had encountered a concentration of early Bronze Age pots but they led into the unexcavated area. It would surely be interesting to follow them up. A fortnight before departure, I received a final email. The company had run out of money and would not be coming. I was delighted. I could have a final excavation with no distractions, and on the 22nd October, I again set off for Ban Non Wat.

As always, Rachanie had everything organized. We were just into late Iron Age layers when I got to the site, with an extensive animal butchering floor overlying burials. One man was interred with an iron spear still with a wooden haft in place. On the 1st November we came to burial 600, a figure I had hitherto only dreamed about. Nancy had often written that there were never enough for valid results, and now I thought that she might be satisfied. We had a field day with later Bronze Age graves, and as we went on down, came closer to the point where the superburial should be. On the 9th November we were there, and what a reward was in store! I treated myself to excavating the length of the right arm, and uncovered shell and marble bangles from shoulder to wrist. They never seemed to end, going on and on. A nearby infant wore about 18 bronze bells round the ankles, and a woman right next to the bangle man had numerous shell bead belts. A family, I wondered? We moved on down to a remarkable flexed burial, a women on her back, holding a complete pig's skull. The denouement came on November 22nd. We came across a complete deer's skeleton, an infant skeleton covered in concretions and a shell midden. We sensed something strange and in due course radiocarbon dates proved us right, the midden dated to about 18,000 years ago, a vanishingly rare late Pleistocene open air site?

I did not go straight home as I would have liked, for I had agreed to be a guest expert on a tour of Southeast Asian archaeological sites for a firm called Far Horizons. This began at a luxurious hotel in Bangkok where I met the ten or so American travellers. We spent the first day visiting the Royal Palace in Bangkok before flying to Siem Reap to explore Angkor. I was particularly glad when driving down to Phnom Penh that we diverted to Sambor Prei Kuk, ancient Isanapura, to visit this most impressive of pre-Angkorian centres. This was not my only first on this journey. We then flew to Vientiane, my introduction to Laos, and down to visit Wat Phu. This was one of the great pilgrimage destinations for the kingdom of Angkor, and it was impressive indeed to climb up the many staircases to a sacred spring on the summit, and look back at the view over to the silvery snake of the Mekong River in the far distance. Then it was back to Vientiane and on to Luang Prabang, where we took a river boat to some caverns mentioned and illustrated by Louis de Carné during the Doudart de Lagrée expedition on the Mekong to Yunnan in 1866-8. I was back home in mid December, and so glad to have completed my commitment to Ban Non Wat in the field. Now I again faced the monster responsibility of bringing the seven seasons of excavations, 640 burials, thousands of artefacts, tons of organic remains and the research of an army of colleagues and students to print.

I looked forward to some concentrated analysis of Ban Non Wat at the start of the 2008 new year. Tom was due to visit over the summer, and by now we had at our disposal, 58 radiocarbon determinations, from charcoal and freshwater shells that had been placed as mortuary offerings. My analysis of the site stratigraphy, in particular the relative position of the burials, had led me to recognize 12 mortuary phases. These began with the enigmatic flexed burials, then two Neolithic, five Bronze Age, four Iron Age and an early historic phase. Tom was with us in New Zealand, and he undertook a Bayesian analysis on the internet, linking directly into the Oxford Lab website. The results were promising, there was internal consistency to the results whether from charcoal or shell. We drafted a paper, in which we concluded that our results "radically shortens the duration of the prehistoric period from the initial settlement of farmers to the foundation of early states". Our initial Neolithic farmer settlement took place from the 17th century BC, the transition into the Bronze Age in the 11th century, while iron first appeared in the 5th century. We completed our paper on the 17th February and sent it off to *Antiquity*. It was immediately accepted and published in March 2009 (Higham and Higham 2009). Later that year it was awarded *Antiquity*'s Ben Cullen prize.

While we were working on this paper, Dougald O'Reilly, my former student and now colleague at the Australian National University, emailed me to ask if I would join him in a research proposal to the Australian Research Council entitled "From Paddy to Pura: the Origins of Angkor". This, he explained, would take the form of a two-pronged approach to the transition into early states. He would work in Northwest Cambodia, and I in the upper Mun Valley, on late Iron Age and early historic sites in order to identify the factors that led to the transition into early states. I accepted his invitation in the expectation that the application would not be successful, there is a very low strike rate in this competitive area of research funding.

For some years, I had been a visiting scholar at my Cambridge college, St Catharine's. Ahead of my impending visit to England, I emailed the Master, Professor Dame Jean Thomas, to see if I still enjoyed this status. It meant that I could enjoy certain college privileges, such as access to the gym and taking lunch and dinner. On the 21st March she replied in the best letter since I was given a place on June 1st 1957, but it began with a sting. Regretfully, she wrote, the college council declined to extend my visiting scholar status. But then she asked if I would be prepared to accept an Honorary Fellowship. I could barely believe it, a Fellow of my college. I would join Tom, a Fellow of Keble, and Katerina at Brasenose.

A month later, I left home for Phimai once again, to find that Rachanie and Daeng, along with our team of villagers, had worked wonders with the curation of our casting moulds, bronzes, iron and bone artefacts. I spent days going over them all, measuring and taking digital images. The ultimate reason for my trip was to go on to New York to give a keynote speech at the annual meeting of Earthwatch, during which I outlined the contribution made by the hundreds of volunteers who had joined me since the first team in 1985. On my return to Dunedin, I settled down for a concentrated effort to put together the first, introductory volume on our work at Ban Non Wat. This involved taking our many plans drawn in each square as we dug deeper, harmonizing them across an area of 854m2 in the main square, and describing the entire cultural sequence. I used the programs Indesign and Freehand MX to do this, and worked all day in my study at home. This also involved the complete description of the sequences in X and Y, our two satellite squares, and summary chapters on the material culture. It all went well, thanks in large part to all the lab work organized in Phimai by Rachanie. Indeed, in August I was back in Phimai for more of my own lab work and photography of the bone tools, bronzes and the stone and shell bangles, hundreds of them. This trip involved moving on to Angkor for another session filming a documentary programme before flying to Leiden to the next conference of European Archaeologists working in Southeast Asia.

The conference went well, and I then went to Cambridge, where in a ceremony unchanged since the college was founded in 1473, and all in Latin, I was inducted as an Honorary Fellow in the college chapel, followed by a dinner in hall. My guest was Maru Mormina. She and I had communicated over the previous months on a matter of great interest to me, the potential of ancient DNA. We found a common interest, and we discussed a joint paper linking her work on population history and mine on climate change for a meeting to be held in Philadelphia that autumn. I asked the organisers if they would invite her and they agreed, so in November, we coincided there for a most interesting meeting that resulted in a book containing our chapter (Mormina and Higham 2010). On my return to New Zealand, I began putting together another research proposal to the Marsden Fund, to reinvestigate and excavate the site of Non Nok Tha. I wanted once and for all to sort out the basic chronology and social structure, having had such a breakthrough with the dating of Ban Non Wat. The procedure required a preliminary proposal and it was all set to go by mid-January 2009.

In early 2009 I formatted the text and illustrations for the first volume reporting on Ban Non Wat, and turned to other commitments. These involved the 2nd edition of *Early Thailand* for River Books, and researching the Bronze Age of Ban Non Wat for the 3rd volume of reports on that site. This drew on contributions from several of my colleagues. Tom had undertaken all the radiocarbon dating, and Nancy and her team identified the age and sex of most of the adult burials. Judith Cameron reported on the spindle whorls and Cathleen Hauman undertook a detailed analysis of the pottery vessels from the Bronze Age 2 superburials and the much poorer individuals at Ban Lum Khao to show that their forms were identical and therefore almost certainly contemporary. Carmen Sarjeant had been a tower of strength when supervising one of the most complex squares we encountered, and she summarised for this volume, her M.A. dissertation on the ceramic fabrics.

Oli Pryce, who had also supervised one of our squares during the actual excavations, now turned to the lead isotopes to identify the sources of the copper and changes over time. Hayden Cawte had been a stalwart in the field, and then gained a prestigious Marie Curie Fellowship to undertake doctoral research at the Institute of Archaeology in London on the *chaîne opératoire* of the copper-base technology, and he provided a summary chapter as well. Bryan Manly had been working with me on statistical analyses of burials based on the variable mortuary offerings since Khok Phanom Di days, and he again contributed massively to our conclusions on social organisation at this site, comparing change over time and with every published or available other Bronze Age site sample in Thailand. I contributed with a description of each Bronze Age burial and an overall summary of the period in the final chapter.

All this writing and editing was interrupted throughout the year by other commitments. In March I was away to China to work on two more television documentaries, one on the great city of Xian that involved visiting the Tang Dynasty Palace and Western Market. Then we flew down to Chengdu and drove to Leshan to film the colossal Buddha that towered over a particularly dangerous stretch of river. I took my editing with me, thanks to my trusty laptop and stored images, to Cambridge in August to work on the issue of Bronze Age mortuary feasting before we flew to Athens to join Minerva on another Swan Hellenic cruise. This took us to Mycenae, the Volos museum and Skyros before sailing again into the Black Sea for some new destinations that included a Scythian tomb near Kerch. As summer came to New Zealand I flew into bitter cold in Beijing for another television documentary. I crossed Tiananmen Square the day before President Obama came, past squads of tall and superbly drilled soldiery to visit the Forbidden City again, before we drove the 870 km to Xuzhou to film in the Han Dynasty royal rock-cut tombs there, and to feature a spectacular miniature terracotta army that few people have heard of. This preceded a visit to a conference in Hanoi, where for the last time I had the chance to catch up with a visibly aged Bill Solheim. On my return to Bangkok, Amphan Kijngam was waiting with a copy of volume 1 of the Ban Non Wat series reports, hot off the press, and I came across an article published in the *Journal of World Prehistory* by Joyce White and Elizabeth Hamilton that offered a new model for the establishment of the Bronze Age in Southeast Asia. It proposed a rapid movement south through Sichuan and Yunnan from the Seima Turbino culture of the Altai Mountain region, that brought copper-base technology to Ban Chiang by about 2000 BC. Several colleagues and I felt that we should respond. The root problem was that White and Hamilton's chronology was based on half a dozen radiocarbon determinations from the organic temper teased out of pottery vessels associated with burials. *Prima facie*, this seems to be an acceptable approach, but unfortunately, the experts have pointed out many sources of potential contamination that discourage acceptance of the results.

I had all the Ban Chiang faunal remains stored in my Department, so I selected a handful of pig bones associated as mortuary offerings with human burials and sent them to Tom for radiocarbon dating, just to see how they would pan out. This was a sideline in my many other more pressing commitments as 2010 got under way. I was contributing my bit to the application to the Australian Research Council for the Paddy to Pura project engineered by Dougald O'Reilly and Louise Shewan. There were two invited named lectures to prepare for, the Golson Lecture in Canberra and the Keble Lecture in Oxford, and Bryan Manly's results from his statistical analyses of the Bronze Age burials were flooding in and needed to be digested and prepared for publication. Some more good news came from Rachanie, that six million baht had been allocated to build a site museum directly over our excavated area at Ban Non Wat.

It was now time for editing, writing and formatting the second volume of our Ban Non Wat report, this one concentrating on the Neolithic period. I was very fortunate once again to call on my team of contributors. Warrachai Wiriyaromp had come to Dunedin with a Thai scholarship to work on the ceramic vessels, and his results were a mainstay in our interpretation of the mortuary and occupation data. Kim McClintock wrote a section on the ceramic tempers and Judith Cameron on the spindle whorls. Tessa Boer-Mah had joined us in the field over several seasons, and her excellent dissertation on the stone adzes was distilled into one of our chapters. Rachanie worked on the fish and shellfish, Amphan Kijngam on the animal bones. My description of each burial called once again on the sex and age designation provided by Nancy Tayles and Sian Halcrow. I printed out the final version in April and sent it off to Amphan in Bangkok, after incorporating the foreword by Somsuda Leyavanija, the Director-General of the Fine Arts Department, who had been such a promising member of my fieldwork team in Mahasarakham Province in 1980.

In April, just as we were setting off for the Golson lecture, Tom emailed to say that the pig bones from Ban Chiang were datable. We flew to Sydney on the back of this promising news, and drove to our booked accommodation in the Blue Mountains. My topic for the lecture was the Bronze Age of Southeast Asia, and to pay my respects to Gordon Childe, I wanted to visit Govett's Leap, where he had leapt to his death in 1957, just as I was starting my studies at the Institute of Archaeology. Our accommodation turned out to be a mansion and we occupied rooms labelled the Gordon Childe Suite. I enquired why and was told by the owner that this house had been the holiday base for the Childe family. He showed me a picture of the infant Vere Gordon in his mother's arms in the garden. Polly took a photograph of me in exactly the same spot. Our visit to Govett's Leap was sombre. He must have been in deep despair to summon up the courage to jump into oblivion. It was excellent to meet so many old friends in Canberra. Jack Golson himself was on fine form. He had been our first dinner guest in Dunedin back in 1967, and had promised me a position in the Australian National University a year later had I not been appointed to the foundation chair. Angela Calder was there and Jean Kennedy, both of whom worked with me in the field in the early 1970s in Thailand.

A new museum was constructed at Ban Non Wat, directly over our excavation.

We flew directly to London and on to Oxford, where I gave the Keble Lecture, before flying to Istanbul for another Swan cruise that took us westward to Epidaurus, Delphi and on to Malta. By now I had received the Ban Chiang pig bone dates from Tom, and we were writing an article intended for the journal *Antiquity*. This was received by the editor in late June and accepted in September (Higham et al. 2011). It was really the first attempt to get the chronology of Ban Chiang on a firm footing, and the results firmly supported the much larger set of results from Ban Non Wat. However, we had only dated half a dozen samples. To do a proper job, we needed a lot more that covered the entire sequence, and to analyse them with the OxCal Bayesian program. Tom suggested that we turn to the human bones, then still housed under the care of Mike Pietrusewsky in Hawaii. So in October, I sent letters to Somsuda Leyavanija and Richard Hodges, Director of the Penn Museum, seeking permission to sample the human bones for radiocarbon dating. Both replied with enthusiastic agreement, Somsuda concluding "May I acknowledge the importance of obtaining a proper chronology for Ban Chiang and send my best wishes for the success of this initiative". Mike extracted multiple samples of bone and dispatched them to Tom in Oxford. The ball was set rolling.

As always when travelling to Europe, I stopped over in Phimai in September to work this time on the Iron Age midden bone analyses before attending the Berlin meeting of the European Association of Southeast Asian Archaeologists. On my return home, I spent some time putting together a paper destined for the *Journal of World Prehistory* that responded to White and Hamilton's article on the timing and social implications of copper-base metallurgy in Southeast Asia. Our team included Roberto Ciarla, who is fluent in Chinese and conversant with this issue through his doctoral dissertation on the southward expansion of metallurgy from the Central

I stand in the same spot as Gordon Childe's mother, holding the future Director of the Institute of Archaeology in her arms at their home in the Blue Mountains of Australia.

Plains of China to the Bangkok Plain. Fiorella Rispoli likewise was the leading authority on the transmission of technical knowledge into Southeast Asia from northern sources. Tom and Katerina contributed new radiocarbon determinations and Amphan Kijngam lent his expertise on Thai sites. Our model was based on a wealth of hard data that saw copper-base metallurgy reaching Southeast Asia in the last century or two of the 2nd millennium BC, that at Ban Non Wat at least, had a significant correlate in the rise of a social elite. Our paper was published towards the end of 2011.

By the end of 2010, I had done all I could to complete the third volume on the Bronze Age at Ban Non Wat, a 600-page monster, and was turning to the Iron Age. This took on a rather unexpected turn, when on the 25th October, Dougald emailed to say that he had landed $A340,000 to pursue the Paddy to Pura project over three years. I was very surprised to think that I was going to return to the field and excavation square. There was no doubt as to where I wanted to dig. We had found a really beautiful double-moated site called Non Ban Jak, set alone in the rice fields about 10 km west of Noen U-Loke and Ban Non Wat. Rachanie went out to see the headman for local permission, and I applied to the Thai authorities for the necessary permits.

I was working in January 2011 on a new Marsden application, entitled "The Passage of Time: Dating the Prehistory of Southeast Asia and Southern China". If successful, Tom and I planned a major assault on getting the chronological scaffolding in place so that we could proceed with the interpretation of the cultural sequence unfettered by uncertainty and rather arid controversies. In March, I heard that we had made the cut into the finals. There was also an email from Tom on the 22nd. His first result from the human bone sample from Ban Chiang had just come off the wheel. It came from burial 76, the male interred deep down in a flexed position in association with a socketed bronze spear. This has always been seen as the earliest undoubted presence of bronze at this site, and the radiocarbon date is 1056-919 BC. This was very timely, because I was preparing to give a lecture on Ban Chiang at the Penn Museum, and could incorporate it in my powerpoint just three weeks before leaving on the 17th April.

I arrived in Philadelphia jet lagged and suffered an awful sleepless night before having breakfast with Richard Hodges and a brisk walk to the Museum. I met for lunch with Brian Rose and Joyce White before returning to my hotel for a much-needed siesta. I gave my lecture at about 5.00 pm with Richard Hodges presiding. I began with a simple fact. The latest radiocarbon revolution involving Bayesian analyses is transformational. One now needs multiple samples from certain contexts in a tightly defined stratigraphic sequence. A handful of samples, or worse, samples from mixed deposits, must be viewed with extreme caution. To illustrate the latter point, I showed a movie I had taken of Jean Kennedy combining a sample of charcoal fragments as she excavated in grave fill at Ban Chiang in 1975. I went on to stress that those adhering to poorly derived dates will experience choppy seas. Being in America and as a light-hearted aside, I said that if anyone ever claimed that raising the flag on Mount Suribachi at Iwo Jima was earlier than Betsy Ross stitching together the first stars and stripes, then they would be in trouble. I then showed an image of burial 76, and announced our new date derived from the human bone. This result and its other new dates, I suggested, harmonized so perfectly with the dates for Ban Non Wat, that the long chronology for Ban Chiang needed to be consigned to history.

The following day, I arrived by arrangement at 9.00 am at the front desk of the Museum. Elizabeth Hamilton, who was then working on the metal remains, arrived to escort me down into the windowless basement to discuss progress. I hadn't been there since 1982, when I was investigating how to proceed with the analysis and report preparation. It was a depressing place, and seemed little changed. Nothing of significance came of this exchange of views, and it was a relief to get back to Dunedin and forge ahead with my many commitments.

First and foremost was working on the new Marsden application, and getting on with the final volume on Ban Non Wat, the Iron Age and overall synthesis. I was also putting together the McDonald lecture for delivery in November. Dr McDonald was a generous benefactor of archaeology at Cambridge, his donation funding a new building with fine laboratories, the *Cambridge Archaeological Journal*, and an annual lecture. I had been to one or two of these, and remember in particular that delivered by Svante Pääbo on ancient DNA. It is a full-on University occasion with a convivial drinks reception after, and a dinner for the speaker and selected guests. I chose as my theme, the origins of Angkor, based very much on the social changes our team had tracked down at Noen U-Loke and Ban Non Wat, not to mention the definitive chronological framework within which to weigh when social inequality arose.

A visit to China in May added a further string to my bow. It involved the celebration of the discovery of Hemudu, the iconic site documenting the early uptake of rice farming in the region of the lower Yangtze River. I flew to Shanghai and in a ritual I was to grow accustomed to, was met at the airport and driven to our destination. This involved crossing the Hangzhou River as we drove south. After about 20 minutes, we were still on the bridge and virtually out of sight of land. I viewed the GPS on my mobile and found to my astonishment that the bridge is about 36 km long, typical of China where everything is on such a massive scale. The meeting was fascinating. We visited Hemudu and the site museum before driving to the related site of Tianluoshan. A large domed roof appeared first, under which lay exposed a massive excavation of an early rice-farming site with the foundation posts of houses in place, even a bridge over a creek and remains of a

The size of Chinese excavations is a source of great envy. Here I visited Tianluoshan.

boat. It had been waterlogged and organic remains were legion. Close inspection revealed caches of acorns. Outside, we inspected excavations of rice fields, and in the site lab, there were loads of artefacts, while Dorian Fuller, who was the inspiration behind the recovery and analysis of the rice and other plant remains, gave us his views on the origins of rice domestication. I was so envious of the enormous area that the Chinese were able to open at this site, and the industrial-scale roof that sheltered them and the site.

I returned home to some good news. Somsuda agreed to fund the publication of Ban Non Wat, the Bronze Age, and the referees' reports on my Marsden application were uniformly positive, fingers crossed. The good news then turned to excellent. In August, Tom emailed to tell me that all the Ban Chiang human bones contained the collagen needed for successful radiocarbon dating, and the following month, a trickle of results turned into a flood. With each set, I calibrated them and by degrees, the chronology for this site began to take shape. The excitement of finally achieving this might have impaired my judgement, for I decided to accept an invitation from the Oxford University Press to join Ian Glover as co-editor of the proposed Oxford Handbook of Southeast Asian Archaeology. This was to prove a far greater undertaking than I imagined possible. Nevertheless my *annus mirabilis* continued unabated. On the 5th of October, I received a phone call from Wellington advising me that the Marsden committee had allocated $818,000 to my research project on the passage of time. The following day Rachanie emailed to say that all permits for excavating Non Ban Jak were signed.

Pamela Smith in Cambridge has been instrumental in recording interviews of Cambridge archaeologists as they describe their experiences. She also organizes day-long meetings where topics are discussed by leading scholars. For example, a day might be devoted to the contribution of Jane Goodall, made even more interesting were she in Cambridge at the time. In November, the day was devoted to the life and career of Eric Higgs and, as his first PhD student, I began proceedings by describing how I became hooked on economic prehistory, and went on to describe our experiences hunting down the Neanderthals in Greece. I was followed by another half dozen speakers before proceedings ended with a convivial tea party before I then retired to St Catharine's to prepare for my McDonald lecture that same evening. I put on my MA gown and proceeded to the Mill Lane lecture theatre that was packed to the rafters, and included many friends and members of my family. I think it went down well and certainly it impressed the Disney Professor, Graeme Barker, who said after that any one of my Bronze Age superburials, if found in Europe, would feature on the front page of *The Times*. We then trouped up to the McDonald Institute for drinks, before a splendid dinner was laid on in the Wordsworth Room in St John's College. It had been quite a day.

I looked at the image and saw the hint of structures to come. A day or two later
and we had a lane flanking town houses.

Thirteen | An Unexpected Return, Non Ban Jak

The day after delivering the McDonald Lecture, I was up at 6.00 am and took the train to Heathrow for Bangkok. The following day I was in Phimai and out to the site. Rachanie had recovered our roof from a local temple and there it was waiting. Non Ban Jak has two distinct mounds, an eastern and a western. We had chosen to open an area 8 by 8 metres on the former and already I could get down into the square now about 80 cm deep and find Phimai Black Late Iron Age occupation in front of me. It wasn't long before we came across an infant burial and an adult, not to mention pits and evidence for occupation. About a week after we began, I had one of those eureka moments that defined our season, and beyond. I took an image of the surface of our excavated area and, as was my custom, I downloaded and looked at the daily take that evening. When I came to the surface image, I was able to make out very faint straight white lines that ran parallel to each other and turned at right angles. I thought at once of the images of houses at Çatal Höyük that Jimmy Mellaart had showed us back in 1960 at Cambridge.

The following day we revealed more and as the days added up, so we began to uncover rooms and plastered clay floors. We had, beyond doubt, come across the houses and lanes in a late Iron Age town. One of the rooms was in microcosm, its own voyage of discovery. Working down and exposing its floor first involved recording and removing a length of collapsed wall. Then another surprise hove into view. A row of postholes, probably to support the roof, ran across the surface of the floor, beside a rectangular area of dark fill contrasting with the white floor itself. In one corner, was a much smaller rectangle and nearby, a third of intermediate size. Lidded pots had been placed in the angles of the walls. We recorded and photographed these rectangles, and then went into them. The soft fill continued until we came across a human skull and then, by degrees, the complete skeleton of a female. The smallest contained a tiny infant skeleton, while the third was the grave of a child interred with the head in one large pot and the feet in another. Since the largest grave was sealed by the collapsed wall, we concluded that the dead were interred while this house was occupied. And what a fine town house it was, with thick clay wall foundations incorporating the circular holes that would have supported the wall studs.

Having recorded everything and exhumed the skeletons, we carried on down. Floors and walls, and pathways between houses continued, some rooms containing hearths and internal buttresses against the walls that looked like items of furniture. The occupants were fastidious, there were no accumulations of rubbish or occupation debris on the living floors, but quite a concentration of broken potsherds in the lanes. Behind one wall however, we came across the skeleton of a rat. We were unable to reach the natural substrate that season, so we bedded down the square and counted the season a complete success. In early December I flew to London, in order to be at the 50th anniversary of the 1961 University Rugby Match. Only one of our team, known as "The Invincibles", was missing as we attended the Hawks Club dinner at the Savoy, followed next afternoon by the match itself. I then returned to Phimai to catch up with the post excavation arrangements, and show Dougald and Louise what we had found out at Non Ban Jak before returning home.

On January 2nd 2012, I finished the final report on Ban Non Wat. It described the Iron Age occupation and provided a synthesis of all our results. In all, there were four volumes, 1,500 pages, 1,634 illustrations, 147 tables and 32 contributors. I then turned to a new volume for River Books. Narisa and I had discussed this, and I decided to cover not just the mainland as currently configured, but also the islands that were part of Sundaland, drowned by the post-Pleistocene rise in sea level. This meant extending it to what is now island Southeast Asia. I also began not with anatomically modern humans but with the first hominins to reach our region from their African homeland. This entailed a fair bit of reading. My research was set aside in February when I embarked for Hanoi, and a meeting including Ian Glover and Peter Bellwood that contributed to the organization of a major exhibition in Germany reflecting Vietnamese cultural heritage. Two cruises rapidly followed, one from Auckland to Norfolk Island, New Caledonia and Australia, the second beginning in Kuala Lumpur and taking in Sri Lanka before ending in Mumbai. Both required the preparation of new lectures and both were very rewarding in terms of site visits and new friends. We flew from India to London and Cambridge, where Colin Renfrew had invited me to contribute to one of his symposia on death rituals. The theme of his several such meetings was pushing back the edges of knowability, and this meeting was no exception.

There was a welcome and unexpected surprise on our return to Dunedin when the British Academy wrote to say that I had been awarded the biannual Grahame Clark Medal for "for academic achievement involving recent contributions to the study of prehistoric archaeology". Many memories rolled back the years, of the rather remote Grahame's lectures, his presence at Nea Nikomedia, his many encouraging and insightful letters to me as a graduate student and as he mellowed with time, his warm welcomes when I returned to Cambridge. I think I became a bit of a favourite of his. When ill in hospital in 1992, he asked for no visitors but me. I couldn't attend the annual awards meeting at the Academy but on the advice of our dear friend Alan Battersby, Tom went down and accepted the medal on my behalf. However, I was back in Cambridge again in August. With my new Marsden grant for dating secured, I sampled the human bones from the important site of Gua Cha, and then went over to Paris to attend a fascinating meeting on the Negritoes of Southeast Asia.

My paper was the first to be delivered and covered the prehistoric hunter-gatherer occupation of the areas where they survive to this day. Other papers I particularly valued related the latest information on their ancestry based on DNA. The following month I flew to Dublin to visit Ireland for the first time. It was the next meeting of the European Association of Southeast Asian Archaeologists, held in Dublin Castle. The meeting was most valuable and when it was over, Polly joined me and we drove down to Castlecomer. We wanted to visit the estate where my Great x12 grandfather Sir Christopher Wandesforde had lived while Governor of Ireland under Charles 1st. It was a fascinating visit, and the stable block survives though his great house has been demolished. There was an exhibition showing the history of the Wandesforde's from which I learned that a distant relative, Geoffrey Prior-Wandesforde, was living near Oxford. I rang him for a chat when we returned to England.

Our second season at Non Ban Jak began on the 1st November, and I had a spring in my step: there were no Earthwatch volunteers. This might seem ungrateful, but

Daeng and I are exploring the walls and floors as we progressed downward.

Rachanie and Daeng are excavating infant jar burials next to a kiln.

I try and figure out the layout of the early houses, with little rooms and ephemeral wall foundations.

Rachanie and Daeng here have opened the kiln. A socketed iron ploughshare lies beside the abandoned pots.

for me it meant a much more serene time digging, and a far more relaxed evening after the long and hot day in the field. No longer did I have to organize local transport and accommodation and, more importantly, find interesting tasks without the possibility of inexperienced hands damaging anything fragile, particularly human remains. No longer too, did I need to spend my evenings entertaining and lecturing. Indeed, I enjoyed an absolute armchair ride. On my arrival at the airport, I went straight to the hotel for a good night's sleep and hearty breakfast. Our driver, Mr Chob, was there at about 8.00 am to take me straight to Non Ban Jak, where Rachanie had arranged everything. The roof was up, locals had been engaged for making tea and cooking lunch under the shade of a tree, and even a proper flushing loo had been installed. On arrival, I ducked behind the car to change into my digging outfit, wielded Sheppard Frere's trowel and climbed down into the square to get going. I was timekeeper. Tea and lunch breaks were signaled by my banging my trowel on a scaffolding roof support.

At the end of each day, I drove the team back to Phimai, about 35 minutes, and went for a swim at the Phimai Inn. What a feeling it was to jump into that pool. Then back to our house to enjoy a gin and tonic with lime, laid on by the trusted

Eo, then another. Dinner followed, then I played my guitar for a bit before going to my air-conditioned room to watch a Netflix and catch up with internet news before lights out at about 9.00 pm. In the morning I awoke at about 6.00 am and went downstairs to make my morning cup of tea before checking my emails and ringing Polly for home news. Daeng was already preparing lunch. Up at 6.45 am to find my breakfast laid out by Daeng. I always took a suitcase containing sufficient home-made bread, honey from our own hives, a kg of Colombian coffee beans, muesli for the duration of the dig and yoghurt mix. Rachanie's nephew Note was a tower of strength, he loaded the pickup and we all set off for another day digging.

We had left the 8 by 8 m square on the eastern mound unfinished, and began at once going down. It was a season of surprises, and the excavation was technically very demanding that drew on all the skill of Rachanie, Daeng and my wonderful village workforce. The thick clay walls and floors were no longer in evidence, and in their place we encountered much more ephemeral wall foundations and floors. We were able to map rooms, one being a kitchen with a pot still on the hearth and floor littered with charred rice grains. One room in this house had an infant jar burial cut through the floor. Right up against the exterior wall we found a large oval pit, that turned out to be a kiln filled with charcoal and the collapsed daub cover. A huge pot was still in place within, and it might well have been the heat or flames from this kiln that set fire to the house we were uncovering, because it had been destroyed in a conflagration. However, a new house was built over the old, on a slightly different orientation. I looked back at my experiences at Verulamium, uncovering the burnt daub foundations of houses destroyed by Queen Boudicca. This took a lot of careful excavation and recording, but once achieved, we carried on down.

We began to identify a concentration of large, broken Phimai Black potsherds, mixed with chunks of red burnt daub. As we moved across this feature in an eastern direction, a circle of daub and charcoal appeared. It was another kiln associated with the rake-out of wasters and charcoal. It had once been covered with a clay dome. We delved down into it, and reaching the base, came across eight pottery vessels abandoned by those doing the firing for some unknown reason. But there was also a definite hint of red, the colour associated with rusted iron. Delicately revealing it, we could see the identical form of a winged socketed and very heavy artefact that we had described

My workers crowded round and declared that we had found a ploughshare, identical with that from a burial at Noen U-Loke seen to the right.

as a spade when we found it in a grave at Noen U-Loke. My villagers crowded round as we examined it. All were rice farmers, and all the men had spent hours behind a buffalo-drawn plough. They looked at its profile, and were unanimous, this was no spade, it was a ploughshare. A huge penny dropped in my head, as I raced through the implications of this, probably one of the most significant artefacts I have ever found. I immediately thought back to Jack Goody's book *Production and Reproduction* (1971), that had pinpointed the social implications when ploughing took over from hoeing fields in Africa.

We were now getting down pretty deep, and the layers were very damp. Then we found that a pit dug down further still one afternoon was filled with water by the morning. We had hit the water table. Fortunately, we also reached the natural substrate. This square was now finished, and my final task was to record the sections.

Meanwhile, we had started a small test square on the western mound. The sequence here was nowhere near as deep, and the deposits were quite different. No floors, no walls, but lying on the laterite substrate, a collection of Iron Age adult graves and some infant jar burials. We earmarked this area for an extended excavation the next season. As we were finishing, Hiro Matsumura arrived, in order to measure some of the human skulls now stored at the Fine Arts Department. I welcomed him with open arms to get this job done not only for the bottle of whisky he gave me, but also for his results, as he revealed that the prehistoric people were surely incoming rice farmers ultimately from the Yangtze Valley. I then went down to Bangkok to visit Siriraj hospital. Some of the human bones from Non Nok Tha were stored there, and I sampled them for my new Marsden dating programme.

We flew up to Hong Kong early in the New Year of 2013 to join Minerva for a Swan cruise down to Bangkok. It gave me the opportunity to visit some of the major Cham civilization sites, beginning with Mi Son, that had suffered badly from American bombing during the Vietnam War. This is the largest and most impressive of all Cham centres, and the focus of much fieldwork during the French colonial period including recording of the temples by one of my heroes, Henri Parmentier. We also visited Po Nagar, and in Saigon I met with Vietnamese colleagues to catch up with their fieldwork on the Mekong Delta, and give them a seminar on our own work in the upper Mun Valley. During quiet times on board I worked on writing the new book on Southeast Asia.

On the 21st March, I received a most welcome invitation to become involved in the new initiative from China, the Shanghai Archaeological Forum. I was asked to prepare a keynote lecture on the comparative origins of civilizations. This required a lot of reading, because I chose to cover many areas: Mesoamerica, the Near East and Egypt, China and Southeast Asia. I also, at this juncture, became better informed on the application of Lidar at Angkor, following phone calls with

Rachanie I and were invited to the first Shanghai Archaeological Forum, where our fieldwork was voted one of the top ten projects in the world. Here I give a summary of our findings.

Po Nagar is one of the major Cham centres on the coast of Vietnam.

Roland Fletcher in Sydney. The results of this initiative were astonishing. Angkor Thom, the walled city of Jayavarman VII, is almost entirely covered by jungle. But Lidar has penetrated and provided a detailed map of the streets, canals, the palaces and temples, ponds and houses following a few overflights by a helicopter. Beyond this city, the internal layout of Angkor Wat and the water distribution system has emerged crystal clear. In my view, it is the most profound advance in understanding this civilization ever. At a meeting in Bang Saen, Thailand, in May, I listened to a presentation on the results of the first Lidar survey given by Damien Evans.

After this meeting, Rachanie and I visited the excavations of Supamas Doungsakun at Nong Ratchawat in Suphanburi Province. My mouth watered at the possibility of digging such a site as this, a beautiful Neolithic occupation and cemetery site with the most remarkable pottery vessels embellished with ceramic breasts and horns. The

We were confronted with awful problems with the high water table. We had to wade through the mud.

radiocarbon dates, too, were entirely in line with the short chronology.

Just over a month later, I set off for the Shanghai Forum. It was a splendid occasion, with a host of friends and luminaries, and typical Chinese hospitality. The meeting began with an award ceremony for the 10 top fieldwork programmes in the world. This involved being nominated, and then adjudicated by a selected panel of authorities. Our Ban Non Wat research was voted in the top ten, and Rachanie and I went on stage to receive our award. Colin Renfrew was selected for the Lifetime Achievement Award at the Forum, and richly deserved it was. The field trip took us to Liangzhu, a site I had always wanted to see. It is the earliest state centre in the Yangtze valley, renowned for the remarkable jade mortuary offerings recovered from elite burials. We were taken to the city walls and one of the fine new museums that are springing up all over China. And one evening, we had a boat trip along the Bund, and drove past Shanghai Cathedral where my grandparents were married in 1908. I wanted very much to visit Bubbling Spring Road, where my parents met for the first time in 1936, but it is now covered by an elevated expressway.

One word summed up our third season at Non Ban Jak: mud. My grandson Joe and I arrived on the 1st November, to find that the water table was high as we extended our excavation from the previous season on the western mound. I had anticipated that the concentration of adult graves in our test square would expand into a cemetery like that at Ban Non Wat, but this was not to be. We did find quite a few infant jar burials, and some adult graves, but no walls, nor floors. As we progressed downward, it became almost impossible to excavate with any accuracy, even though we had a pump going to remove the constant upsurge of water. So we decided to extend further and hope that conditions would soon dry out sufficiently for us to complete our work where we had started.

A week into the season, Tom and Katerina arrived to sample the Ban Non Wat and Khok Phanom Di human bones for our dating programme, so for a few days there were three generations of Highams on the dig. The extended area immediately paid dividends with five adult graves very close to the modern surface, and rather drier conditions. In due course we waded across the mud to recover quite a few infant jar burials, one of these containing miniature bronze belts. When we neared completion, we also came across adults wearing silver and gold. Nigel Chang was keen to continue after we left in mid-December, so we cut down a large tree that stood in the way and extended further for him to continue the good work. Naturally on this our last season with Australian funding, we wanted to get as much information as possible, and ended with 65 burials, sufficient I hoped, to enable us to make a significant contribution to the findings of the Paddy to Pura project.

It wasn't long before I was back in Southeast Asia. In mid-January I met Rachanie in Bangkok and we took our car to Aranyaprathet before entering Cambodia, hiring a car and driving to Siem Reap for the next meeting of the Indo-Pacific Prehistory Association. Narisa was there with a boot load of copies of my book on Mainland Southeast Asia, and we enjoyed a successful book launch. I was on the committee of IPPA so I attended various meetings, and the conference itself was a great success, including a field trip to Angkor Thom and a dinner out with all participants in the Paddy to Pura project organized by Dougald O'Reilly. On my return to Dunedin I heard from Nigel of his successful season at Non Ban Jak, we were now up to 108 burials, one of which contained two bronze belts. He sent me all his plans and images for me to integrate with my own as I turned my mind to a final report.

I also thought it an opportune time to work with Fiorella Rispoli on a paper integrating the prehistoric sequences of the Mun Valley with that of the Lopburi region of Central Thailand, where she and Roberto Ciarla had been working for years with the Pigott and Natapintu's Thailand Archaeometallurgy Project (TAP) and on their own sister project, the Lopburi Regional Archaeology Project (LoRAP). This turned out to be an innovative effort, one of, if not the first, to try and mesh sequences from two regions, and we found much common ground.

Three generations of Highams at Non Ban Jak, me, Tom and Joe.

We sent it to the Society of Antiquaries of London, of which I was a Fellow, to see if they would publish it in their Proceedings as they had with a previous effort of mine on the Iron Age. Two referees' reports were sent me, along with acceptance from the editor in London. Both were very positive, and we made a few minor improvements and sent the text back to be published. A couple of months elapsed before another email arrived from the editor. It said that they had consulted a third referee, and the paper was now declined. Naturally I asked her for a copy of the new report, but my request was refused. I sent the paper to another journal and it was soon accepted and published. Six years later, I mentioned this incident to my friend Norman Hammond, and he encouraged me to contact the Secretary of the Antiquaries to ask again for a copy of that opinion, but again it was declined. I resigned my fellowship.

As the months unfolded, so Rachanie sent images of the restored pots from Non Ban Jak, and the radiocarbon determinations came back from the Oxford and Waikato laboratories. My colleagues, bioarchaeologists Hallie Buckley and Sian Halcrow and I met and decided that our work at this site was by no means finished, but the Australian money was spent. So we decided to apply to the University of Otago for a one-year grant as seed money for another Marsden application a year later. We were successful, and laid our plans that further progressed in August when I made my annual trek to Phimai to photograph the restored artefacts, this time including close-up images of the fabric attached to iron mortuary offerings, the glass beads, adzes and spindle whorls. I combined this trip with a conference I had been invited to attend in Hong Kong.

The following month we returned for what was becoming an annual visit to Cambridge, where my college was generous in providing us with Fellow's accommodation. We visited Sheppard Frere, now 98 and just as incisive in his comments on my excavations as ever, and conferred with Tom and Katerina as a flood of radiocarbon dates from Ban Chiang, Ban Na Di and Non Nok Tha were coming off the AMS accelerator at Oxford. All of them were internally consistent and we applied OxCal Bayesian analyses to each. We decided that we would report on them to the journal *Plos One* and in November, we began our article, sending if off to the editors on the 2nd December, along with lengthy and comprehensive supporting information. Two days later, Polly and I took passage to Colombo to join a cruise that visited Sri Lankan sites before crossing the Andaman Sea to Rangoon, and so down the coast of Thailand and Malaysia to end in Singapore.

On the 1st of January 2015, our paper on the chronology of Non Nok Tha was published. I first encountered this site in 1967, when Donn Bayard and Ham Parker were discussing it in our Department, and I studied and published the faunal remains. The site received much attention when Bill Solheim claimed the

Cristina Castillo (in white shirt) faced a massive task of sorting and analysing our botanical remains, with fascinating results.

earliest bronze in the world, and a socketed axe was nicknamed WOST, "the world's oldest socketed tool". Tom had dated the human bone samples I had assembled from Bangkok and their resting place in Nevada, and the results revealed initial Neolithic occupation in about 1500 BC, with the transition into the Bronze Age five centuries later. It all now made sense and I was glad to have set it all to rights.

It was good to have this out before I departed for our third season at Non Ban Jak in the middle of January. I was very pleased to have my last graduate student in archaeology, Helen Heath, with me as we flew up to Bangkok. She was beginning her research on the pottery. It was a really excellent season. Thankfully the mud and slime of the previous year was not repeated. We began to uncover well-preserved walls and floors again, and the dead had clearly been interred within the rooms we found ourselves tracing. One male wore gold earrings and agate beads. In one case, a wall abutted a living floor still with broken pots in place, through which a grave had been cut. An infant jar burial nestled in the corner of this room, and beyond it, another adult had been interred. We also welcomed Cristina Castillo, who had come to undertake flotation to recover the plant remains. Two or three kilns appeared, and they were associated with many carbonized rice grains as well as, significantly, rice field weeds that were to prove vital in interpreting the nature of the agricultural regime. During our rest day, I turned to drafting yet another Marsden application, in the hope that we could continue our involvement with this remarkable site.

This application, and working on the final text for our major paper for *Plos One* on our radiocarbon chronologies, dominated the first few months of 2015. The substance of the latter we worked into a paper for the July meeting of the European Association of Southeast Asian Archaeologists in Paris. With Katerina in the chair, flanked by Tom and me, we gave the plenary address. I began with a summary of the new Ban Chiang, Ban Non Wat and Non Nok Tha chronologies, followed by Tom describing the technical backdrop to dating human bone and shell in conjunction with charcoal. The auditorium was packed. Katerina then asked for any questions, and, as is often the case, there was an element of disagreement from Joyce White, who rose to support a rather earlier uptake of bronze technology. On the last day of this conference, she was scheduled to give her presentation, read in her absence by Oli Pryce. Given the extreme rarity of bronze mortuary offerings, other complete bronzes and virtually no moulds at Ban Chiang, she stressed the importance of fragments from occupation contexts. These were dominated numerically by broken pieces of bronze bangles. Turning to our report on Ban Non Wat, she found that we had not provided detailed data on the number and form of bronze fragments. This was not to be the last time that this issue was to surface, one that I felt, overlooked the importance of moulds rather than surviving fragments that inform on what was cast. We recovered about four fragmentary moulds at Ban Chiang none of which revealed what they had cast. At Ban Non Wat we recovered about 400. They had been used to cast axes, spears and bangles but naturally, axes and spears on account of their size, are more likely to have been melted down and recycled.

Barbara Wohlfarth gave a fascinating paper on her research at Lake Kumphawapi, scene of our fieldwork and excavations at Ban Na Di in 1981. She and her team had taken cores from the lake bed for the sediments that reflected the environmental history over the past three millennia. She identified a period of marked weakening in the monsoon, leading to an extended period of aridity. The crucial issue was that this dry period coincided with our dates for the construction of moats round Noen U-Loke, Non Ban Jak and Ban Non Wat. A seed for a new model on social change was sown in my mind, that was to germinate into a most interesting and I hope, influential publication (Wohlfarth 2016).

From Paris, we flew to Greece to celebrate Tom and Katerina's wedding, and then down to Athens for dinner under the Acropolis just as Richard and I had done back in 1960. It was there that the referees' reports on the latest Marsden application arrived. Our proposal centred on excavating on both the western and eastern mounds at Non Ban Jak on the premise that those interred on the latter were the elite in a community displaying social inequality. The reports were positive and encouraging. On my return to Dunedin, my then Marsden expired on September 1st and with it, my employment in the University. That week I went to the University Library to borrow a book and was told I was no longer able to. I thought this a little much after being the longest-serving Professor in the history of the University. Even more irritating was my checking in at the airport on the 10th September for a meeting in London. I was told that my ticket, issued from a travel agency in London, named me as Higham Charles instead of Charles Higham, which did not match the name on my passport and I could not board. A telephone call when London awoke got me onto a flight the following day, and I attended a vital and fascinating meeting hosted at the Institute by Dorian Fuller, on the origins and implications of rice domestication. Here, a paper by Cristina Castillo and Katie Miller added further fuel to the model I was working on that involved a late Iron Age agricultural revolution following the weakening monsoon.

There was so much happening. On the 30th September I joined a group of Oxford and Cambridge alumni for a river cruise from Angkor to Saigon, as the guest speaker. There were only about 10 couples on board a little boutique vessel with creaking internet access. Having spent several days at Angkor we set off across the Tonle Sap, the Great Lake, and I finally got into my emails. One immediately stood out, it was from Hallie Buckley. We had landed another Marsden for two seasons at Non Ban Jak. I was reinstated as a Research Professor and with a light heart, returned to borrow library books and set off on the 13th December for the second Shanghai Archaeological Forum. The year ended on another high, when in the New Year's Honours list, I was awarded the Order of New Zealand Merit for services to education and archaeology.

And so in mid-January 2016, Helen and I set forth for another tilt at Non Ban Jak. Rachanie had laid out a 10 by 10 m square on the top of the eastern mound, about 30 m from our first season's opening, and I anticipated a similar, deep sequence. I was joined by my Uncle Strachan's great grandson Richard, then studying archaeology at Bournemouth University. My uncle had been so supportive of my early ambitions, and it was a great opportunity to have this link strengthened in the person of my first cousin twice removed. We were also helped in this with the arrival of half-a-dozen former Earthwatch volunteers who had formed themselves into a group to help Nigel over the previous few years. Our lunch time breaks were now punctuated with talk of Trump's chances the following November. I also hosted Glenn Scott, a graduate student of Dougald O'Reilly, whom I allowed to incorporate our mortuary data into his doctoral dissertation. We spent the first week uncovering an historic occupation phase that involved walls and floors, and a clay statuette of the Buddha. Two very late inhumation graves, burials 144-5, were associated. Then we excavated down into essentially sterile deposits, as if this part of the site had been unoccupied. We did come across a row of hearths, but little else and I am sorry to say that I grew frustrated and this time not even Rachanie could prevail on me to keep going. So our workforce had literally to pick up the roof, walk it over to the western mound, a distance of about 200 metres, and set it up next to our previous year's excavation.

Within 24 hours we were uncovering another nice complete late Iron Age burial of a man with multiple iron mortuary offerings, and so on down through a familiar sequence that extended the plans of our walls and floors, and accumulated more adult and infant burials that as I now had concluded, fell into four phases. We completed this extension by the 20th February, whereupon the roof was returned to the eastern rise, and we continued on down, finally exposing a floor and walls before it was time to cover up and await our final excavation a year hence. Overall, it had been another good season.

Early in 2016, I received a rather unexpected invitation from the Director General of the Fine Arts Department. He asked if I would be able to attend in May, a celebration at Ban Chiang for the anniversary of its "discovery". I wrote a presentation incorporating my results from Ban Non Wat to paint a portrait of dynamic cultural change and rise of social elites during the initial Bronze Age. This model of course, is rooted in the short chronology we had now identified.

I arrived for the meeting on the 24th May and met Rachanie. We drove up to the meeting hotel in Udorn Thani, and the day prior to the meeting we drove out to Ban Chiang. I had not been back since 1975 and could barely believe what I was seeing. A broad highway had replaced a rutted track as we left the main road, and signs announcing the world heritage status were festooned across the highway. Gift shops lined the main street, and a large new museum was in place. We entered, and the first exhibit particularly intrigued me. It recorded a conversation at Ban Chiang on the 20th March 1972 between HM King Bhumibol and Professor Sood Sangvichien, and it went like this:

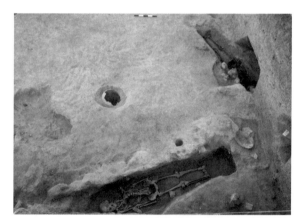

The adult grave lies right up against a room wall. Another grave follows the line of another wall of this room, and an infant jar burial lies at the wall junction with another in the middle of the room.

We found a statuette of the Buddha, just 6 cm tall.

We simply moved the roof 200 metres and continued extending the excavation area on the western mound.

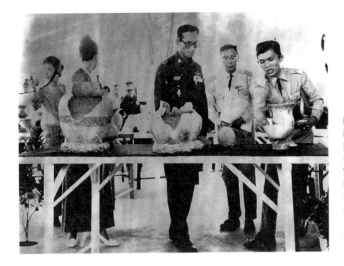

HM King Bhumibol at Ban Chiang in 1972. Pote Geangoon points to a pot, and Professor Sood Sangvichien stands between them. They had a very significant conversation on dating the human bones, which we accomplished over 45 years later.

The King: "Have the bones been dated?"

Professor Sood: "Bone dating has been done in other countries, but we have never sent these in because it might be too costly, your Majesty."

The King: "It should not be considered too costly, since this is of international interest, and Ban Chiang has attracted attention world wide. Everyone would like to cooperate and participate in dating procedures, and they would be more reliable."

I was thunderstruck by this conversation. I had often read how the King was well informed and insightful, but here was a truly remarkable prescient exchange. I immediately incorporated this into my lecture and began with the King's very words when I rose to speak the following day. Then I presented our complete set of new radiocarbon determinations from the bones of those who had lived at Ban Chiang. I had followed the King's advice and with Tom's vital input, provided the now almost universally accepted chronology for this site. The following day Rachanie and I went back to the museum. It is so distressing that the vast majority of exhibits came from looting. I did, however, find a corner where some of our finds from Ban Na Di were on display, including the superb cattle figurines that remind me so of the Cycladic art.

Very interesting matters were now on my immediate horizon. In June, I enjoyed the first of many skype meetings with Eske Willerslev and Hugh McColl. At long last, they were extracting aDNA from some prehistoric Southeast Asian bones. The basis for this breakthrough came when Ron Pinhasi found that the very hard petrous bone in the ear was far more likely to preserve DNA than any other bone in the human body. Eske heads one of the world's top ancient DNA labs at Copenhagen, and is also a Professor at Cambridge, so when as usual, we spent summer months in Cambridge, I had lunch with him in St John's College and we forged a cooperative approach to his findings and future explorations in bones from my excavations. His graduate student, Hugh McColl, was the key scientist in this exciting new departure, but one that for me had begun, also in St. John's, in 1991 when I first met and discussed this with Erika Hagelberg.

Two more ventures that I look back on as being highly significant were initiated at the same time. Cristina Castillo had given a fascinating presentation at the London meeting on early rice, that described the preferred habitats of the weeds recovered from Ban Non Wat and Non Ban Jak. These revealed a transition from the species adapted to dry land rice fields, and those that prefer a wet habitat. I noted that the transition from one to the other took place during the later Iron Age at Ban Non Wat, and by the occupation of Non Ban Jak, there were virtually no dry-land weeds at all. This dovetailed perfectly with the first presence of ploughshares and iron sickles, the construction of moat/reservoirs and the rise of social elites, a situation that again pinpointed the absolute necessity of bolting down the chronology. I said to Cristina that we should integrate all these findings into a paper and submit it to *Antiquity*. Katie Miller had undertaken much of the identification of the weed species so she and Dorian Fuller contributed to this article, as did Tom and Katerina, because the seed samples from Ban Non Wat came from one of Nigel Chang's excavation squares and the rice grains had to be radiocarbon dated. It turned out to be a very concise paper drawing on several sources of information, and in due course it brought to the authors the Ben Cullen prize for 2018 (Castillo et al. 2018).

The second venture involved the sites in the Khao Wong Prachan Valley (KWPV) of Central Thailand excavated in the late '80s and '90s by the Thailand Archaeometallurgy Project (TAP) directed by Vince Pigott and Surapol Natapintu. Non Pa Wai and Nil Kham Haeng were two enormous copper smelting and casting sites with some occupation evidence and burials. A third site, Non Mak La, was mainly occupation and mortuary contexts with some copper smelting evidence. These are absolutely key sites for identifying when copper technology was firmly established, for what better context could there be than mines and smelting site?

I make a point at the Fine Arts Department meeting to celebrate the 50th anniversary of discovering Ban Chiang.

Given the resistance from the Ban Chiang project to accepting the burgeoning evidence for the short chronology as supported by our evidence from southern Northeast Thailand, I emailed Vince offering funding from my Marsden dating grant for about 100 TAP radiocarbon dates. He consulted his colleagues, and came back with enthusiastic agreement. This set in train a long and sometime very stressful enterprise. Flotation at these sites, under the direction of the late archaeobotanist Steve Weber, had retrieved samples of prehistoric seeds and grains, including millet and *Spilanthes*, not to mention loads of charcoal. Two of the millet grains identified by Weber had been dated to the late third millennium BC, both being derived from the initial Neolithic occupation of Non Pa Wai (Weber et al. 2010). These are currently the earliest identified millet grains from anywhere in Southeast Asia. Further identification of the plant remains was undertaken by Jade d'Alpoim Guedes with the assistance of Sydney Hanson (d'Alpoim Guedes et al. 2020).

The late Andy Weiss, whom I had last seen at the conference in Chiang Mai in 1996, had, early on, curtailed his TAP involvement for a career as a top-flight GIS specialist outside archaeology. But his heart was always with TAP, and, as he had been the on-site director of excavations with unique insight into the selection of samples, Vince encouraged him to return to the fold. Fiorella Rispoli and Roberto Ciarla, long time TAP excavators and co-directors of LoRAP, which has excavated several additional related sites in the immediate Lopburi area, offered cautionary advice about contextual issues arising from the unique, disturbed and bioturbated strata at Non Pa Wai and Nil Kham Haeng. They, with Pigott, had been driving forces behind the important preliminary report on TAP and LoRAP fieldwork providing the first ever comprehensive chronology for and dating of early copper production in the greater Lopburi region (Rispoli et al. 2013). At Oxford the dating was undertaken by Tom and Christopher Bronk Ramsey. We hoped to cross date the Lopburi sites with Ban Non Wat, where Oliver Pryce's pioneering Southeast Asian Lead Isotope Project (SEALIP) has provided, thus far, the only link between KWPV copper production and copper-base artefacts from Ban Non Wat (Pryce 2012).

Over the next two years we tracked down the appropriate samples, and progressively dated them. One of the problems we faced seemed to be insurmountable. Naturally, the thick deposits of smelting and casting debris were disturbed by a combination of centuries of continuous copper smelting activity, extensive bioturbation and the impact of monsoonal deluges. Tom and Christopher then suggested that we apply a new analytical tool, known as kernel density estimate

This little terracotta disc reveals a lion on its haunches, looking at us.

modelling. This is predicated on the fact that a millet grain date shows that humans were at the site. When our results were all formulated, we came to the conclusion that at Non Pa Wai, the Neolithic settlement began in the late 3rd millennium BC, just like Khok Phanom Di on the coast. There was then a hiatus before the site was reoccupied by a community versed in copper smelting with a peak about 1000 BC extending well into the first millennium BC. There was a slight overlap in copper smelting between Non Pa Wai and Nil Kham Haeng, the latter site spanning much of the 1st millennium BC. Non Mak La was occupied from about 1600 BC during the later Neolithic, the dates showing a double peak with the Bronze Age presence falling between about 1100-600 BC. The harmony between the initial onset of copper mining in the KWPV and indications of its copper having been used in the casting of artifacts in the early Bronze Age burials at Ban Non Wat, was pleasing.

We authors were unanimous in finding that this joint enterprise added yet another strong foundation to the chronological scaffolding we sought to erect in order to weigh judiciously the later prehistoric sequence. We sent our paper to *Antiquity* on the 5th September 2019 and our anonymous referees agreed with us. It was soon accepted with minor revisions and published in 2020 (Higham T. et al. 2020).

On January 10th 2017, 1 set off for another 'final' excavation season, and this time I think it really was. It was a double-pronged campaign. Nigel further extended our big opening on the western mound, and continued to trace walls, floors and burials. Most significantly, he also came across some Bronze Age potsherds, and at the base of his area, incised and impressed Neolithic pottery and a good haul of stone adzes. Over on the eastern rise, a year earlier we had drawn a veil over the 10 by 10 m square just as we had uncovered at last, some late Iron Age structures, and for the first several weeks of the new season, it was indeed dominated by floors, walls, one building phase stratified over the next. Several of these buildings had been destroyed by fire, and we uncovered charred wooden posts still in position, and the wattle structures of the walls. One remarkable find came when Daeng brought to my attention a small circular terracotta disc. I cleaned the surface and found myself looking at a little face. More cleaning and there was a crouching lion looking at me, so delicately fashioned that even its minute claws were visible. I took this to mean that Buddhism was spreading during this late prehistoric period, since the Buddha was in the early days often represented as a lion. Some of the floors were still littered with broken pots, hearths were still in place, rice grains and animal bones were left as if there had been a last meal before a conflagration. It was such a refreshing experience to find such clear evidence for domestic life, including another iron ploughshare. What was missing, were the remains of the occupants. No graves were in evidence.

This all changed on the 6th February. Marc Oxenham came to visit and I

Marc Oxenham found an infant jar burial, then they popped up like mushrooms.

invited him to wield a trowel and deal with a large ceramic vessel that was emerging. Before long he came across an infant skeleton, and this began a veritable tsunami of burials. One of the finest grave cuts I have ever seen was cut through a clay floor. The excavation square was soon littered with infant jar burials. As we began to scrape the surface of the natural laterite down 4.5 metres, we came across graves cut into it. The man in burial 190 wore a bronze belt. Infants popped up with multiple bronzes and agate jewellery. I began to wonder if we would ever finish before my return ticket to New Zealand. Then I re-booked, giving me another week. Finally, with burial 200, we finished. I returned home on March 1st with a bittersweet feeling, glad to be back but sad that it was the end of the line for my 50 years of excavating in Southeast Asia. I had a big responsibility now, to draw together all the specialist contributions and publish a final report on my contribution to the Paddy to Pura project.

There was much to do in order to complete my commitment to Non Ban Jak. There were masses of field plans that we recorded as we progressed downward, all of which had to be assessed, integrated and drawn using my preferred program, Freehand MX. Every one of the 200 burials had to be described and illustrated, and all associated mortuary offerings photographed and incorporated. I was supervising Helen Heath for her Master's dissertation and when available, distilling it with her into a chapter. Hallie Buckley and her team were working in Phimai on the human bones. Once I had tabulated all the mortuary offerings, I turned once again to Bryan Manly to apply his statistical analyses to evaluate change and make comparisons with other sites, in particular Iron Age Noen U-Loke and Ban Non Wat. Tom and Fiona Petchey were reporting on the radiocarbon chronology.

Although the site had been occupied during the Neolithic and the Bronze Age, we had very little further evidence for either. Essentially the best documented occupation corresponded to the final Iron Age phase 4 at Noen U-Loke, but at Non Ban Jak we were able to subdivide it into four sub-phases that developed into an early historic occupation closely akin to the Dvaravati states of Central Thailand. The Paddy to Pura project that initiated this research for the first three seasons, and our Origins of Inequality project that funded the last three, sought the roots of the transition into early states with particular reference to Angkor. I think that we have now generated a model for further evaluation. Its central feature is climate change.

We came across burials cut into the natural substrate, here Stacey Ward and Christina Stantis are recording one of them.

Above: About the clearest grave cut I have seen, severing a burnt house floor. Below, the skeleton uncovered.

Left: We found some of the best evidence yet for the domestic houses, with clay wall foundations, floors and hearths.

The onset of aridity placed stress on early Iron Age communities that relied on rice for a significant component of their diet. The reaction was to construct moat-reservoirs fed by the streams that flowed past their settlements. These were massive earthworks requiring much labour. There was a major technological innovation: the hoes we found in early Iron Age graves were replaced by ploughshares and the dead were now often interred with their iron sickles. Ploughing in irrigated fields is much more efficient than hoe farming in rain-fed fields. Those who own the best land can produce wealth surpluses. But health is greatly affected by standing water. It can increase the likelihood of malaria and a host of water-borne pathologies, particularly when poorly cooked fish and shellfish are consumed. Wealth and health are manifested in the rise of some very wealthy individuals, and a remarkable surge in the death of the newly born and pre-term infants.

Once these variables coalesced, the transition into early states was rapid, perhaps in only a handful of generations. The inscriptions in the upper Mun Valley were describing kings and Buddhist communities even as Non Ban Jak entered its final period of occupation. We drew all these variables into an article for the *Cambridge Archaeological Journal*, and were given permission to reproduce it as the final chapter of our Non Ban Jak report (Higham et al. 2019; Higham and Kijngam 2020).

Editing and writing occupied much of my time in the quiet of my study, but I did venture forth as well. In June, I was back to Cambridge, and on to the next meeting of the European Association of Southeast Asian Archaeologists in Poznan. Visiting Poland was a new experience for me, and I was particularly keen on the field trip, which took us to Biskupin. This is one of the sites I had read about as an undergraduate. The visit certainly lived up to expectations, particularly the reconstructed Danubian 1 long house, and the guide dressed as a Neolithic immigrant. In November, I flew to Xiamen in China to give a paper at a meeting on the Neolithic maritime expansion into Southeast Asia, and was back in China again for the third Shanghai Forum, where I gave a public lecture to an audience that filled to capacity within half an hour of the admission tickets going on line.

This was, sadly, my last dig. It was all such an incredible journey of discovery.

Helen Heath and me as we finished the last square at Non Ban Jak. She was great company and we recorded all the sections together.

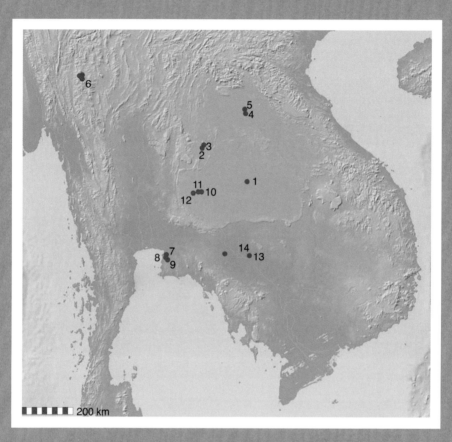

Sites in Southeast Asia where I have been involved in excavations.
1. Non Dua, 2. Non Nong Chik, 3. Non Nok Tha, 4. Ban Na Di, 5. Ban Chiang,
6. Banyan Valley Cave, Spirit Cave and Steepcliff Cave, 7. Khok Phanom Di,
8. Ban Bon Noen, 9. Nong Nor, 10. Ban Lum Khao, 11. Noen U-Loke and Ban Non Wat,
12. Non Ban Jak, 13. Baksei Chamkrong, 14. Phum Snay.

Fourteen | An Ongoing Quest

I enjoyed my first experiences of excavating. Roman Verulamium and Palaeolithic Arcy-sur-Cure stand out for the combination of teamwork and excitement of discovery. I was incredibly fortunate to be 19 days too young and therefore exempt from two years of military service. Aged 17, I left school to study the course for the Postgraduate Diploma in Archaeology at the University of London. This combined practical archaeology – photography, surveying, conservation – with, in my case, concentration on the Western Roman Empire. Still very much under the influence of its founders, Mortimer and Tessa Wheeler, we were encouraged to engage in fieldwork, and imbued with the importance of publishing what we might one day, dig up. Two particular lessons of my happy two years there have always influenced my own fieldwork. I learned a great deal on how to dig from Sheppard Frere, and all my photographs bear the stamp of Maurice Cookson.

I went up to Cambridge well primed to launch myself into the Archaeology and Anthropology Tripos. The Department lacked the egalitarian and convivial tearoom I had enjoyed at the Institute, and there was no practical instruction at all. It was simply assumed that if you wanted to excavate, it was up to you to sort it. I was able to learn more in Malta and Greece, and as the course progressed, I grew increasingly interested in the European Neolithic, Bronze and Iron Age option. This field in general was in a state of change. The chronology had traditionally been tied to artefact parallels with the dynastic sequences with the Near East and Egypt. Hence, an Egyptian faience bead in a Mycenaean context would date the latter, and a Mycenaean bronze north of the Alps would take the dating a stage further north. This framework was exemplified in a then much-quoted article by Christopher Hawkes and Gordon Childe. We also learned how the Iron Age of Germany was dated by Müller-Karpe on the basis of minute changes in the morphology of iron swords, each stage being given one century.

Glyn Daniel was our principal lecturer on this subject, and there were times when he would announce a new "radiocarbon date" to herald a new dawn in dating. The differences between the traditional and the new methods, although in retrospect we had to await major refinements in the latter, have long stressed to me and many others, the importance of getting your chronology right. During my second year at Cambridge, I was greatly attracted to the economic prehistory approach espoused by Eric Higgs. Based on the recovery and interpretation of the plant and animal remains in prehistoric sites, this seemed to me a very necessary avenue for illuminating prehistoric societies, and I was more interested in this than artefact typology.

I worked consistently and intensively towards my successive University examinations for several reasons, one of which was to follow in a family tradition and another, to secure a State Scholarship to fund doctoral research that would come with first class honours in my finals. Having achieved this, I moved directly into my doctoral research that concentrated on the Neolithic to Iron Age economies of the Swiss Lake Villages. It was during this period of my life that I met Polly Askew. She joined me in Switzerland for a holiday after a brief acquaintance, and after a month together I came to the inescapable conclusion that I could not possibly envisage life without her. It was my wisest decision of all, and without her constant support, even to the unenviable task of typing my entire doctoral dissertation, I could never have achieved a fraction of my archaeological ambitions.

By now married with an infant son and a completed PhD, in 1966 I was short listed with two others for a lectureship in European Prehistory at the University of Birmingham. I went to the interview with an offer of a lectureship in far off New Zealand in my back pocket, but I was not wanted. At the time, this was a very hard blow, we were happily settled in our new home in the Cambridgeshire village of Barrington. With the benefit of hindsight, I was so fortunate not to go to Birmingham, but it did not seem like that at the time. We spent five weeks on board the Rangitane, and arrived into an entirely new world for us in January 1967, I as a lecturer in the tiny Department of Anthropology, the University of Otago.

One of my luckiest breaks was that a colleague, Ham Parker, had been involved in the 1966 excavation of a prehistoric site in Northeast Thailand called Non Nok Tha (translated as "Partridge Mound). Donn Bayard, his co-excavator and PhD student of Professor Wilhelm G. Solheim II (Bill) in Hawaii, visited the Department and learning of my interest in faunal remains, asked me if I would care to analyse the animal bones from this site. Thus came my introduction to mainland Southeast Asian prehistory.

What was known about this area then? If you include the southern provinces of what is now China, it covers 2000 by 1700 km, or about the same area as from Brittany to the Carpathian Basin and from Sicily to Denmark. In his first summary of World Prehistory, Grahame Clark described the Southeast Asia funnel through which people passed. Since much of Southeast Asia had been colonized by the French, most of our knowledge came from the scholars attached to the École française d'Extrême Orient, centred in Hanoi, and the Geological Service of Indo-China.

A century ago, Madeleine Colani and Henri Mansuy fanned out from Hanoi into the hinterland of the Red River valley to identify and publish the hunter-gatherer cave sites that they excavated. While not aspiring to the heights of the European Upper Palaeolithic in their eyes – the prehistoric occupants did not manufacture impressive blade stone tools – they documented an indigenous hunter-gatherer complex named after two provinces, the Hoabinhian and the Bacsonian (Colani 1927, Mansuy 1924).

The Cambodian site of Samrong Sen had been the focus of the realization that Southeast Asia had a prehistoric Bronze Age, since explorations there in the late 19th century had found bronzes, including a socketed axe, bangles and a fish hook. Indeed, there was a lively debate in French scholarly circles over the dates and the status of this period (Noulet 1879, Cartaillac 1979). Fuchs (1883) suggested that these bronzes dated in the first millennium BC, which they almost certainly do. Further excavations at Samrong Sen by Henri Mansuy (1902, 1923) revealed at least one mould for casting a socketed axe, matched later by Lévy (1943) at sites near Mlu Prei in northern Cambodia.

Prehistoric bronzes were also being excavated in Guangdong Province of southern China by the Jesuit priest Father Rafael Maglioni. His fieldwork in the vicinity of Hong Kong led him to propose prehistoric phases beginning with the Neolithic, which he dated between 4000-3000 BC, then a final Neolithic from 3000-1500 BC, followed by the Chalcolithic and then the Bronze Age (Maglioni 1975). Between 1911 and 1938, Walter Schofield in this same region was finding bronzes and bivalve casting moulds for axes (Schofield 1975).

The later Bronze Age coincided with the first knowledge of iron forging, and is particularly notable for the large bronze drums. Heger (1902) described as many as 165, and more were being found, their decoration analysed by Henri Parmentier (1918). In 1924, the École française organized excavations at the site of Dong Son, on the right bank of the Ma River, where Louis Pajot encountered graves containing a range of bronze mortuary offerings. This site has since given its name to the chiefly late prehistoric societies that were to be overrun by the predatory Han Empire.

The early states of Southeast Asia, and in particular that centred on the northern bank of the Great Lake at the complex known as Angkor, were a prime target for early French research. Visited by 16th-century Portuguese missionaries as a deserted stone city in the jungle, the early research into its nature and origins rested very much on the translation of the corpus of stone inscriptions in Sanskrit, by the leading luminary George Cœdès. It was self evident, given the presence of an Indic script and language, not to mention the worship of Hindu deities, that there was a strong infusion of influence from South Asia. What Cœdès was not able to identify, for lack of information, were the formation processes of Angkor. Indeed, he adopted a pessimistic view of the contribution of the indigenous inhabitants, referring to them as poor savages. In the 1940s, earlier state societies were being

I greatly admired Helmut Loofs-Wissowa for his excavations and contribution to evaluating the Southeast Asian Bronze Age (Loofs-Wissowa 2009).

Bill Watson was a personal friend and outstanding scholar. He was a pioneer in Southeast Asia with his excavations at Khok Charoen

revealed in the Mekong Delta by the excavations at the city site of Oc Eo by Louis Malleret, that illuminated a maritime trading network linking this nodal location with India and China.

In 1969, I followed in the footsteps of those then scratching the surface of the prehistory of Thailand. Bill Watson and Helmut Loofs-Wissowa had excavated the Neolithic site of Khok Charoen, and Chet Gorman was active in the far north at Hoabinhian rock shelters. Per Sørensen had excavated Ban Kao and Donn Bayard had put in his two seasons at Non Nok Tha. The late 1960s were a time of effervescence, that, as in most cases of opening a new frontier in prehistory, had its fair share of debate. Was there, for example, an early and independent Bronze Age? Where and when was rice domesticated, how did the great civilization of Angkor arise? It was to this background that I rolled up my sleeves and set forth on a remarkable voyage of discovery.

I have contributed little to documenting the prehistory of the hunter-gatherers of Southeast Asia. My principal findings come from Nong Nor, where we documented a mid-third millennium BC settlement on the shore of a marine embayment. I think that this is probably the correct interpretation of this site, as there was no evidence for rice cultivation or of domestic animals. The biological remains revealed intensive shellfish collection, fishing and hunting of marine mammals. Over the past decade, much has been learned of the complex and sedentary hunter-gatherer communities found on raised beaches in northern Vietnam, as at Con Co Ngua. It is likely that the occupants of these sites were descended from those who had long been adapted to the marine habitat but whose settlements are now lying under the vast tract of Sundaland drowned by the rising Holocene sea. I also contributed to Chet Gorman's endeavours in the karst uplands of Mae Hongson Province by identifying and reporting on the faunal remains from three Hoabinhian caves, and helping in the excavation of one of them, Banyan Valley Cave.

Identifying where and when rice was first domesticated was a major issue, for this plant today is the staple food for over half the world's population. When I began excavating Khok Phanom Di, we had no knowledge of the prehistory of rice cultivation, and I even formulated a model that identified domestication on the coastal tracts of Southeast Asia. We now know, as archaeology in China has opened up, that there was a long process of domestication in the middle and lower lowlands of the Yangtze River. What we found at KPD owes much to Jill Thompson, who identified domestic rice, and Hiro Matsumura, whose analyses of the human crania has revealed a very close match with the Neolithic inhabitants of the lower Yangtze. We also now know from the isotopes in the bones of the first occupants, that they came to KPD from a different environment, but thereafter, nearly all the population were locally born.

Occupied from about 2000 BC, KPD was a pottery-making and trading community strategically placed at a commanding river estuary. Over about 20 generations, women potters made superb ceramic vessels embellished with complex incised and impressed designs. They imported marine shell from coral seas, showing a preference for a range of beads, discs and bangles. These may have been imported ready made, but some at least were locally manufactured. The people were adaptable, turning to the locally abundant marine resources for much of their food, and showing very little interest in maintaining domestic animals. Health was a problem in what must have been a habitat swarming with mosquitoes. Adults seem to have had a gene that gave resistance to malaria at the expense of suffering from thalassaemia, a blood disorder that increases anaemia and reduces energy levels. This might well have caused the very high incidence of infant mortality. The community at KPD incorporated some individuals of high social standing, if this is a reflection of mortuary wealth. A woman potter interred wearing clothing embellished with over 120,000 shell beads stands out in this context.

My second contribution to exploring the establishment of food-producing societies centres on Ban Non Wat. It came as a welcome surprise when Per Sørensen and I espied some incised potsherds there that could only be Neolithic. We went on to identify two phases there. In the earlier of these, there was an association between occupation middens and human graves. As at KPD, we came across a lot of stone adzes fashioned as Tessa Boer-Mah found, from imported stone. There were rice grains in the occupation and mortuary contexts, and trade in exotic shell was under way, perhaps from coastal sites like KPD because one young male wore cowrie shell ear pendants. While revealing local preferences in terms of pottery form and decoration, there was also an underlying similarity in the syntax of preferred motifs, a point strongly made by Warrachai Wiriyaromp in his doctoral dissertation. His expert paintings of these pots underscores the expertise of the potters at this site.

When the Marsden Fund declined to support my application to seek ancient DNA from Non Ban Jak, Eske Willerslev said he would. I am enormously grateful.

The second Neolithic phase involved much plainer pottery vessels matched in the initial settlement we found at nearby Ban Lum Khao.

We dated charcoal from the deep and early Neolithic middens and hearths, finding that they formed in the 17th century BC, 300 years or so after the first rice farmers occupied KPD. The first burials we dated to the 15th century BC. We found too, that the dates for the later Neolithic at both Ban Non Wat and Ban Lum Khao fell between about 1400-1100 BC.

These pieces fit into a rather neat jigsaw. Anatomically modern humans reached mainland Southeast Asia at least 60,000 years ago. They encountered and interbred with the indigenous and still mysterious Denisovans, whose ancestors originated, again surely in Africa, much earlier (Higham T. 2021). There may also have been an independent movement of anatomically modern humans north of the Himalayas who infiltrated into the region of the Yellow and Yangtze rivers far to the north. We can now turn to the evidence of archaeology, human biology and ancient DNA. Long since, Per Sørensen was arguing for a route that brought early farmers to Central Thailand from the north, possibly via the Salween River route. For me, it has been rather surprising to find that some incoming farmers brought with them domestic millet that originated in the Central Plains of the Yellow River. There must also, surely, have been intrusive movements down the rivers and coast of Lingnan into northern Vietnam, where the cemetery at Man Bac contained the graves of both incoming farmers and indigenous hunter-gatherers, to judge from the distinct skull forms and their DNA.

Ancient DNA has made a late entry into Southeast Asian archaeology, because the hot and wet conditions do not preserve it as well as in colder and drier habitats. However, the breakthrough that found that DNA survives best in the very dense petrous bone found in the ear has opened up this field, one that I began to explore in 1991. I have been involved with Eske Willerslev's group in Copenhagen, where Hugh McColl has led an initiative to extract and interpret DNA from modern and prehistoric Southeast Asians (McColl et al. 2018). Numerous skype sessions were involved in bringing our results to publication, and our paper took its place alongside another from the Harvard group that covered the same subject with parallel results (Lipson et al. 2018). What these showed was that there is an underlying genetic population of hunter-gatherers with close African affiliations, some of whom remain to this day hunters and gatherers surviving in the remote forests of peninsular Thailand and the Andaman Islands. The DNA of the incoming rice and millet farmers is quite distinct, providing convincing evidence for two populations that were to meet and interbreed.

Austroasiatic is the name given to related languages that stretch from the Munda of India to Vietnamese and Khmer with many widely dispersed enclaves in between. I have been fascinated by the evidence that can be drawn from cognate words, those with the same proto-word. In particular, the names given to rice and many aspects of its cultivation (but not ploughing), are widely related. What this means is that there is strong supportive evidence for the expansion into Southeast Asia of farmers. They founded their settlements, grew their rice and made artefacts after a common tradition as well as introducing their languages and genes. Mark Alves (2020) has recently pointed out that there is a cognate word for a conical hat, not an artefact that readily survives. On reading this, I thought of the beads found only on the skulls of the wealthy elites at Bronze Age Ban Non Wat that could have been stitched onto a hat, and the bell that rang in my head of Iron Age paintings on Ban Chiang pots of - conical hats.

When Mark Alves told me that there was a cognate word in Austroasiatic for conical hat, I immediately thought of this painting on a pot from Ban Chiang.

The Bronze Age in Southeast Asia

How people learn to turn distinctively coloured stones into a cast metal object has an enduring fascination. It involves finding a source of the stone, in our case the ores of copper-base and tin, mining and smelting it, and, if an alloy is involved, mixing two or more metals, and casting the metal when it has been heated beyond melting point. Since these skills are thought to have originated in the Old and New Worlds independently, it is evident that there need be no single origin.

When I attended Colin Renfrew's 80th birthday party in the summer of 2017, a number of his friends successively gave a ten-minute talk on how they came to know him and his contribution to prehistory. I was the first in line, and later that morning I listened to Miljana Radivojevic give her presentation. She was then a post doctoral researcher at Cambridge. I was fascinated when I heard her describe how she had identified an early centre of the origins of copper-base base metallurgy in her native Serbia, and gravitated towards her to find out more during the tea interval. Until then like so many others, I assumed that the first steps on the road to metallurgy took place in the Near East.

I have always tried to document and understand the impact of metallurgy on the prehistoric societies of Southeast Asia on the basis of fully evaluated excavations. It all began for me at Ban Na Di. A first priority is securing a well-founded chronology, but just as important to me is to identify the social impact of metallurgy. Graves at Ban Chiang and Non Nok Tha were poorly equipped with mortuary offerings. At Ban Na Di I concluded that there was possibly some distinction in social standing between burials in one part of the site compared with another, but that it was not of great moment.

My next two excavations in Bronze Age sites, at Nong Nor and Ban Lum Khao, also failed to identify evidence for a social elite. True, some were interred with marginally greater wealth than the majority, but there was no evidence for an elite burial place. So far, my summary as far back as 1996 that there was little social differentiation with the Bronze Age held firm. But all this changed with the excavation of Ban Non Wat. I count our excavation at this site central to an entirely new interpretation of the social impact of copper-base metallurgy. There was already a wide gulf between the ritual intensity and mortuary offerings when comparing the late Neolithic as it morphed into the initial Bronze Age. This was further magnified with the cemetery that contained the next two phases. This is easily demonstrated by sheer numbers, as well as by the quality and variety of the pottery vessels placed with the dead. In my earlier excavations, the Bronze Age graves might contain up to half-a-dozen pots, but some of the Ban Non Wat elite were accompanied by more than 80. No exotic shell bangles were found at Ban Chiang, compared with near on 1,000 at Ban Non Wat. Moreover, the graves were far larger than was necessary to contain the coffin, even for tiny infants.

My second contribution to understanding the Southeast Asian Bronze Age has involved the chronology. I have been very fortunate to have a son who is Director of the Oxford University Radiocarbon Dating Laboratory, and a very large Marsden Grant to date hundreds of samples. These advantages coincided with significant advances in radiocarbon dating that now make it possible to date a single rice grain, and with multiple samples from a secure stratigraphic sequence, to apply Bayesian analyses to refine the conclusions. We first undertook this with Ban Non Wat. The determinations come from charcoal, freshwater shells and rice grains from the 12 phases we identified, and were sufficiently internally consistent to obtain what colleagues have referred to as the basic sequence dated for the region. There was a hunter-gatherer occupation about 17,000 years ago, before the first farmer settled in the 18th century BC. The initial presence of copper-base base metal from assured contexts dates to the 11th century BC.

Dating the sequence at Ban Chiang then hove into view. I owe it to Tom when he suggested that we try and date the human bones from that site, in order to settle its chronology once and for all. Gaining access was an issue. The bones were stored under the charge of Mike Pietrusewsky in Hawaii. I secured permission to access the bones from the Directors of the Fine Arts Department and the Penn Museum, and Mike sent over 50 samples over to Oxford. As the results filtered through to me in batches, I increasingly realized that, at last, this problem was solved. The initial settlement by Neolithic pioneers took place a couple of centuries later than at Ban Non Wat, in the late 16th century BC, and the first copper-base base metal precisely matched the 11th-century date from Ban Non Wat.

Getting the chronology right is the essential platform for assessing cultural change over time. One of our research objectives has been to define and understand social change over a period of about three millennia, from first farmers to early state formation. And this has also concentrated our attention on the period when Southeast Asia became a component of an extensive trading network. It is possible that this introduced the know-how on smelting iron. I say this because if my interpretation of this part of the sequence at Ban Non Wat is correct, we have come across the transition from the late Bronze Age cemetery into graves containing iron, and very rare carnelian, glass and agate ornaments. These ornaments almost certainly indicate ultimate contact with India. Progressively, we have unraveled some knotty questions regarding the Iron Age in the upper Mun Valley.

There is no doubt that one of these relates to the date and the purpose of the moats that surround the many Iron Age settlements there. This is an issue that had long foxed me, but we contributed to understanding their purpose in one afternoon. At Noen U-Loke, my geomorphologist colleague Bill Boyd and I decided that we really needed to section through the moats and banks. The problem was that the five moats and banks extend to about 200 metres and the deposits are like concrete in the dry season. After a desultory day digging at the end of which our workers had sore wrists, Amphan made a radical suggestion: hire a back hoe and get the job done. So we did, the digger cut a four-metre deep trench right through the moats and banks and Bill got into it before the water table rose up and half filled it. There was then a revelation. The profile of the moat was flat. There was no V-shaped cut, no hint of defensive measures. We took charcoal samples from the bank layers and resolved the dating at this site to the first few centuries AD. This we repeated at about five other sites with similar results.

In aerial photos, one can detect at some sites, straight lines emerging from the moats. With remote sensing, Scott Hawken has even identified the ghostly outlines of bunded rice fields (Hawken 2011). A pattern began to emerge, one that was to be reinforced by three further discoveries. The first came when we found an iron socketed object in a pottery kiln at Ban Non Wat. My village workers crowded round and declared it to be a ploughshare. The chances of finding an iron ploughshare are very rare, because the smith can so easily recycle the valuable metal. Now I have found three of them, one in a grave at Noen U-Loke. Ploughing is so much more productive than hoeing, and any person or family that owns improved irrigated rice fields cultivated with a plough is on the path to wealth and status. This was made clear to me by Jack Goody, who had interviewed me for admission to St Catharine's College in May 1957, and became a lifelong friend. His book *Production and Reproduction* sets out the impact of ploughing on the social order in parts of Africa (Goody 1971).

Another piece of the jigsaw fell into place during a conference in Paris in 2015. Barbara Wohlfarth told me of her fieldwork at Lake Kumphawapi. She had taken cores through the lake sediments to examine the plant remains that had accumulated, and dated them. She came to a fascinating conclusion, that the monsoon had faltered and a period of aridity had set in just as the moats and banks were being constructed, and some individuals were interred with great wealth (Wohlfarth et al. 2016).

A final piece came at another conference, this time in London at the very Institute where I had studied as a keen young teenager. Cristina Castillo and her student Katie Miller told me that their analysis of the plant remains from Ban Non Wat had revealed a transition from a dominance of dry rice-field weeds to those adapted to wet conditions that took place as the dry period took over. This transition was confirmed when Cristina found that during the late Iron Age at Non Ban Jak, virtually all the weed seeds came from wet habitats (Castillo et al 2018).

Our research objective at Non Ban Jak was to trace how early states were formed from about the 6th century AD. It has been very satisfying to feel that our fieldwork has, at least, generated a model to illuminate what might well have happened (Higham et al. 2019). The saga began with dense clusters of Iron Age townships. The inhabitants made and traded salt, made pots, had iron smiths and traded in exotic valuables. People lived in substantial houses with thick clay wall foundations and stud walls incorporating wattle and daub finish, divided by town lanes. These communities were faced with a drying climate as rainfall fell away. This is likely to have stimulated the leaders to marshal labour and construct water-control measures. Much work went into the banks to corral the local streams, and dig canals out to the newly embanked rice fields. These leaders would have owned the best rice land, and accumulated prestige and wealth, that is reflected in their mortuary rituals.

The really interesting point about this transition, is that it all took place on the brink of a big change in the archaeological sequence. In the upper Mun River region, this is seen in the expansion in the area of one of the moated sites, called Muang Sema. Here, additional moats and banks evidence a huge expansion of the site, within which Buddhist monuments were built and inscriptions refer to kings who made merit by donating to the new religious foundations. I find it intriguing to ponder that the new aristocratic elite in the late Iron Age towns saw in the new exotic religion, a means to lay the foundations to a whole new social format rooted in inequality and an enduring dynastic establishment. Tracking all this down has been intellectually very rewarding.

I cannot help but, from time to time, reflect on my good fortune to land in Southeast Asia after first becoming so closely involved in studying and then undertaking research on the Neolithic to Iron Age of Western Europe. In effect, I entered a scene in which I was one of only a handful of western prehistorians trying to fathom what happened in Southeast Asia, and finding some intriguing parallels as well as contrasts between the two regions. They are similar in area. Both in the mid-Holocene had experienced occupation by hunter-gatherers stretching back millennia. We did not know this even three decades ago, but rice and millet were progressively domesticated, along with cattle and pigs, in the Yangtze and Yellow River regions, from which farmer communities proliferated and spread south by several routes into Southeast Asia. We know this on the basis of the archaeological, linguistic and human biological evidence. A similar demographic expansion took place in Europe, in that case with stimuli from Anatolia and the Levant. As new analyses of ancient DNA come on stream, so we can evaluate the interactions between incoming farmers and indigenous hunter-gatherers, and compare how this varied between east and west. In Southeast Asia, it is becoming evident that there was considerable social and biological interaction between the two.

I feel some sense of achievement that, along with son Tom, we have generated a scientifically rooted and consistent chronological framework. I find tracing the dissemination of the knowledge surrounding metallurgy fascinating. A scenario shared with my friends and colleagues sees progressive southerly movements that began in far northwest China with Eurasian origins (Higham et al. 2019). What was cast, and how, very much turned on the aspirations and the requirements of the communities that came face to face with copper-base ores, tin and their properties. In the Central Plains of the Yellow River and Sichuan, rapidly developing state societies sponsored specialist workshops dedicated to the piece-mould casting of sumptuary bronze vessels, along with bivalve tools and weapons. Casting far and wide for new ore sources, specialist metalworkers reached the great Yangtze copper-base ore deposits, and further south, tin. My current thinking, based on as-yet-unpublished lead isotope data, is that some socketed copper-base axes travelled along established trade routes into Southeast Asia. Perhaps simultaneously, as the 2nd millennium BC was drawing to a close, miners tracked down massive deposits of copper-base ore at Vilabouly in Laos, and the Khao Wong Prachan Valley in Central Thailand.

I find it interesting to compare aspects of this take-up of copper-base metallurgy with what happened as this occurred in Europe. For example, Earle et al. (2015) have employed a political economy model in which to weigh the comprehensive information available for the European Bronze Age. Its essence is this. Copper-base and tin, together with other desirable materials such as salt, amber, and shell and high quality ceramics, have restricted distributions. Exchange in these goods is constrained by geography. Rivers, the coast and passes through uplands involve constriction points the control of which give social advantages to strategically positioned communities. In the Carpathian Basin, it has been noted that sites were occupied over multiple generations, giving corporate groups the opportunity to own and maintain the local resources necessary to engage in reciprocal exchange, and gain wealth and prestige by ownership of exotic valuables that passed of necessity through the constriction points they controlled. This is a model that has not been adopted or applied with any rigour in Southeast Asia, but it is one that has the potential to illuminate and better understand the key changes in the three millennia I have been involved in.

In this approach, the location of a site relative to a potential constriction point is a central issue. Domestic houses are very rare in prehistoric Southeast Asia: excavated areas have hardly ever been extensive enough to identify residential plans. This has led to a reliance on human burials as a source of social information, particularly the degree to which presumably prestigious items, or the sheer number of mortuary offerings were in question. This brings me to my incredible luck at Ban Non Wat. The wealth of the early Bronze Age elite we encountered there is matched only at nearby Ban Prasat. Both are located in what I see as a constriction point, east of a pass that bisects the Petchabun Range, a location that would have given the occupants the potential to control exchange in and access to prestigious goods, such as marine shell and copper-base artefacts. I am very aware that interpretations can change with new findings, but as things stand, the relative wealth of the Ban Non Wat elite presents a sharp contrast to the poverty of their contemporaries in the remote settlements to the north, at Ban Na Di, Non Nok Tha and Ban Chiang.

There are some interesting parallels in the later prehistory of both regions as well. Just as Julius Caesar was conquering Gaul, and Claudius was establishing a new Roman Province in Britannia, so the Han armies invaded northern Vietnam. Boudicca rose up in revolt, just as did the Trung Trac sisters. My own interest in the rise of social inequality has been greatly influenced by the evidence for climate change and the agricultural revolution involving ploughed and irrigated wet rice. It is remarkable how rapidly this seemed to have stimulated the rise of early states with dynastic rulers. I would like to explore this issue further in the field.

However, my digging days are over. It is sad. I miss the excitement of discovery but the responsibility to analyse and publish what I find means that under present circumstances this is not possible. This situation does not rule out a lot of research activity. I have for long, explored possible ways of extracting aDNA from the human skeletons unearthed on my excavations. With the discovery that the petrous bone in the ear has a far greater likelihood of retaining DNA than any other bone, my colleagues Eske Willerslev and Hugh McColl in Copenhagen have had the most welcome results from the site of Non Ban Jak. This now involves about 25 individuals with sufficient DNA to work on their remote and proximal ancestry, and for me of great interest, their relationships. Thus, when a male and female were interred in adjacent graves, imagine finding out if they were brother and sister, father and daughter or mother and son or, if they were not consanguinally related and were in fact more likely to have been affinal. We have some DNA from infants, and I would like to know if they were interred with their parents. Multiply these results several times for the available sample, and we are getting into realms of prehistory one once thought quite beyond reach.

It is not only human DNA that I am interested in. As new analytical techniques are developed, so my archived data can be used as vehicles for further research. With Roz Gillis, I am hoping to solve a problem that has attracted me for years. What is the origin of domestic cattle in Southeast Asia? As far as I know, one does not find cattle bones in early Neolithic sites along the coast of Vietnam. However, they are abundant in the contemporary early settlements of Northeast Thailand. Were the domestic animals locally domesticated from one of the three indigenous species of bovid - the gaur, banteng and kouprey – or were they introduced by the first farmer settlers?

I should know something about ploughing, having done it myself at Ban Chiang. This is a still from a 1975 movie taken by Chet Gorman.

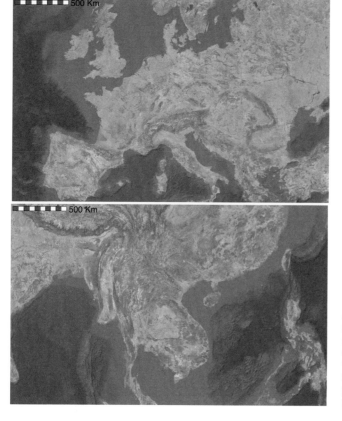

Europe and Southeast Asia at the same scale. I began my research in the former and finished it in the latter. There are many fascinating parallels between their prehistories.

At Noen U-Loke, Barbara Anderson undertook flotation to extract the microscopic biological remains from our excavation. No one has ever examined those samples over the past 23 years, and the big box that contained them has lain in our store of archived material in Dunedin. I remember when digging, coming across pits and surfaces containing many carbonized rice grains. I have extracted half a dozen of these from our flotation samples for radiocarbon dating and all the rest has gone to Cristina Castillo and Dorian Fuller for analysis. They date from the millennium of the Iron Age, and if any seeds from ricefield weeds have survived, it will be fascinating to see if they confirm our findings that there was a transition from dry to wet rice fields during the occupation span of this site.

Oli Pryce has a major research project that traces exchange between copper-base mines and consumer sites reliant on identifying matches in the values for lead isotopes. Cyler Conrad has been re-analysing the faunal remains from Spirit Cave and Banyan Valley Cave. With Mattia Foschetto and Amy Bogaard, we are calculating the Gini Coefficient to lay the groundwork for following social changes over the later prehistoric period. There remains, indeed, much to do.

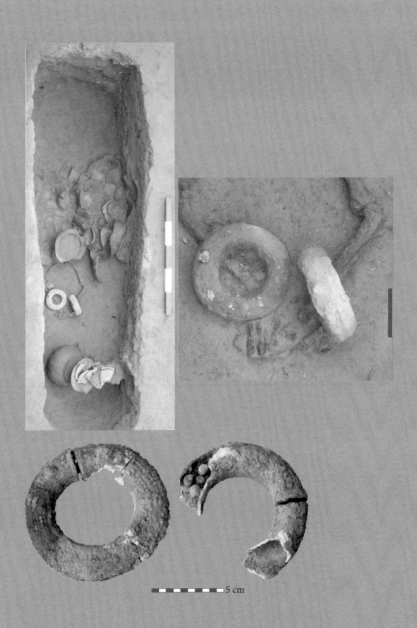

5 cm

Sometimes we reveal an unexpected and evocative glimpse into our prehistoric communities. Here, an Iron Age infant was buried wearing bronze anklets. They contained little clay balls that would have rattled as he walked and ran through the village of Ban Non Wat and out into the rice fields.

Bibliography

Alves, M. 2020. Historical ethnolinguistic notes on Proto- Austroasiatic and Proto-Vietic vocabulary in Vietnamese. *Journal of the Southeast Asian Linguistics Society* 13.2:xiii-xlv.

Bayliss, A.C. and Whittle, A. eds. 2007. Histories of the dead: Building chronologies for five southern British long barrows. *Cambridge Archaeological Journal* 17(1) Supplement.

Cartaillac, E. 1879. Review of Noulet, J-B. "L'Age de pierre polie et du bronze au Cambodge d'après des découvertes de M. Moura. *Matériaux de l'Histoire de l'Homme* X:315-23.

Castillo, C.C., Higham, C.F.W., Miller, K., Chang, N., Douka, K., Higham, T.F.G. and Fuller, D.Q. 2018. Social responses to climate change in Iron Age Northeast Thailand: new archaeobotanical evidence. *Antiquity* 92:1274-91.

Colani, M. 1927. L'Âge de la pierre dans la province de Hoa Binh. *Mémoires du Service Géologique de l'Indochine* I XIII:1.

Earle, T.J. Ling, C. Uhnér, Z. et al. 2015. The political economy and metal trade in Bronze Age Europe: Understanding regional variability in terms of comparative advantages and articulations. *European Journal of Archaeology* 18:633–57.

Fuchs, E. 1883. Station préhistorique de Som-Ron-Sen, au Cambodge, son âge. *Materiaux de l'Histoire de l'Homme* XIII:356-65.

Goody, J.R., 1971. *Technology, Tradition and the State in Africa.* Hutchinson: London.

Gorman, C.F. and Charoenwongsa, P. 1976. Ban Chiang: A mosaic of impressions from the first two years. *Expedition* 8(4):14-26.

Hawken, S. 2011. *Metropolis of Ricefields: a Topographic Classification of a Dispersed Urban Complex.* Unpublished Ph.D thesis, University of Sydney.

Heger, F. 1902. *Alte Metaltrommen aus Südost Asian.* Leipzig: K. von Hiersemann.

Higham, C.F.W. 1975. *Non Nok Tha: The Faunal Remains.* University of Otago Monographs in Prehistoric Anthropology 1, Dunedin.

——1977. The prehistory of the southern Khorat plateau, N.E. Thailand, with particular reference to Roi Et province. *Modern Quaternary Research in SE Asia* III:103-43.

——1984. The Ban Chiang Culture in wider perspective. *Proceedings of the British Academy* LXIX:229-61.

——1996. *The Bronze Age of Southeast Asia.* Cambridge: Cambridge University Press.

——2017. First farmers in Southeast Asia. *Journal of Indo-Pacific Archaeology* 41:13-21.

Higham, C.F.W. and Bannanurag, R., 1990. *The Excavation of Khok Phanom Di: Volume I, The Excavation, Chronology and Human Burials.* London: The Society of Antiquaries of London.

Higham, C.F.W. and Bannanurag, R (eds.) 1991. *The Excavation of Khok Phanom Di: Volume II: The Biological Remains Part 1,* London: The Society of Antiquaries of London.

Higham C.F.W. and Higham, T.F.G. 2009. A new chronological framework for prehistoric Southeast Asia, based on a Bayesian model from Ban Non Wat. *Antiquity* 82:1-20.

Higham C.F.W., Higham, T.F.G. and Kijngam, A. 2011. Cutting a Gordian Knot: The Bronze Age of Southeast Asia, timing, origins and impact. *Antiquity* 85:583-98.

Higham, C.F.W. and Kijngam, A. 1984. *Prehistoric Excavations in Northeast Thailand: Excavations at Ban Na Di, Ban Chiang Hian, Ban Muang Phruk, Ban Sangui, Non Noi and Ban Kho Noi.* British Archaeological Reports, International Series 231(i-iii), Oxford.

Higham, C.F.W. and Kijngam, A. eds. 2020. *The Origins of the Civilization of Angkor volume VII. The Excavation of Non Ban Jak.* Bangkok: The Fine Arts Department.

Higham, C.F.W., Manly, B.F.J., Thosarat, R., Buckley, H.R., Chang, N., Halcrow, S.E., O'Reilly, D.J.W., Domett, K. and Shewan, L.G. 2019. Environmental and Social Change in Northeast Thailand during the Iron Age. *Cambridge Archaeological Journal* 29(4):548-69.

Higham, C.F.W., Halcrow, S.E, Ward, S., O'Reilly, D.J.W., Domett, K. and Shewan, L.G. 2019. Environmental and Social Change in Northeast Thailand during the Iron Age. *Cambridge Archaeological Journal* 29(4):548-69.

Higham, C.F.W. and Message, M. 1971. The assessment of a society's technique of bovine husbandry, In Brothwell, D. and Higgs, E.S., *Science in Archaeology* (2nd edition) 315-30, London: Thames and Hudson.

Higham, C.F.W. and Thosarat, R. eds. 1993. *Khok Phanom Di: Volume III: The Material Culture Part 1.* London: The Society of Antiquaries of London.

——1998. *The Excavation of Nong Nor, a Prehistoric Site in Central Thailand.* University of Otago Monographs in Prehistoric Anthropology 18, Dunedin.

——2004. *The Excavation of Khok Phanom Di: Volume VII. Summary and Conclusions.* London: The Society of Antiquaries of London.

Higham, C.S.S. 1962. *Wimbledon Manor House under the Cecils.* London: Longmans Green.

Higham, T.F.G. 2021. *The World Before Us. How Science is Revealing a New Story of Our Human Origins.* London: Penguin.

Higham, T.F.G., Weiss, A.D., Higham, C.F.W., Bronk Ramsey, C., d'Alpoim Guedes, J., Hanson, S., Weber, S.A., Rispoli, F., Ciarla, R., Pryce, T.O.

and Pigott, V.C. 2020. A Prehistoric copper-base-production centre in central Thailand: its dating and wider implications. *Antiquity* 94:948-65

Leroi-Gourhan, A. 1961. Les fouilles d'Arcy-sur-Cure (Yonne). *Gallia Préhistoire* 4:3-16.

Lévy, P. 1943. Recherches préhistoriques dans la region de Mlu Prei. *Publications de l'École française d'Extrême Orient* XXX. Lévy, P. 1943. Recherches préhistoriques dans la region de Mlu Prei. *Publications de l'École française d'Extrême Orient* XXX.

Lipson, M., Cheronet, O., Mallick, S. et al. 2018. Ancient genomes document multiple waves of migration in Southeast Asian prehistory. *Science* 361:92-5

Loofs-Wissowa, H.H.E. 1986. The rise and fall of early bronze in Thailand. Paper read at the XXXII International Congress for Asian and North African Studies, Hamburg.

Loofs-Wissowa 2009. A Peaceful Legionnaire: An Indochina Sketchbook 1948-1954. Canberra: Veritas Publishers.

Maglioni, R. 1975. Archaeological discovery in Eastern Kwangtung. *Journal Monograph II.* Hong Kong, Hong Kong Archaeological Society.

Maloney, B. 1991.Khok Phanom Di: the physical environment. In Higham, C.F.W. and R. Bannanurag eds. T*he Excavation of Khok Phanom Di Volume II. The Biological Remains (part 1).* London: the Society of Antiquaries of London,

Mansuy, H. 1902. *Stations Préhistoriques de Samrong-Sen et de Longprao (Cambodge).* Hanoi: F.H. Scheider.

——1923. Contribution a l'étude de la préhistoire de l'Indochine. Résultats de nouvèlles récherches effectuées dans le gisement préhistorique de Samrong Sen (Cambodge). *Mémoires du Service Géologique de l'Indochine* XI(1): 5-24.

——1924. Stations préhistoriques dans les cavernes du massif calcaire de Bac-Son (Tonkin). *Bulletin de la Service Géologique d'Indochine* 11.2.

Matsumura, M, Oxenham, M, Simanjuntak, T. and Yamagata, M. 2017. The biological history of Southeast Asian populations from Late Pleistocene and Holocene cemetery data. In P. Bellwood. *First Islanders: Prehistory and Human Migration in Island Southeast Asia* 98-106. Oxford: Wiley Blackwell.

Matsumura, M., Hung, H., Higham, C.F.W. et al. 2019. Craniometrics reveal "two layers" of prehistoric human dispersal in Eastern Eurasia. *Scientific Reports* 9:12-24.

McColl, H.M., Racimo, F, Vinner, L. et al. 2018. The prehistoric peopling of Southeast Asia. *Science* 361:88–92.

Mormina, M. and Higham, C.F.W. 2010. Climate crises and the population history of Southeast Asia. In A.B. Mainwairing, R. Giegangack and C. Vita-Finzi eds. *Climate Crises in Human History* 197-212. Philadelphia: American Philosophical Society.

Nelson S. and Rosen-Alyalon, M. (eds.) 2002. *In Pursuit of Gender. Worldwide Archaeological Approaches*. Oxford: Altamira Press.

Noulet, J.B. 1879. L'Âge de la pierre polie et du bronze au Cambodge d'après les découvertes de M.J. Moura. *Arch. Mus. Hist. Nat. de Toulouse* 1.

Parmentier, M.H. 1918. Ancient tambour de bronze. *Bulletin de l'École française d'Extrême Orient* 24:325-43.

Pryce, T.O. 2012. Technical analysis of Bronze Age Ban Non Wat copper-base -base artefacts. In Higham, C.F.W. and Kijngam, A. (eds.) *The Excavation of Ban Non Wat, Part 3. The Bronze Age*. Bangkok: The Fine Arts Department

Rodden, R., Pyke, G., Yiouni, P. and Wardle, K. A. 1996. *Nea Nikomedeia I: The Excavation of an Early Neolithic Village in Northern Greece* 1961-1964. Athens: The British School at Athens.

Schofield, W. 1975. An archaeological site at Shek Pik. In Meacham, W., ed. *An Archaeological Site at Shek Pik*. Journal Monograph I, Hong Kong Archaeological Society, Hong Kong.

Solheim W.G. 1968. Early bronze in northeastern Thailand. *Current Anthropology* 9:59-62.

Solheim, W.G. 1972. An earlier agricultural revolution. *Scientific American* 226/4: 34-41

Spriggs, M. 1989. The dating of the island Southeast Asian Neolithic: an attempt at chronometric hygiene and linguistic correlation. *Antiquity* 63:587-613.

Spriggs, M. and Anderson, A.A. 1993. Late colonisation of Polynesia. *Antiquity* 67: 200-17.

Tayles, N.G. 1999. *Khok Phanom Di. The People*. London: Research Report of the Society of Antiquaries of London LXI.

Thompson, G.B. 1996. *Khok Phanom Di, Subsistence and Environment: the Botanical Evidence (The Biological Remains Part 2)*. London: the Society of Antiquaries of London.

Thomas, N. 2005. *Conderton Camp, Worcestershire : A Middle Iron Age Hillfort on Bredon Hill*. York: Council for British Archaeology.

Thomas, N. and Thomas, K. 2005. *Snail Down Wiltshire*. Wiltshire Archaeology & Natural History Society Monograph no. 1.

Thosarat, R. and Kijngam, A. 2004. *The Excavation of Ban Suai, Amphoe Phimai* (in Thai). Bangkok: Fine Arts Department.

Trump, D. 1966. *Skorba. A Neolithic Temple in Malta*. London: Society of Antiquaries Research Report No. 22.

Vickery, M. 1998. *Society, Economics and Politics in Pre-Angkor Cambodia*. Tokyo: The Centre for East Asian Cultural Studies for Unesco

Vincent, B.A. 2004. Khok Phanom Di. The Pottery. London: Research Report of the Society of Antiquaries of London LXX.

Weber, S., Lehman, H., Barela, T., Hawks, S. and Harriman, D. 2010. Rice or millets? Early farming strategies in prehistoric central Thailand. *Anthropological and Archaeological Science* 2: 79-88.

White, J.C. 1982. *Ban Chiang: Discovery of a Lost Bronze Age*. Philadelphia: University of Pennsylvania Press.

Wohlfarth, B., Higham, C.F.W., Yamoah, K.A., Chabangborn, A, Chawchai, S. and Smittenberg, R.H. 2016. Human adaptation to mid- to late-Holocene climate change in Northeast Thailand. The *Holocene*, 26(4): 614-26

_____ 10 cm

Many of the thousands of pots we have found accompanying the dead tell their own story. A, found
with an early Bronze Age infant at Ban Non Wat, reveals an ancestral human face with eyes looking
from a distance of three thousand years. B, also from Bronze Age Ban Non Wat, has a scene of
dancers. Was there dancing at the funeral of this aristocrat? C is an Iron Age vessel from Non Ban Jak.
The decoration looks very like canals linked to channels leading water into the rice fields. Above, do we
see a row of growing rice plants? D At Ban Non Wat, we anticipated an Iron Age settlement. Finding
magnificent decorated Neolithic pots came as a stunning and welcome surprise.

Index

Charles Higham has been exploring Southeast Asia's past for over fifty years. In this book, he first describes how he found a passion for archaeology while still a teenager in England. During his studies at London and Cambridge Universities, he learned to excavate in a wide range of sites, from Palaeolithic caves in France to Knossos in Crete, a Maltese temple and the Roman city of Verulamium. His doctoral research took him to Switzerland, where he studied the economies of the famous Swiss Lake Villages. In 1966, he and his wife travelled round to the world to New Zealand and a lectureship at the University of Otago. Two years later, he was appointed the first Professor of Prehistoric Archaeology in Australasia, and began his fieldwork in Thailand in 1969. Working first with Chester Gorman, he joined excavations on Banyan Valley Cave before working for two seasons at Ban Chiang. He then branched out on his own initiative and with his to long-time Thai colleagues Amphan Kijngam and Rachanie Thosarat, he has directed excavations at some of the key sites in Southeast Asia. At Khok Phanom Di, he uncovered a remarkable early Neolithic settlement, and Ban Non Wat has required a complete re-evaluation of the start and impact of metallurgy. Noen U-Loke and Non Ban Jak have contributed to new insight into the foundation of early states. His excavations have all been fully published, and he has authored influential overviews with River Books.

In this book, Charles describes above all, the excitement of discovery, how it feels to reveal the past through uncovering the graves of prehistoric people, their homes, their relationships through ancient DNA, their migrations, the environments they adapted to, how civilizations began. He recounts how our understanding of timescales and cultural changes have developed, along with the trials and tribulations, the debates and disagreements.